# A Handy Book On the Law of Husband and Wife

You are holding a reproduction of an original work that is in the public domain in the United States of America, and possibly other countries.You may freely copy and distribute this work as no entity (individual or corporate) has a copyright on the body of the work.This book may contain prior copyright references, and library stamps (as most of these works were scanned from library copies).These have been scanned and retained as part of the historical artifact.

This book may have occasional imperfections such as missing or blurred pages, poor pictures, errant marks, etc. that were either part of the original artifact, or were introduced by the scanning process. We believe this work is culturally important, and despite the imperfections, have elected to bring it back into print as part of our continuing commitment to the preservation of printed works worldwide. We appreciate your understanding of the imperfections in the preservation process, and hope you enjoy this valuable book.

PRICE **2s. 6d.** NET.

WILSON'S LEGAL HANDY BOOKS.

A HANDY BOOK ON THE LAW OF

# HUSBAND AND WIFE.

BY

JAMES WALTER SMITH, Esq., B.A. (Oxford), LL.D. (London),

OF THE INNER TEMPLE, BARRISTER-AT-LAW.

*Author of Handy Books on the Law of "Private Trading Partnership;" on the Law of "Bills, Cheques, Notes, and I O U's;" on the Law of "Master and Servant;" on the Law of "Joint Stock Companies;" and of "Legal Forms for Common Use."*

ELEVENTH THOUSAND. NEW AND REVISED EDITION.

EFFINGHAM WILSON, 11, ROYAL EXCHANGE.

# NORTH BRITISH

— AND —

# MERCANTILE

## INSURANCE COMPANY.

**TOTAL FUNDS**

*At 31st December, 1894.*

**Over Eleven and a half Millions Sterling.**

INCOME FOR 1894—

**£2,906,678.**

## Life Department.

Most Policies are World Wide from date of issue.
Policies free from vexatious conditions.
Claims Paid on Proof of Death and Title.
NINETY PER CENT. of the Profits in the Life Department is reserved for distribution among the Assured on the Participating Scale. The Profits are divided every Five years.

**Annuities** of all kinds granted on the most favourable terms.

## Fire Department.

Property of nearly every description at home and abroad insured at the Lowest Rates. Losses by Lightning, Damage by Explosion of Gas in buildings not forming part of any Gas Works, made good. Rents of Buildings insured.

**SECURITY, LIBERALITY, & PROMPTITUDE**
**in Settlement of Claims**
**are characteristics of this Company.**

*Prospectuses and every information can be obtained at the Chief Offices:*

London ... { 61, THREADNEEDLE STREET, E.C.;
(West End Branch): 8, WATERLOO PLACE, S.W.

Edinburgh: 64, PRINCES STREET.

[ENTERED AT STATIONERS' HALL].

# A HANDY BOOK ON THE LAW OF HUSBAND AND WIFE.

ENGAGEMENTS TO MARRY.
PROPERTY & SETTLEMENTS.
WIFE'S SEPARATE RIGHTS.
THE SPOUSES' LIABILITIES.
PROTECTION & MAINTENANCE.
DIVORCE & SEPARATION.
CHILDREN.


BY

JAMES WALTER SMITH, Esq., B.A., (Oxford), LL.D. (London).

OF THE INNER TEMPLE, BARRISTER-AT-LAW,

*Author of Handy Books on the Law of "Private Trading Partnership;" on the Law of "Bills, Cheques, Notes, and I O U's;" on the Law of "Master and Servant;" on the Law of "Joint Stock Companies;" and of "Legal Forms for Common Use."*


"Were the state of the law known to all, no one, unless on the ground of knowingly false evidence, would venture to institute an illegal claim or defend himself against a legal one."—BENTHAM.

ELEVENTH THOUSAND.

NEW AND REVISED EDITION.

LONDON:

EFFINGHAM WILSON,

11, ROYAL EXCHANGE.

1897.



NEW YORK PUBLIC LIBRARY

THE NEW YORK
PUBLIC LIBRARY
68010
ASTOR, LENOX AND
TILDEN FOUNDATIONS.
1897.

## PREFACE TO THE EDITION OF 1891.

THIRTY-TWO years ago I wrote the first edition of this book, thinking it important that the public should have at hand a short and plainly written treatise on the subjects dealt with.

The respective rights of husband and wife as to property; their contractual and other liabilities towards the world and one another; the various proceedings in the Divorce Court, with their results; and the relations of parent and guardian to child and ward appeared to me to be matters in which any family might at any time come to be concerned.

The first edition was followed by several others, two of which were necessitated respectively by the Married Women's Property Acts of 1870 and 1874. Since then the Married Women's Property Act, 1882, has increased the area of property which a wife can deal with as her own, and has gone further towards setting her free in commercial and other business and employments.

This Act is so defective both in expression and arrangement, that one would imagine it was hurriedly introduced, and was afterwards amended, by various hands in its passage through Parliament.

This, however, was not the case. It was first introduced into the Commons by Mr. Hinde Palmer in 1880, but after discussion was withdrawn. In 1881, it was again brought in and referred to a select committee, but was once more withdrawn owing to pressure of business. In 1882, Lord Selborne, then Chancellor, brought the bill into the House of Lords almost in its present shape, and it passed through both Houses with little change. But, in spite of the length of time occupied, the statute is marked with many serious defects: and though it was not altered in the Parliament, it shews as a patched piece of work, and lacks so much of unity of design and uniformity of expression as it would have had if left wholly to one draftsman, even though not one of the best.

But, such as it is, I have tried to explain it. I have also endeavoured to state the effect of those other recent statutes, which affect wives in regard of their property, and those which give them summary remedies when they suffer desertion, or are the victims of their husbands' violence, and those which relate to the guardianship of children.

These additions to the Law and changes in it, have made it necessary to almost wholly re-write the book.

If these subjects are treated briefly, I hope they are not treated only superficially, and that the book may serve to teach the student and articled clerk, an outline of the law which he may afterwards have to apply; and to give the non-legal reader, who takes the requisite pains, some definite ideas on a set of subjects, which, some time or other, are pretty sure to concern him.

Since the earlier portions of this work was sent to the press, the Intestates Estates Act, 1890, has become law, and it is treated of in the latter chapters, where they are concerned with the rights of the widow, and is printed in the Appendix.

## PREFACE TO THE EDITION OF 1897.

Since the edition of 1891 was published, the Married Women's Property Act, 1893, has introduced important amendments, which have gone far to reconcile the law of the wife's property and obligations with the standard of common sense, and have required the omission of many passages in the edition of 1891, and the substitution of other matter. The Custody of Children Act, 1891, the Voluntary Conveyances Act, 1893, and the Summary Jurisdiction (Married Women) Act, 1895, have also been noticed.

J. W. S.

# CONTENTS.

# THE LAW OF

# HUSBAND AND WIFE.

---

## CHAPTER I.

### OF ENGAGEMENTS TO MARRY AND OF CONTRACTS TO BRING ABOUT A MARRIAGE.

1. *Who may marry?*
2. *Engagements to marry. Must be reciprocal.*
3. *Where one party is a minor.*
4. *How soon the promise should be fulfilled.*
5. *Marriage never enforced by law. Actions for breach of promise. Damages.*
6. *Evidence.*
7. *Circumstances that will excuse the marriage. Fraud as to property or character. Unchastity. Dissipated habits. Conviction for crime. Violence. Physical incapacity.*
8. *Loss of property or health after engagement.*
9. *Long engagements. Engagement abandoned for a long time.*
10. *Promise by person already married. By infant.*
11. *Seduction after engagement.*
12. *Engagement put an end to by consent.*
13. *Of contracts by deed to marry.*
14. *One-sided promise by a woman by deed.*
15. *Contract to bring about a marriage between other persons.*
16. *Security given as the price of a marriage.*

1. Any man or woman may marry who is of full age, and not within the prohibited degrees of relationship with the intended husband or wife. A person under

age cannot lawfully marry unless he or she is a widower or widow, or has the consent of his or her father, guardians, or mother, or has no parents or guardians at all. But the male must not be under fourteen, or the female under twelve years of age.

If there is no parent or guardian, a petition may be presented to the Lord Chancellor to appoint a guardian to consent; and if the parent, guardian, or other person whose consent is required is *non compos mentis*, or beyond the seas, or refuses consent from improper motives, the consent of the Chancellor, Master of Rolls, or Vice-Chancellor may be obtained on petition. (4 Geo. 4, c. 76, ss. 16, 17).

The marriage of a minor, however, who does not come within any of the above exceptions, though unlawful, and subjecting him or her to certain penalties, is yet valid when solemnised, and the issue will be legitimate.

2. Engagements or agreements to marry are seldom expressed in any way but by word of mouth or by letters written during courtship. Whether such agreement be merely verbal or contained in letters, it is binding, provided the parties be unmarried, of full age, of sound mind, and not within the prohibited relationships.

If an offer of marriage be made and not accepted within a reasonable time, neither party will be bound unless the offer be kept open and subsequently accepted, in which case the engagement will be as binding as if at once acceded to.

3. If one party is a minor, he or she is not bound by the agreement, though it receive the assent of parents or guardians, and may put an end to it at once, and on arriving at full age is not bound by it, or by any ratification of it after full age. The Infants' Relief Act, 1874, enacts that no action shall be brought, whereby to charge any person upon any promise made after full age to pay any debt contracted during infancy, or upon any ratification made after full age, of any promise or contract made during infancy, whether there shall be any new consideration for such ratification or not.

So that, where an infant falls in love and continues

the intimacy after full age, and then breaks it off and is made defendant in an action for breach of promise, it is a question of fact whether the continuance after age was a new promise or a ratification. This question will be left to the jury, if the case is tried by a jury, and a very little will satisfy the jury that there was a new promise.

I say "though it receive the assent of parents or guardians," for an engagement to marry a minor other than a widow or widower, whose parents or guardians have not consented, is of course not binding, for it is a contract to do an unlawful act.

The case of a minor is an exception to the common rule, namely, that the bargain, to be binding upon either, must be binding upon both. For though a minor on receiving a promise of marriage, makes a reciprocal promise with parental sanction, the promise is not binding upon the minor, and yet the latter may bring an action, even before twenty-one, for the breach of the promise made *to* him or her, if the proper time for performing it has arrived.

4. I have said "if the time has arrived," because, if any time is fixed, that is the time when either party is entitled to have the marriage take place, and if *no* time is fixed, then each party is understood to promise to marry within *a reasonable time*. What is a reasonable time will of course depend upon the circumstances of each case, which the jury, or the judge sitting without a jury, will decide, if the defence is that a reasonable time has not elapsed for the fulfilment of the promise.

Sometimes, however, the promise is to marry upon the happening of a certain event, as on an estate in reversion falling into possession, and in such case, of course, no action can be maintained for the breach of the promise until the event in question has taken place.

5. Where one party refuses to marry the other, an action for breach of promise of marriage is the only remedy. Down to the year 1753 a promise to marry at once was as binding as an actual marriage; so far at least that neither party could, without committing adultery, cohabit with anybody else, though united with such latter person in church. So that a woman who

had a long time supposed herself married and had children, might find the marriage dissolved and the children bastardised by reason of her husband having before promised to marry some other woman. And the husband was liable to a similar surprise. This state of things was in that year abolished by "Lord Hardwicke's Act."

Since that Act the only remedy for a breach of an engagement to marry is by an action, in which the injured person can recover damages or compensation for what he or she may have lost by the non-fulfilment of the promise. The promise or contract to marry is thus on the same footing with the large majority of other contracts; for there are only certain classes of contracts which the law will compel to be actually carried out.

The damages to be awarded in such actions are to be measured by the loss which the plaintiff (male or female) has sustained in a social and pecuniary point of view by being disappointed of the marriage; and juries are always informed that the law does not intend the damages to be a solace for the plaintiff's injured feelings.

6. By the "Evidence further Amendment Act, 1869," sec. 2, the parties to any action for breach of promise of marriage shall be competent [but not compellable] to give evidence in such action; provided always that no plaintiff in any action for breach of promise of marriage shall recover a verdict unless his or her testimony shall be corroborated by some other material evidence in support of such promise.

The plaintiff's case must, therefore, be partly made out by other evidence than his or her own, such as the evidence of friends as to the conversation and conduct of the parties, by the letters which may have passed between them, and by anything said or written by either of them to anybody else about the engagement.

It must appear from the evidence adduced by the plaintiff, that there was a promise made, and that it was accepted, and if conditional that the condition has been performed. In order to fix *a man* with liability, the woman's promise or acceptance need not be in words, but may be in acts and behaviour. But if *a woman* be defendant in the action, there must be distinct evidence of a promise or consent on her part. Before bringing an action, the plaintiff must have been prepared to marry the defendant, and a refusal on the defendant's part must be proved; but this, like the female plaintiff's original acceptance of the promise, may be by acts and behaviour as well as by direct words. It must also appear that a reasonable time for the marriage has elapsed, or that the time fixed is passed, or else that defendant has married another person, and has therefore rendered it impossible to perform his or her promise.

It will be observed that it is respecting the promise itself, that the statute requires the plaintiff to be corroborated, and not as to the breach or the damages.

7. There follows a short statement of some circumstances which will excuse the marriage, and, when proved in evidence, will amount to a defence to an action for breach of promise.

If any fraud is practised upon either party by the other, as an inducement to the marriage, the fraud being with reference either to property or to those points of character which the world regards as essential to respectability, the party so deceived may break off the engagement.

For example, if false representations are made by a girl and her friends in collusion with her, as to her circumstances in life, and the amount of her fortune, the intended husband will have an answer to an action for breach of promise of marriage. But it must be shown that the plaintiff herself connived at the fraud or herself made some false representation or wilful suppression of the truth. A similar fraud as to the circumstances of the man, would entitle the woman to break off the match.

Any other fraud practised by one party upon the other as to what was considered material between them, would be a proper reason for breaking off the match.

And if an unanimity as to religious creed had been insisted on as necessary, either by the man or his intended wife, a want of such unanimity, discovered after the engagement, would be good ground for one party to break off the match if the other had concealed his or her views.

If a man, knowing a woman to be or to have been unchaste, engage to marry her, he is liable to an action if he refuse; but if, after the engagement, her conduct, without his connivance, becomes immoral, or if, after the engagement, he discovers for the first time that she has previously been unchaste, these matters will constitute a defence to an action brought by the woman. The same may be said of other loose habits, such as drinking and keeping profligate company. But the bad conduct complained of, if relied upon as a defence to an action, must be distinctly proved, or else evidence must be given of a *general reputation* for immorality of character.

If one party had been convicted of a felony, and the other did not know of it until after the engagement, the latter may break off the match.

If the man has behaved with brutality or violence to the woman she may break off the match.

If a man who had appeared and had been represented as a man of steady habits, after the engagement entered into a drunken, dissipated, or profligate career, and in fact showed that he was not the man he appeared to be, that would no doubt be a defence for the lady if he brought an action against her for breach of promise. But the law would not require that a man should preserve the same rigorous propriety as would be expected in a woman.

Where either the man or woman becomes affected by an accident or illness rendering him or her phsically unfit for the marriage state, the engagement may be broken off.

8. But though a fraud or a concealment of material circumstances practised by one party on the other will enable the latter to put an end to the engagement, yet no such right arises merely because a misfortune takes place which entirely alters the position of the parties. For example, sickness, the loss of personal beauty or of fortune, or the death of an influential friend, would not give either party the right of breaking off the match.

But if the person who was being sued in an action for

breach of promise had become very poor, that fact, if made apparent, would tend to reduce the damages to a very trifling amount, inasmuch as the damages are principally measured by the loss of comfort and of social position.

9. If the parties are young, an engagement, not to be fulfilled for a long time, will be valid in law, but if they are elderly it will be void as being "in restraint of marriage," and therefore regarded by law as contrary to public policy.

If both parties lie by for a considerable period and do not treat the contract as subsisting, it will be held to be abandoned; and if an action were brought, a jury would be directed that, if they so found the facts, they should give their verdict for the defendant.

10. If a person already married engages to marry another, such an engagement is not binding on the other party; and if the person to whom the promise was made was ignorant of the former marriage of the other, the latter will be liable to an action for breach of promise.

With reference to an infant, not being a widow or widower, it has already been stated that he or she is unable to maintain an action without the consent of parent or guardian, having been obtained to the proposed marriage. That is, the absence of such consent will be a defence in case the infant bring an action.

11. A woman cannot complain that her intended husband abandons her if she has been seduced by another person; but the fact of her being seduced by her intended husband, so far from constituting a defence to an action by her for breach of promise, would only tend to enhance the damages.

12. Persons who have mutually promised to marry may, at any time before the performance of the ceremony, put an end to the engagement by mutual consent. But actions are often brought, after engagements have been broken off, under a pretence that they have been resumed.

An offer may be retracted at any time before acceptance.

13. Though engagements to marry are usually made

by word of mouth, or evidenced by letters passing between the parties during courtship, yet one or two remarks shall be made on contracts entered into a more formal manner.

If a man and woman were to enter into *mutual* covenants to marry by a *deed*, or writing under seal, they would both be bound unless one of them was defrauded by the other. In this case, as where the engagement is by word of mouth, the party defrauded has the option of declaring the contract void, but the other has not the same choice.

The contract by deed is so formal and solemn that it is not necessary in this, as in the ordinary contract above treated of, that there should be any *consideration* for the covenant of one party, or any mutual engagement binding upon both parties. So that, if one party covenant by deed to marry the other, the former will be bound though the latter do not execute the deed or enter into any corresponding covenant.

14. But, women being usually unversed in business, and peculiarly liable to be imposed upon where their affections are concerned, the Courts will regard with extreme jealousy and suspicion, any deed by which a woman binds herself to marry a man who is not bound to her by any corresponding obligation. On application to a Court of Equity, such a deed would certainly be set aside if clandestinely obtained from a lady, without the knowledge of her parent, or of any person acting as parent to her, whether the lady were a minor or not, if she had expectations from her parent or such other person. But if the deed were given by the lady, with the knowledge of her parent, as a pledge of her good faith, and as an inducement to her suitor to keep himself free from other engagements, the deed would be held good.

The actual performance of the covenant would not be enforced any more than the actual performance of a verbal engagement to marry, but the remedy would be by action for damages.

15. But as marriages are intended by the law to be the result of the mutual esteem and affection of the

parties to them, a contract between third parties to bring about a marriage is wholly void.

Thus a contract between A and B, whether with or without valuable consideration, that a marriage shall take place between C and D, is void, and none the less so though A and B are each a parent or *in loco parentis* to C or D. I am not now speaking of contracts to make settlements in the event of a marriage, as to which see chapter xi., but of contracts actually to bring about a marriage.

16. So also a contract by which A agreed with B to pay him a certain sum of money or perform some service for him upon a marriage being brought about between A and C is void. All such contracts known as "marriage brokage contracts," will be cancelled by the Court.

A bond given by the lover of a young lady to her maid to secure to her £1,000 if the marriage took place, was set aside by the Court as being a bribe to the maid to bring about the marriage. The same thing was done where the bond had been given to the wife's father, to induce him to consent to the match. And a bond by which a man bound himself to execute to the mother of his intended wife, within two days after the marriage, a release of all accounts between him and the mother in respect of certain rents which she had received and improperly applied, was set aside by the Court after the bond had been put in suit, on the ground that the lady had abused her parental authority; and had taken a price for the marriage.

In fact it may be stated broadly that any security which has been extracted, directly or indirectly, from the man or his wife by a parent or any other person as the price of consenting to or procuring the marriage, will be cancelled by a Court of Equity; and in case any money has been paid in pursuance of such security or otherwise, the Court will order the money to be returned.

It is not, however, to be supposed that an innocent holder for value, or his indorsee, would fail to recover upon a bill or note merely because it was originally given as the price of the marriage.

## CHAPTER II.

### WHEN A MARRIAGE ONCE SOLEMNIZED MAY BE DECLARED VOID.

1. *The Court may declare that there has been* no *marriage, but will not set aside a real marriage.*

2. *Marriage cannot be impeached by showing want of parental consent, or non-residence within the parish.*

3. *But male must not be under* 14, *or female under* 12.

4. *Certain marriages altogether void for disobedience to law.*

5. *Otherwise where only one party was to blame and has deceived the other. Marriage in false name. Banns in false name. Sham licence. Licence obtained by fraud. Sham priest.*

6. *Decree of nullity on ground of sexual incapacity.*

7. *Grounds on which, and persons by whom, the petition should be presented.*

8. *Jurisdiction to enquire into the validity of marriages solemnized in England between foreigners domiciled abroad.*

1. There is a seeming contradiction in the title to this chapter, for wherever what has taken place amounts in law to a valid marriage, it can never be declared *void*, though a divorce may be decreed. But what I mean to state in this chapter is, in what cases, where a marriage ceremony has been performed, the Divorce Court will declare that nevertheless there was no marriage. And the reader will observe that this decision will sometimes be given on the application of one party but not of the other.

2. Although it is unlawful for a person under age to marry without consent of parent or guardian, where he or she has any; and though no person can be married unless by special licence) except within the parish or

chapelry where one of the parties has resided fifteen days; and though the guilty parties, and the minister who colludes with him or them, are subject to certain penalities for disobedience to this law; yet when, in either of these cases, the marriage has once been celebrated it remains a valid marriage; and not only is no evidence of consent or of residence necessary to prove the validity of the marriage if disputed, but the party disputing the marriage will not even be allowed to show that there was *no* residence or *no* parental sanction.

In other words, if a boy and a girl can manage to get married without parental consent, or any other persons can manage to get married without the required residence, the fraud or perjury they may either of them have committed does not invalidate the marriage itself, but only subjects the guilty party to punishment, and to a forfeiture of all estate and interest in any properties accruing by the marriage. (On this punishment nothing will be said, as it is not within the scope of the book).

Some people go to Scotland to marry clandestinely, because by the Scots law a marriage may be effected by both parties expressing their present intention to marry, or an acknowledgment that a marriage exists; but by Statute 19 and 20 Vict., c. 96, s. 1, no irregular marriage by declaration, acknowledgment or ceremony can be contracted in Scotland, unless one of the parties had at the date thereof, his or her usual place of residence there, or had lived in Scotland for twenty-one days next preceding such marriage. And so where a couple went to Scotland, and arrived there at 4 a.m. on the 1st of July, and remained there till the 21st, and then went through a ceremony of marriage at 11 a.m. on that day, the marriage was declared void, because neither party had lived in Scotland for twenty-one days "next preceding" the marriage.

3. Subject to the requirement of the consent of parent or guardian, a boy at fourteen and a girl at twelve are capable of contracting a valid marriage. But if before that time they go through the ceremony of marriage, though with parental consent, they may either declare

the marriage void on their arriving at the respective ages above mentioned, or may ratify and confirm it by cohabiting *after* that period.

4. All marriages celebrated in England or Ireland after the 31st of August, 1835, between persons within the prohibited degrees of consanguinity and affinity are absolutely void; (Lord Lyndhurst's Act, 5 and 6 Will. IV., c. 33, s. 2). Wife's sister and husband's brother are within the degrees, but all cousins may intermarry; the popular opinion to the contrary being erroneous. The Statute 32 Henry VIII., c. 38, legalises marriages between first cousins.

If any persons knowingly and willingly intermarry in any other place than a church or chapel of the Church of England, without special licence from the Archbishop of Canterbury, unless it be in a registered building, or registrar's office, and upon licence, or due publication of banns, or due notice to the superintendent-registrar, or certificate of notice duly issued, or intermarry in the absence of a registrar, or superintendent-registrar, where the presence of a registrar or superintendent-registrar is necessary, the marriage of such persons is absolutely null and void.

The Marriage Act, 6 Geo. IV., c. 76, s. 21, makes it felony for a person to solemnize a marriage in an unlawful place, or without the authority of banns or licence, or according to the rites of the Church of England, falsely pretending to be in orders, or in unlawful hours; but the Marriage Act, 1886, has extended the lawful hours to from 8 a.m. to 3 p.m.

5. But if the disobedience to law was on one side only without the knowledge of the other party, the marriage will remain good.

Where a man has concealed his true name when banns were published, or has had them published in a false name without the woman's knowledge, the law will not enable him to turn round and annul the marriage and bastardise the issue on the ground of his own fraud and disobedience to law.

Where the husband gave a wrong name as that of his intended wife to the clergyman for the publication of banns, and the woman was married in the wrong name, but never found it out till after the marriage, the marriage was held good notwithstanding the mistake of the name.

But if the husband, by some fraud, had deceived his wife as to the *person* she was about to marry, the marriage might then be declared void on the ground of fraud on *her* application, but not on *his*.

As with banns published in a false name, without the woman's knowledge, so it will be where a licence is granted in the wrong name; the mere misdescription will not make the marriage void.

If the man has imposed a sham licence and a sham clergyman upon the woman, he cannot apply to have the marriage declared void, though the woman may.

But if any fraud or intentional deception were practised with the knowledge and connivance of *both* parties upon the bishop or archbishop, as if a licence were obtained for one person with the intention that it should be used for another, the licence will be void, and any marriage taking place upon it will be void also.

If persons professing to marry according to the rites of the Church of England, knowingly or wilfully consent to or acquiesce in the solemnization of such marriage by any person not being in holy orders, the marriage is null and void. (See note * at end of chapter.)

A woman, prostrated in body and mind by sickness and anxiety, was induced by a threat of being shot, to accompany a man to a Registrar's office, where she went through a ceremony of marriage with him, after which they immediately parted, and the marriage was never consummated. It was held that there was not sufficient consent to the marriage and, on the woman's petition, it was declared null and void.

Where a decree of nullity is sought on the ground of the insanity of one of the parties, the burden of proving it rests on the party asserting it, and the Court has to determine whether the person was capable at the time, of understanding the nature of the contract and the duties and responsibilities which it creates, and was free from the influence of morbid delusions on the subject.

6. When either party to the marriage is found to have been at the time of the marriage physically incapacitated from sexual intercourse, the Divorce Court will, on the petition of the other party, but not of any third person, declare the marriage null on the ground that a necessary element to a valid contract of marriage was wanting. Where it is the woman who seeks a decree of nullity on the ground of the impotence of the man, the Court usually requires him to have had opportunities during three years of cohabitation to perform his marital duties and proof that the woman, if a spinster at marriage, is *virgo intacta*.

The Court always gives the man an opportunity of submitting to a medical examination, which he can refuse if he so pleases. If the examination takes place, it may tend to establish impotence without resulting in evidence of malformation.

7. A suit for nullity of marriage must be founded on grounds existing at the time of the marriage, and not on any grounds arising afterwards, as insanity or impotence may do, and the suit must be instituted and concluded while both parties to the marriage are alive. Apart from this, the person seeking to have a marriage declared null should not slumber on his or her rights, for the Court will make every presumption in favour of a marriage where the couple have long cohabited or have had children.

In suits on the ground of sexual incompetency of one of the parties, the petition must be presented by the other; but in other cases other persons having interest, are entitled to petition, for example the father of a female minor married *by banns*, in a wrong name, and persons entitled to property on one of the parties dying without issue. In cases of marriage within the prohibited degrees, as where the wife is niece, or a deceased wife's sister, either party may petition.

As to the right of the Queen's Proctor to intervene in a suit for nullity, and as to the decree being *nisi* in the first instance, and as to the right to shew cause against the decree, and as to appeal, and at what time the parties may marry again, see c. xix., s. 81, *et seq.*

8. A word must be said as to the jurisdiction to declare void a marriage between two foreigners, or a foreigner and an English person, solemnized in England.

The rule is that the law of the country where the marriage is solemnized, governs the forms and ceremonies requisite for the marriage and also the personal capacity of the parties. This may be illustrated by what happens where a domiciled Englishman marries his deceased wife's sister in a country, or a colony, where such a marriage is lawful, and by the forms proper there. In that country the Courts will treat the couple as husband and wife; but the English Courts will not.

So where a domiciled Frenchman who, by the law of France, was incapable of marrying without parental consent; but being twenty-one years of age, was capable in England, married a Frenchwoman in England, the French Courts pronounced the marriage bad, but the English Court pronounced it good. So where a Portuguese boy of fourteen, domiciled in England, married his first cousin of sixteen, who, though temporarily living in England, retained her Portuguese domicile, the marriage was held good in England, although, by the law of Portugal, it was incestuous unless authorized by a Papal dispensation.

Where both parties are foreigners, with a foreign domicile, but the marriage is in England, the English Courts have jurisdiction to enquire into its validity. Where the marriage is void according to English law, our Courts will declare it to be so; but the Courts of no country hold a marriage bad, merely because the parties are the domiciled subjects of another country by whose laws they are under a personal incapacity to contract. Although the result may be that the parties are legally husband and wife in England, but in their own country are unmarried, such consequences do not concern us.

---

* NOTE TO s. 5.—As to forfeiture of property, where a valid marriage is procured by the false means mentioned in 4 Geo. IV., c. 76, see also 6 and 7 Will. IV, c. 85, s. 43; and 19 and 20 Vict., c. 119, as to marriages by Registrar; and 12 and 13 Vict., c. 68, s. 15, as to marriages abroad; and 7 and 8 Vict., c. 81, as to marriages in Ireland.

## CHAPTER III.

### EFFECT OF MARRIAGE UPON PERSONAL PROPERTY APART FROM A SETTLEMENT, AND APART FROM THE MARRIED WOMEN'S PROPERTY ACTS.

1. *Unity of husband and wife by the common law.*

2. *Rights conferred on husband and wife by the common law.*

3. *Most of the husband's common law rights abolished by the Married Woman's Property Acts.*

4. *Husband's common law rights to property of wife differed according as it was real or personal.*

5. *What real property is.*

6. *What personal property is.*

7. *The latter is either in possession, or in action, or reversion. Importance of the distinction.*

8. *Husband keept his own personal property in possession and takes absolutely his wife's.*

9. *Husband only took* choses in action, *and* in reversion, *by reducing them into possession, or selling to some one who does so.*

10. *Unless he had done so the property would belong to his wife on his death.*

11. *If husband survived wife her choses in action and reversion would belong to him on his taking out administration.*
*reversion will belong to him on his taking out administration.*

12. *Examples. Money due to the wife on bond. Her trust funds. Legacy.*

13. *Bankruptcy of husband no bar to wife's right by survivorship.*

14. *Debts due to wife and her reversionary interests. Malins's Act.*

15. *Wife's chattels in the hands of a third person.*

16. *What amounts to reduction into possession by husband.*

17. *Release by husband of debt due to wife.*

1. By the common law the husband and wife became one person, and so continued during the marriage. So

much were they one person, that a bequest to A. and B. his wife, and C., a stranger, in equal shares and proportions, was held to give only half the property to the married couple.*

2. By the common law certain rights were, on the mere fact of marriage, acquired by the husband and wife in one another's property. The wife acquired the right of dower out of all the estates of inheritance of which her husband died possessed, unless the right of dower had been barred. And the husband acquired absolutely all the personal property of the wife or the right to possess himself of it, the rents and profits of all her real property during the marriage, and the right to a life estate in the whole of it after her death if issue had been born of the marriage capable of inheriting. This life estate was called an estate by the courtesy of England, or briefly "by the courtesy." These rights of dower and courtesy will be again referred to.

The rights of the husband shortly above described are what the common law gave him, in relation to all property of the wife, except what was the subject of some settlement, or agreement for a settlement, between the man and his wife, or was derived to the wife through some gift, deed or will, whose words restricted the husband's dominion (see chapter xi).

3. These rights of the husband were very much modified by the Married Women's Property Act, 1870, and except as to "courtesy" wholly abolished by the M.W.P. Act, 1882, as regards property accruing to people marrying on or after the first of January, 1883.

The chief of those Acts are four known respectively as the Acts of 1870, 1874, 1882, and 1893. Further on will be found a Table in which I have endeavoured to shew in respect of what marriages and what property these Acts affect the rights of the husband.

But, inasmuch as, before any of these Acts were passed, husbands had by the favour of the common law, acquired rights in the property of their wives, it is

* And the same unity continues since the Married Women's Property Act, 1882 (see chap. ix., s. 1). *Re Jupp*, 39 Ch. D., 148 (but see *re Dixon*, 42 Ch. D., 306). *Re Gue*, W.N. (1892) 88.

proper to explain the rights of the man and the wife in property unaffected by any settlement—say briefly, "unsettled property"—and unaffected by the M. W. P. Acts.

4. Property is divided into two large classes, real and personal. The husband's rights over his wife's property differed according as it belonged to the one or to the other of these classes.

I propose in this chapter to treat only of the rights of man and wife in personal property, unsettled and unaffected by the M. W. P. Acts, and will deal in a subsequent chapter with the rights in real property, unsettled and unaffected as aforesaid.

But I must first explain carefully the difference between real and personal property.

5. Real property consists of all interests in land other than that which a lessee has in a lease.

It sometimes happens that a lessor who grants a lease holds the land under a lease himself, and then he and the lessee who holds under him have both of them only a personal estate in the land. If A holds land or houses for 1000 years at a penny rent, and underlets to B for 999 years at three half-pence, they have both nothing but personal estates in the land, and the only owner whose property in the land comes under the class *real* property, is that person whose descendants or assignees will be entitled to the land when A's 1000 years are expired.

Real property cannot be transferred by word of mouth and delivery as a chattel can; and if the owner dies without a will it descends to his *heir*, whoever he or she may be, instead of being distributed.

The only way in which it can ever be said to be distributed is when it descends to several daughters (or other female relatives of equal degree), who altogether make but one heir, and may part the land among them, or to sons or male heirs of equal degree in gavelkind, who share the land between them.*

6. Personal property consists of all moveable chattels, of money (whether in specie or in negociable securities or bonds, or invested in funds, railways, banks, joint-

* See note as to gavelkind lands, chap. iv. s. 9.

stock companies, or mortgages), and of lessees' interests in land held under leases, for however long a term, and at however small a rent.

The interests of the tenant who holds under that kind of lease for three years or less, usually called an agreement comes under this class of property.

Personal property, upon the owner dying and leaving a will, is vested in his executor, by whom it is employed in paying debts and bequests; and whatever is not disposed of by the will is distributed to the wife and among the next of kin of the deceased, according to their degree of relationship to him.

Where there is no will, the personal property of the deceased goes to the person who is appointed by the Court of Probate administrator of the deceased's personal estate, and it is then distributed and applied by him in the same manner as by the executor.

This distribution, and the payment of legacies, must in every case be preceded by the payment of debts.

Land built upon with houses is the same as land covered with grass or water. Whether the interest of a particular owner of the land comes under the class *real* or *personal* property, depends on the rules above given. The man who pays rent—however small—for it (except a quit-rent or a rent-charge), who holds it under a building lease for however many years, or the man who has bought it subject to a ground-rent, has in each case only a *personal* estate or interest in the land and the houses with which it may be covered. Whereas the man who has a freehold interest in it, whether to him and his heirs for ever, or only for the life of an old man of ninety, possesses a *real* estate in it. It is *personal* estate to the one, and *real* estate to the other (see chap. iv., sect. 2).

7. Personal property is further divided into things in possession and things not in possession, the latter being called in legal language *choses* (*i.e.* things) *in action*.

The former class, however, includes a great many things not in the actual manual custody of the owner, as, for instance, articles lent by the owner to others, or placed in the hands of others for repair or sale.

The latter class includes debts and arrears of rent

due, legacies, reversionary interests in personalty, the residuary personal estate of a testator, bequeathed and unpaid, trust funds, stock, balance at a bank, money on deposit, &c., and to these may be added bills of exchange and promissory notes; as to which, however, see sect. 12.

This distinction between personal property in possession and *choses in action*, is so important, that the reader will have to keep it continually in mind in order to understand the relative rights of husband and wife, which I am about to explain.

8. The personal property in possession and specific chattels in the hands of third parties, which, before the marriage, belonged to the *husband*, continue to belong to him after the marriage.

But all such chattels of the kinds above mentioned as belonged to the *wife* at the time of the marriage (except her wedding gifts which were always her separate property), and all that come to her since (excepts gifts from strangers of personal ornaments, apparel, and the like, which were always her separate property) belonged at common law, by virtue of the marriage exclusively to the husband. From the time of the marriage, or of the wife becoming possessed of such chattels, they belonged absolutely to the husband, just as much as if they had always been his.

And after her death they were, and still are, his without his taking out administration.

He might therefore sell, pawn, or leave them by will, as well during the life of his wife as after her death. And at *his* death, though his wife survived him, the property did not return to her but remained part of his estate, and she would only be entitled to such portion of it as was bequeathed to her, or if there were no will to the share which was given her by the law. And though the husband died without having got his wife's specific chattels into his own hands, out of the hands of third parties, such property would at his death form part of his personal estate.

This kind of property would still, on the wife's death, belong to the husband in his marital right and without his becoming her administrator.

Bills of exchange and promissory notes belonging to the wife had this resemblance to her chattels in possession, that instantly upon the marriage the husband alone could negociate and pass them away by indorsement. The wife was incapable of doing so. (See sect. 12).

The husband might transfer stock and shares standing in his wife's name to himself or any other person. (See sect. 12.)

The wife, however, might acquire a separate right to personal property during the marriage with the consent of her husband; but the most conclusive evidence would be required to show that he meant to give her the property out and out and exclude himself from all dominion over it. He could only do this either by transferring it to a trustee for her, or showing a clear definite intention to hold it in trust for her himself.

9. But while, by the mere fact of the marriage, the husband became, by law, possessed of all his wife's chattels in possession, from the date of the marriage or from the time when she acquired them, the law was different as regards her *choses in action.*

This term, though technical, is the only one we can use. It includes, as above stated, debts and arrears of rent due to the wife, her legacies, and the residuary personal estate bequeathed to her and unpaid, her trust funds, stock, balance at a bank, and money on deposit. It also includes bills of exchange and promissory notes of which she is the holder, but as to these the rules are practically of little importance. (See last preceding section).

Property of this kind the husband was entitled to reduce into his possession, and when he had done so, he was as absolutely entitled to it as if it had been originally his own. The marriage gave him the right of obtaining possession of his wife's *choses in action* by process of law or in any other lawful way, and so to make them his own as much as if they had always been his.

He might also assign them; and his assignee might, if he could reduce, them into possession.

10. If the wife survived the husband, and neither he nor his assignee had actually reduced the *choses in*

*action* into possession during his lifetime, the property would belong to the wife, and the assignee who had bought it would derive no benefit from his purchase.

Whether the wife consented to the sale, or actively promoted it, or signed the document by which the interest was transferred, is quite immaterial; her rights at her husband's death would be just the same. Whoever, therefore, purchased this kind of property, did so at the risk of losing his purchase if the wife survived the husband. But see next section.

11. But if the husband survived the wife, then the property would belong to him upon his being appointed her administrator, and if he had assigned the property the assignee's right to it would be good.

[There is a difference, it will be observed, between the wife's personal property in possession and her *choses in action*, in this respect, that, at her death, a grant of administration was necessary, as it still is, to vest the latter in the husband, but not the former.]

What amounts to a reducing of property into possession shall be afterwards explained; but here some examples shall be given to illustrate the law.

12. Suppose the wife was, at the time of her marriage, or afterwards became, entitled to a sum of money upon a bond; if the husband died in her lifetime without receiving the money or suing upon the bond, the bond and the money due on it formed no part of his estate and could not be bequeathed by his will, but remained absolutely the property of his wife as if she had never been married.

The receipt of interest by the husband made no difference. If he had wished to reduce the property into possession and was unable to get the principal, he might have taken a new bond to himself for whatever was due, and might have cancelled the other bond.

If the wife at her marriage possessed, or afterwards became possessed of Government stock, or a share in a company: whether placed in her own name or in that of a trustee for her, if the husband did not procure it to be transferred to him and placed in his name, it remained at his death the property of the wife as much as if she had never been married. (I am here speaking of the fund itself, not of the dividends, which, of course, the husband would be entitled to receive, unless the fund was settled to the wife's separate use (see chap. xi). At the husband's death the stock or share, if not reduced into possession, would be in the same predicament as the bond above mentioned. If the husband desired to reduce the property into his possession he must, if it stood in his wife's name, procure her to transfer it to him, or if it stood in the name of a trustee the husband had to get the trustee to transfer it to him; but, if the wife or the trustee refused, application had to be made to a Judge of a Court of Equity.

The same law as to the necessity of a reduction into possession by the husband applied to a legacy of personal property (not to her separate use), *whether in possession or reversion*, to which the wife might have become entitled, whether before or after marriage. Until it was paid, the husband's right to it was not perfected, and it would survive to the wife if he died first. If paid during the husband's lifetime it must of course be paid to him, for the wife's receipt would be no discharge, and if she had received the legacy without his consent he could make the executor pay him over again.

The above are only mentioned as examples of the general rule that if the wife's *choses in action* were not reduced into possession by the husband or the person to whom he had assigned them, they would survive to her if she lived the longer.

If the wife died first, the property would, as has been said, belong to her husband upon his obtaining a grant of administration.

Bills of exchange and promissory notes, whether in the hands of the wife at the time of the marriage or coming into her possession after, are *choses in action*, and were liable to the above rule. The rule was, however, of little importance, because the husband was held to have reduced the bill or note into possession by merely transferring it to another party.

Taking interest on an overdue bill or note would not be a reduction of the principal into possession. Receiving the value of the bill or note in money or goods, or by a renewal bill or note *to the husband*, would of course be a reduction into possession; so would bringing an action and issuing execution. But if the bill or note was not somehow reduced into possession it would be the exclusive property of the wife if she survived.

13. The right of the wife on surviving her husband to all her *choses in action* not actually reduced into possession by him or by a purchaser from him, was not interfered with by his having become bankrupt or having assigned his estate for the benefit of the creditors. The particular assignee who purchased of the husband, and the general assignee who came in by the operation of bankrupt laws, thus stood on the same footing, and neither of them interfered with the rights of the wife.

14. The cases where the husband assigned and neither he nor his assignee reduced the property into possession, and the wife survived the husband, so that the assignee got nothing, were mostly cases of reversionary interests in personal property, of which it was impossible to obtain possession until some prior interest in it had ended.

As, for instance, if a testator by his will directed that £1000 Consols should stand in the name of trustees upon trust to pay the dividends to his widow for life, and after her death to pay the principal to his daughter A. Here A would have a reversionary interest which, if she married, her husband might take when it fell in. But if he were to sell her interest under the will and then die, while the testator's widow was alive, neither the husband nor the purchaser could obtain a transfer of the stock, but it would remain the property of the wife. Whether it was through the testator's widow surviving A's husband (as in this case), or through the negligence of the latter or his assignee after the widow's death, that the property had not been obtained possession of, would not have mattered.

Hence the difficulty of getting anything like the value for this kind of property belonging to the wife, either by mortgaging, *i.e.* pledging it, or selling it out and out.

But by a statute called Malins's Act, a married woman is empowered with her husband's consent to dispose of any "future or reversionary interest, whether vested or contingent," which she, or her husband in her right, may have to any personal estate to which she may be entitled under any deed, will, or other instrument, made after the 31st December, 1857, and which did not restrain her right of alienation (see chap. xi). The disposition is to be made by a deed in which her husband concurs, and which the wife must acknowledge after being examined apart from him as in the case of a sale of her freehold estate. (See chap. iv., s. 12).

The Act does not apply to property settled, or agreed to be settled on her marriage.

A debt due to the wife might be in the same predicament as her reversionary interest. If, at the marriage, a sum were owing to the wife, whether upon written security or not, and the husband died in her lifetime, and before getting it in, he could not leave it by will, nor would his children be entitled to their share of it at his death, but it would survive to the widow.

15. But if the wife, when married or afterwards, owned a horse which was put out at grass in a neighbour's close, and the neighbour would not give up the horse to the husband till the grazing was paid for, and the husband refused to pay and died; this, not being a *chose in action* but a chattel in constructive (though not actual) possession (see sect. 8), would pass to the husband by the marriage and might be bequeathed by him to any one he pleased, subject to any lien the neighbour might have acquired. And if the husband left no will, the horse would form a part of his personal estate, of which his children, as well as his widow, would come in for their share.

16. Payment to the husband's attorney or agent of a debt due to the wife was the same as payment to the husband himself. But payment of interest was not equivalent to a reduction into possession, nor was receipt of a part equivalent to a reduction into possession of the whole.

Where the husband or his agent received money due to the wife, it would not be considered as reduced into possession by the husband unless it was taken by him in the exercise of his *exclusive control*, and without any view to having it kept in trust for the wife.

If the wife's *chose in action* was already vested in a trustee for her (as in the case of the stock above mentioned), the mere shifting the legal ownership from the trustee to the husband would not necessarily vest the beneficial ownership in the husband, but might simply leave him a trustee for his wife. There must have been evidence of an intention to deal with the property *as his own*, as by spending a portion of it, selling it out and re-investing it in another way, or transferring to a trustee upon other trusts such as would prevent his wife having a title by survivorship.

17. The husband might by deed (*i.e.* by writing under seal), *release* or relinquish a debt then actually due, in whatever way, to the wife.

# CHAPTER IV.

## EFFECT OF MARRIAGE UPON REAL PROPERTY (INCLUDING LEASES) APART FROM A SETTLEMENT, AND APART FROM THE 'MARRIED WOMEN'S PROPERTY ACTS.'

1. *Where there was no settlement, marriage of itself conferred rights as to land.*

2. *Landed property consists chiefly of estates of inheritance and life estates and* chattels real. *Definitions and examples.*

3. *As to chattels real. Husband's lease.*

4. *Wife's lease.*

5. *Wife's lease after her death.*

6. *Husband disposing by will of wife's lease.*

7. *Wife's next presentation to a living.*

8. *Husband's power of selling or mortgaging his wife's chattel real in his lifetime.*

9. *Freeholds. Husband's freeholds. Dower.*

10. *Wife's freeholds. Husband's right to them during her life. His tenancy by the courtesy.*

11. *His power of leasing.*

12. *Ultimate inheritance belongs to wife. Husband cannot sell without her consent. Acknowledgement.*

13. *Wife's freeholds descend to her heir at her death.*

1. I will now pursue with regard to landed property, the same plan as was adopted in the last chapter with respect to personal property, namely, to state the rights conferred by the marriage upon the husband and wife where the property in question stands unaffected by any settlement, or agreement for a settlement, between the husband and wife, or any restriction or qualification imposed by the person from whom the property was derived, and unaffected by the 'Married Women's Property Acts.' (See chaps. vii, viii, ix.)

# TABLE

## TO AID IN BRINGING TO VIEW THE EXTENT TO WHICH THE MARRIED WOMEN'S PROPERTY ACTS AFFECT AND HAVE AFFECTED THE PROPERTY AND LIABILITIES OF

# A WOMAN MARRIED

| I. At any time. | II. On or after 9th August, 1870, and before 1st January, 1883. | III. Between 9th Aug., 1870, and 30th July, 1874. | IV. On or after 30th July 1874, and before 1st January, 1883. | V. On or after 1st January, 1883. |
|---|---|---|---|---|
| 1. May acquire, hold and dispose of by will or otherwise, all real and personal property which the law permits her to acquire, as her separate property, and as if she were single, and without the intervention of a trustee.—Act of 1882, s. 1. (1).<br>2. May enter into (and make herself liable in respect of and to the extent of her separate property, present and future, on) any contract and may sue and be sued on contracts or for wrongs or otherwise as if single, and without her husband being joined as plaintiff or defendant, and may keep as her separate property all that she recovers and is liable to pay out of her separate property, but not otherwise, all that is recovered against her.—Act of 1882, s. 1. (2) (4). | | | | |

| | | | | |
|---|---|---|---|---|
| When she contracts, otherwise than as an agent, is deemed to contract so as to bind her present and future separate property, except what she is restrained from anticipating, and all property that she may have after the marriage is ended.—M. W. P. Act, 1893, s. 1.<br>3. If she, or a next friend on her behalf, brings an action, etc., is liable to pay costs awarded against her even out out of property which she is restrained from anticipating. *Ibid.*, s. 2.<br>4. If trading separately from her husband, is liable to the bankruptcy laws as if single.—Act of 1882, s. 1. (5).<br>5. May have and hold, and dispose of by will or otherwise, as her separate property, all real and personal property, her title to which, whether vested or contingent, and whether in possession, reversion, or remainder, accrues on or after 1st Jan., 1883, including any wages, earnings, money or property gained or acquired by her in any employment, trade, or occupation, in which she is engaged, or which she carries on separately from her husband, or by the exercise of any literary, artistic, or scientific skill.—Act of 1882, s. 5 (and see s. 2). | 5. Might take as her separate property all wages and earnings gained by her, after 9th Aug., 1870, in any employment, occupation, or trade in which she was engaged, or which she carried on, separately from her husband, and also any money, or property so acquired by her | | | 5. May have and hold, and dispose of by will or otherwise all real and personal property, her title to which accrues after marriage, or which she acquires after marriage. [This is given her by the Act of 1882, s. 2, the effect of which is set out in the first column in paragraph No. 5, |

leaving the lease to whomever he pleased, and then, if she happened to die before him, the will would take effect as if she had been dead when it was made, for all wills are treated (in respect of the property disposed of) as having been made immediately before the testator's death, unless the language used indicates a contrary intention.

All the rights of the husband as to his wife's chattels real are rendered obsolete by the Married Women's Property Act, 1882, and will only now apply where the marriage was before the first of January, 1883, and even then only to property the title to which accrued before that date.

7. With regard to the wife's next presentation to a living, severed from the advowson, the husband might present when a vacancy occurred, or might dispose of the next presentation during the lifetime of the present incumbent, and receive the purchase-money. At the death of either husband or wife the same rules applied to this kind of property as to a lease.

8. If the husband during his life agreed to dispose of his wife's chattel real for valuable consideration, the wife after his death would be bound by such agreement as much as the husband himself was.

The husband might dispose of a part of his wife's chattel real; for instance, in case of a lease, he might underlet a part of the lands reserving rent to himself, or he might underlet the whole for a portion of the term.

The husband might sell his wife's reversionary interest, whether contingent or not, in chattels real; and it mattered not that he died before the contingency took place or the reversion fell in.

The husband being able to sell, might, of course, mortgage his wife's chattel real; but after his death the equity of redemption survived to the wife, *i.e.*, the wife had the right to redeem.

If the husband had agreed to mortgage such property of his wife to secure a debt which he owed, the wife would after his death be bound to execute the mortgage or pay the money.

The wife's chattels real were liable to execution for the husband's debts.

entitled during her marriage under any deed or will, and her receipt alone would be a good discharge; but this was without prejudice to any settlement affecting the property.—Act of 1870, s. 7.

5. Might have to her separate use the rents and profits of any freehold, copyhold, or customaryhold property which descended upon her as heiress or coheiress of any intestate, and her receipts alone would be a good discharge, but this was without prejudice to any settlement affecting the property.—Act of 1870, s. 8.

TABLE—*Continued.*

| At any time. | On or after 9th August, 1870, and before 1st January, 1883. | Between 9th August, 1870, and 30th July, 1874. | On or after 30th July, 1874, and before 1st January, 1883. | On or after 1st January, 1883. |
|---|---|---|---|---|
| 6. May hold as her separate property;<br>(1.) All deposits in any bank ;<br>(2.) All annuities, by whomever granted ;<br>(3.) All sums forming part of the public stock or funds, or of any other stocks or funds transferable in the books of any bank ;<br>(4.) *All* shares, stock, debentures, debenture stock, or other interest of or in any corporation, company, or public body, municipal, commercial, or otherwise ;<br>(5.) *All* shares, etc., in any industrial, provident, friendly, benefit, building or loan society, which on 1st January, 1883, stood in her name, or which, after that day, are put into her sole name, and if they are put into her name jointly with any person or persons other | 6. Might have as her separate property.<br>(1.) Deposits in savings' banks and Post Office savings' banks, made after 9th August, 1870, in her name.<br>(2.) Annuities granted after that date by the Commissioners for the Reduction of the National Debt in her name.<br>(3.) Sums forming part of the public stocks or funds in England or Ireland.<br>(4.) *Fully paid* | | | |

than her husband, she may enjoy her part as her separate property. And the fact that any of these interests are put into her name raises the presumption, until the contrary is shewn, that they are her separate property, and that her separate property is solely liable in respect of them.—Act of 1882, ss. 6, 7, 8.

7. May transfer any such interest as is mentioned in the last preceding paragraph without her husband joining in the transfer.—Act of 1882, s. 9.

8. May effect a policy on her own feli or her husband's for her separate use and is entitled to the benefit of

*up* shares, debentures, debenture stock, or any stock of any incorporated or joint stock company *to the holding of which no liability is attached.*

(5.) Shares, benefits, debentures, rights, or claims *to the holding of which no liability is attached,* in, to, or upon the funds of any industrial etc. society (as in Act of 1882, see column 1).—Act of 1870, ss. 2, 3, 4, and 5.

TABLE—*Continued.*

| At any time. | On or after 9th August, 1870, and before 1st January, 1883. | Between 9th August, 1870, and 30th July, 1874. | On or after 30th July, 1874, and before 1st January, 1883. | On or after 1st January, 1883. |
| --- | --- | --- | --- | --- |
| any policy effected by her husband on his own life expressed to be for her benefit, and may effect a policy on her own life expressed to be for the benefit of her husband or her children, or both, so as to entitle those persons to the proceeds.—Act of 1882, s. 11, and see Act of 1870, s. 10.<br>9. May take in her own name, as if she were single, all civil and criminal remedies for the protection of her separate property, and against all persons including her husband, and both husband and wife may give evidence in any such proceeding;* but she must not proceed | | | | |

* And either husband or wife, except when defendant in a criminal proceeding, can be compelled by the other to give evidence. — Married Women's Property Act, 1884.

criminally against her husband while they are living together as to any property claimed by her, nor, while they are living apart, for any act of his done while they were living together concerning any property claimed by her, unless he wrongfully took it when leaving or deserting her, or when about to do so.—Act of 1882, s. 12.

10. Is liable to criminal proceedings for any act done by her to her husband's property, which, if done by him to her property, would render him liable to such proceedings under the Act of 1882.—Act of 1882, s. 16.

11. May sue and be sued as executrix, administratrix, or trustee, whether she is so alone or jointly with any other person, and may, in any of these capacities transfer or join in transferring any property of the sorts mentioned in sections 6, 7, and 8 of the Act of 1882.—Act of 1882, s. 18.

12. If she has separate property and her husband becomes chargeable as a pauper in England or Ire-

TABLE—*Continued.*

| At any time. | On or after 9th August, 1870, and before 1st January, 1883. | Between 9th August, 1870, and 30th July, 1874. | On or after 30th July, 1874, and before 1st January 1883. | On or after 1st January, 1883. |
|---|---|---|---|---|
| land, is liable for his maintenance out of her separate property.—Act of 1882, s. 20.<br>13. If she has separate property, is as liable as her husband is by law for the maintenance of her children and grandchildren.—Act of 1882, s. 21.<br>14. Leaves her executor or administrator with the same rights and liabilities in respect of her separate estate as she herself has, and subject to the same jurisdiction as she was subject to. (This is the jurisdiction provided by s. 17 of the Act of 1882, for settling questions as to whether property belongs to husband or to wife.)—Act of 1882, s. 23.<br>15. Is liable to answer out of her separate property for any breach of duty committed by her before or | | | | |

| | | | |
|---|---|---|---|
| after marriage, as trustee, executrix, or administratrix, and her husband is not liable unless he has intermeddled in the trust or administration.—Act of 1882, s. 24.<br>16. If she lends or entrusts money or other property to her husband, is not allowed to take a dividend, in case of his bankruptcy, till all other creditors for value are satisfied, and the money or property will be treated as part of the estate of the bankrupt husband.—Act of 1882, s. 3.<br>17. By the execution of a general power of appointment by will, makes the property so appointed answerable after her death for her liabilities.—Act of 1882, s. 4.<br>18. Is liable for antenuptial debts, contracts and wrongs to the extent of any separate property to which she becomes entitled by virtue of the Act of 1882, and which she would not have been entitled to but for that Act ; and, as between her and her husband, if there be no agreement between them to the contrary, such separate property | 18. Is solely liable to be sued for her debts contracted before marriage (if the remedies for such debts are still alive) and her separate property is solely answerable for | 18. Is liable to be sued alone or jointly with her husband for all debts contracted by her and wrongs and breaches of contract committed by her before marriage (if the | 18. May be sued alone for debts contracted, and contracts entered into, and wrongs committed by her before her marriage, including her liability as contributory in a Joint Stock Com- |

TABLE—*Continued.*

| At any time. | On or after 9th August, 1870, and before 1st January, 1883. | Between 9th August, 1870, and 30th July, 1874. | On or after 30th July, 1874, and before 1st January, 1883. | On or after 1st January, 1883. |
|---|---|---|---|---|
| will be primarily liable for such debts, etc. She may be sued alone or jointly with her husband, and in the latter case his liability will be restricted as stated in column V., paragraph 18. | | them.—Act of 1870 s. 12. | remedies for such debts are still alive) and must answer out of any separate property which she has, or acquires; but her husband, if sued, is only liable to the extent of any property of hers which has vested in him, or which he has got in, or might with reasonable diligence have got in, or which the wife, in contemplation of marriage with him, has transferred to him or any other person, and the | pany, whether before or after she is placed on the list, and for any liability in damages or otherwise, under any such contract or for any such wrong, and her separate property is answerable for what is recovered against her, and, as between her and her husband, is primarily liable, unless there is a contract between them to the contrary.—Act of 1882, s. 13.<br>18. May be sued |

| | |
|---|---|
| husband is entitled to take credit for any debts of hers which he has paid after marriage and for any judgment already obtained against him in any such action for any such debt.—Act of 1874. | jointly with her husband in respect of the matters mentioned in the last preceding paragraph, and her separate property will be liable for them; but her husband will only be liable to the extent of the property of hers which he shall have acquired or become entitled to through her after deducting any such debts, etc., which he has paid, and any judgments recovered against him for such debts, etc.—Act of 1882 s.s. 14.15.<br>19. Is disabled from protecting her separate property from answering her debts contracted |

TABLE—*Continued.*

| At any time. | On or after 9th August, 1870, and before 1st January, 1883. | Between 9th August, 1870, and 30th July, 1874. | On or after 30th July, 1874, and before 1st January, 1883. | On or after 1st January, 1883. |
|---|---|---|---|---|
| | | | | before marriage, by means of any clause in restraint of anticipation inserted in any settlement or agreement for a settlement of such property entered into by herself. — Act of 1882, s. 19. |

7. The several rights and liabilities are classified by numbers so as to facilitate a comparison where they are altered in the different periods.

It will be observed that most of the enactments of the Act of 1882, apply to married women irrespective of the dates of their marriages.

The rights marked five and six in the second column are spoken of in the past tense because, if the property accrues, or is acquired after the 1st of January, 1883, the wife's rights are now enlarged; see paragraph 5 in first and in last column.

The liabilities marked eighteen in columns, 3 and 4 are of little moment now because, from the lapse of time, most of them will be barred.

The Act of 1882 is printed by way of appendix, but the other two Acts are not set out at length, because their operation has almost wholly ceased.

The Acts of 1882 and 1893 are printed by way of appendix, but the other two Acts are not set out at length, because their operation has almost wholly ceased.

# TABLE

## TO AID IN BRINGING TO VIEW THE EXTENT TO WHICH THE MARRIED WOMEN'S PROPERTY ACTS AFFECT AND HAVE AFFECTED THE PROPERTY AND LIABILITIES OF

# A WOMAN MARRIED

| I. At any time. | II. On or after 9th August, 1870, and before 1st January, 1883. | III. Between 9th Aug., 1870, and 30th July, 1874. | IV. On or after 30th July 1874, and before 1st January, 1883. | V. On or after 1st January, 1883. |
|---|---|---|---|---|
| 1. May acquire, hold and dispose of by will or otherwise, all real and personal property which the law permits her to acquire, as her separate property, and as if she were single, and without the intervention of a trustee.—Act of 1882, s. 1. (1).<br>2. May enter into (and make herself liable in respect of and to the extent of her separate property, present and future, on) any contract and may sue and be sued on contracts or for wrongs or otherwise as if single, and without her husband being joined as plaintiff or defendant, and may keep as her separate property all that she recovers and is liable to pay out of her separate property, but not otherwise, all that is recovered against her.—Act of 1882, s. 1. (2) (4). | | | | |

| | | | |
|---|---|---|---|
| When she contracts, otherwise than as an agent, is deemed to contract so as to bind her present and future separate property, except what she is restrained from anticipating, and all property that she may have after the marriage is ended.—M. W. P. Act, 1893, s. 1.<br>3. If she, or a next friend on her behalf, brings an action, etc., is liable to pay costs awarded against her even out out of property which she is restrained from anticipating. *Ibid.*, s. 2.<br>4. If trading separately from her husband, is liable to the bankruptcy laws as if single.—Act of 1882, s. 1. (5).<br>5. May have and hold, and dispose of by will or otherwise, as her separate property, all real and personal property, her title to which, whether vested or contingent, and whether in possession, reversion, or remainder, accrues on or after 1st Jan., 1883, including any wages, earnings, money or property gained or acquired by her in any employment, trade, or occupation, in which she is engaged, or which she carries on separately from her husband, or by the exercise of any literary, artistic, or scientific skill.—Act of 1882, s. 5 (and see s. 2). | 5. Might take as her separate property all wages and earnings gained by her, after 9th Aug., 1870, in any employment, occupation, or trade in which she was engaged, or which she carried on, separately from her husband, and also any money, or property so acquired by her | | 5. May have and hold, and dispose of by will or otherwise all real and personal property, her title to which accrues after marriage, or which she acquires after marriage. [This is given her by the Act of 1882, s. 2, the effect of which is set out in the first column in paragraph No. 5, |

in the property, the trustee, whether stranger or husband, had to convey the legal estate or interest, or give the manual possession to that person on demand. And now, under the Act, where the property is vested by gift or settlement in a trustee, and the wife disposes of it to a third person, the trustee will still either have to convey or hand over the property to that person, or hold it as a trustee for him. If no trustee, however, is named in the settlement or the gift, or if the wife acquires, as her own, property which is not already held by a trustee, her husband no longer becomes a constructive trustee for her, and when she disposes of the property it passes straight to the recipient as if coming from a man or an unmarried woman.

2. The 2nd sub-section has to do with a wife's power to sue and to make herself liable. It enables her to sue and be sued "in contract, *tort* or otherwise," and these words include every sort of action that can be brought. *Tort* means *wrong*, and so the wife can sue and be sued in actions on contracts, or for wrongs, and every other sort of action. And, whether she is plaintiff or defendant, her husband need not be joined. Whatever she recovers is to be her separate property, and whatever is recovered against her must be paid out of her separate property. The wife may, therefore, sue alone for an injury done to her person or her property; but the power here given does not take away the husband's right to bring an action for an injury done to his wife, joining her as co-plaintiff, and to recover damages for his own loss of her society and services, arising from the injury.

Sub-sections (3) and (4) are repealed by the Married Women's Property Act, 1893, the first section of which replaces them by an enactment which gets rid of certain difficulties that had arisen under them. This section relates to every contract entered into after the 5th of December, 1893, by a married woman *otherwise than as an agent*, which latter words will again be referred to. It says that contracts made by the married woman *not* as an agent are—(1) To bind her separate property, whether at the time she is entitled to any or not; (2)

to bind all that she shall in the future become entitled to; and (3) to be enforceable against all property that she may have after the marriage is ended, and which of course cannot be called "separate." And the section ends with a proviso protecting from such liability all the property which is separate and is subject to a "restraint on anticipation," an expression to be explained further on in this chapter.

There is one thing, however, for which even such separate property as is subject to this restraint may be made liable by the Court's order, and this is (by s. 2) for the costs of the person against whom the married woman, or a next friend on her behalf, has unsuccessfully instituted a legal proceeding, or to which that person has become entitled in the course of a proceeding.

3. The repealed sub-section (3) said that every contract entered into by a married woman should be deemed to be a contract entered into by her with respect to and to bind her separate property, *unless the contrary were shewn*, and the Act of 1893 says that every contract entered into by a married woman *otherwise than as an agent*, shall be deemed, etc. In other words, when a married woman makes a contract, not as an agent, it is to bind her separate property.

No favour is done to the wife by the insertion of the words about agency, for no one is liable on contracts when he makes them only for another, and so expresses himself by speech or writing, according as the contract is verbal or written.

The person for whom the wife is oftenest agent is her husband, and there are few wives who are not agents for their husbands in domestic affairs. Some wives are also agents for their husbands in business matters, and may buy, sell, warrant, give credit, engage and discharge business servants, and draw and accept bills in his name. A married woman may also be an agent, with authority more or less extensive, for a third person in business, and often is so in housekeeping.

A married woman may also be appointed, by her husband or by a stranger, an agent for a special purpose, as to execute a deed or to settle claims or make a particular purchase, in which case the appointment will usually be in writing, and must also be by deed if it is to authorize the execution of a deed.

Where the wife is acting in the management of the domestic affairs usually entrusted to a wife, she will be presumed to be acting as the husband's agent, and, unless there is evidence that she is acting on her own account, a judgment will not be obtained against her on an ordinary housekeeping contract. But the *extent* of her agency may come into question when she orders articles unsuited to her condition in life or to the economy in which her husband makes it his rule to live.

When acting in the ordinary course of housekeeping, the married woman need not proclaim that she is only an agent, but must take care not to say that she is acting on her own account. In dealings beyond this range, especially with persons who are not aware of her extended agency, it will be wise for the married woman to tell the person with whom she is dealing that she is not acting for herself, but as agent for her husband or other principal, and, if writing is employed, she should sign her contracts, letters, or other communications either with her principal's name, adding *per*, followed by her own name, or with her own name, adding, "on behalf of," or "as agent only for," followed by the name of her principal.

If, however, she has contracted in her own name, but really for her husband or some other person, she is, as between herself and that person, only an agent, and that person, as her principal, is bound to indemnify her from liability.

It was proper to say so much here on the subject of agency, but it is treated of more fully in chapters XII. and XIII., in connection with the liabilities incurred by the husband through the wife.

4. Nothing in the Act of 1882 or the Act of 1893 imposes any restriction on the wife's liability for wrongs, independent of contract. If, therefore, a wife is sued for such a wrong committed by her before marriage, and judgment is given against her, any property which

she may have in the present or the future, unless it be subject to the restraint on anticipation, will be liable to answer the judgment. And the like result will follow if judgment is obtained against her for a like wrong committed by her after marriage. For this her husband is also liable, as he was before the Acts, to the extent of all his property; for, it is said, the Acts were not intended for the relief of husbands.

The nature of a liability for a wrong, as distinguished from a liability on contract, may, without attempting a definition, be brought to view by naming as examples such wrongs as defamation of character, assault, trespasses to land and to goods, stopping up another's watercourse, injuring the support to his house, or causing him injury by negligent driving, etc. These are acts which are seldom breaches of any contract, but there are circumstances under which it is hard to say whether an act is a breach of contract, or a wrong independent of it, and there are some acts which may be both.

Before the M. W. P. Acts, the husband could obtain a decree against his wife in respect of her separate estate for breach of a contract made with him by which she intended to bind such estate. The Acts do not deprive him of this right and he may sue his wife for money which he has lent her after marriage, and for money which he has paid for her after marriage, upon a request made by her either before or after marriage.

Returning to the first section of the Act of 1882, sub-section 5 says that a wife carrying on a trade separately from her husband, shall, in respect of her separate property, be subject to the bankruptcy laws as if she were a single woman. Before the Act, a wife could not be made bankrupt at all, except where she was carrying on a separate trade according to the custom of London, or where her husband was in exile, or had been transported, or where she lived apart from her husband under a judicial separation or a protection order. And she can only now be made a bankrupt if she carries on a *trade*, and does so separately from her husband. This does not mean her living in a separate house or ceasing to cohabit; and, if her husband is not concerned in the trading and does not interfere with the business "more than you would naturally expect a person to do who was living in the house, and in the relation of husband to the person who was carrying it on," his living with her does not prevent the trade being a separate one.

Throughout the Act the wife's separate property means that which, if she were single, would be her property, and so does not include property over which she has a general power of appointment. (See remarks on sec. 4 of the Act below.)

6. Sections 2 and 5 should have been put together. The former gives to the wife who is married on or after the 1st of January, 1893, as her separate property, almost every kind of property which she has at marriage or gets afterwards. The latter section gives to a wife married *before* the 1st of January, 1893, all the same kinds of property, her title to which accrues or which she gets *after* that date.

The words of section 5 are "her title to which, whether vested or contingent, and whether in possession, reversion, or remainder, shall accrue after the commencement of this Act." This will seldom apply to earnings, but has to do with other personal property and real property. There have been a great many disputes about these words. If a wife is entitled, under a will, to a sum of money on the return of some one from India, her title is "contingent"; if she is entitled on the ending of a lease, her title is usually a "reversion," and if her father left his land to his widow and after her death to his daughter, the married woman, her title would be one in "remainder." Now it is clear that her title to each of the properties in question can accrue at two times; one when the right is given her, and the other when the event happens on which she is entitled to enjoyment. So, when a woman was married before the Act, having any of these rights, but the event on which she could enter into the enjoyment of them did not happen till after the Act, the question arose whether she was entitled to the property for her separate use by reason of the event happening after the Act. The creditor, who wanted to make the property answerable for her obligations contended that the title had "accrued" after the Act. But the Courts have decided that where before the Act the woman being already married, acquired a title, whether vested or contingent, and whether in reversion or remainder, to any propetty, such property is not made her separate estate under sec. 5, by its falling into possession after the Act.

7. Under section 3, if the husband becomes bankrupt, any money which his wife has lent to him, and any property which she has entrusted to him, for the purpose of any trade or business carried on by him or otherwise, is to be treated as assets in his bankrupt estate, and the wife can get no dividend till every other creditor for value has been paid in full.

Where the wife seeks to prove against the estate of her bankrupt husband for money lent, the burden is upon her to show that it was not lent for the purpose of his trade or business, and, failing this, she cannot prove or vote till all the other creditors for value have been paid 20s. in the pound. No importance seems to be attached to the words "or otherwise."

This section does not apply where the wife lent the money before marriage and married her debtor, for that would not be lending money "to her husband." Nor does the section prevent a wife, who has lent money to her husband, proving upon his estate if he dies insolvent without being made bankrupt. Estates of deceased insolvents, it is true, are administered like bankrupt estates (see Judicature Act, 1875, sec. 10); but the money lent by the wife to the husband is not made assets of his estate when he dies intestate and insolvent without being made bankrupt.

Nor, if the husband is a member of a trading firm which becomes bankrupt, is the wife prevented from proving against the *joint* estate, on an equal footing with the other creditors, for money which she has lent to the *firm*.

The wife lending money to her husband to be used in

his business appears to be just in the same position by the section as by the Partnership Act, 1890, a person is placed who lends money to one who is engaged in a trade or undertaking on the footing of being repaid by a share of the profits. In both cases the lender is postponed to other creditors for value. But, inasmuch as in the latter case, the creditor who has taken a mortgage on the terms of receiving a share of profits, is not deprived by the Act of the security of his mortgage, it is presumed that a wife who has taken a mortgage to secure a loan to her husband to be used in his business, may retain a mortgaged property, though she cannot prove along with the other creditors for the debt.

8. Section 4 enacts that, where a married woman by her will exercises a *general* power of appointment, the property so appointed is answerable after her death for her liabilities in the same way as her separate estate is. A general power of appointment is where, under a will, gift, or settlement, the married woman has power given her to appoint the person who is to take the property in question, and to appoint whom she pleases. When she does this, the property is as much under her power to leave by will as what was her own, and so is made answerable for claims on her estate. But property over which she has a general power of appointment to be exercised by deed or will, does not become her separate property on her bankruptcy; so she cannot be compelled to execute the power in favour of the trustee of her bankrupt estate for the benefit of her creditors.

9. As to the stocks, funds, shares, etc., mentioned in sections 6, 7, and 8, it is to be observed that they are presumed to be the separate property of the wife alone, if they stand in her sole name, and to be her property jointly with another person or persons, if they stand in the joint names. The burden of proving that these investments are not the property of the woman lies upon the person who disputes her title. These sections apply to such investments whether made by the woman herself or by a stranger, or by her husband; unless indeed the husband has put the share fund, etc., in the joint names of himself and his wife, when the Courts will regard it

as only an "advancement" or gift to her in the event of her surviving him.

The Courts will compel a joint-stock company or other corporation to register a transfer to a married woman of any share or stock to the holding of which no liability is attached; at all events where a married woman is not excluded from such a right by the constitution of the corporation.

Section 9, rendering it unnecessary for the husband to join in transferring any stocks, funds, shares, etc., standing in the name of his wife, or of his wife and another, needs no comment.

10. By section 10, if the wife makes any investment in any stocks, funds, shares, or any other of the things mentioned in secs. 6, 7, and 8, with the moneys of the husband without his consent, the Court may order such investment to be transferred, and the dividends thereof or any part thereof, to be paid to the husband. This can be done, the section says, on an application under sec. 17, and the only property spoken of is that mentioned in secs. 6, 7, and 8, but sec. 17 gives power to the Court to settle *all* questions between husband and wife as to the title to or possession of property in general. Under that section, the husband can claim any property which the wife has, without his consent, bought with his moneys, and the wife can claim any property which the husband has, without her consent, bought with her moneys.

Sec. 10 goes on to say that any gift by the husband to the wife of any property which the husband afterwards keeps in his "order and disposition" or his "reputed ownership," and any investment by the husband in his wife's name in fraud of his creditors, shall be invalid, and the property may be followed. The wife being by sec. 4, equally liable to the bankruptcy laws if she carries on a separate trade, the same rule, it is presumed, would apply if she made gifts to her husband in fraud of her creditors.

The invalidity of the gifts and investments here referred to had already, as the statute implies, been established by law; and indeed any gift by a person largely indebted at the time was liable to be set aside as being void as against creditors under the statute 13 Eliz. c. 5.

11. Apart from the claims of creditors, however, there is nothing to prevent either husband or wife making gifts or conveying property to the other. By the Conveyancing Act of 1881, either may execute conveyances of freehold land and may make assurances of "things in action" to the other, either alone or jointly with another person. A "thing in action" or *chose in action* has already been explained in chap. iii. s. 9. As the same section of the Act empowers a person to convey to himself jointly with any other person —which in some cases he could do before—it is presumed that a husband can convey property direct to himself and his wife, and a wife can convey property direct to herself and her husband.

But money and chattels pass by delivery without any writing at all, and either husband or wife can make a good gift of these to the other, if the rights of creditors do not interfere.

The wife may, without any writing, give to the husband any money or chattels which she is at liberty to dispose of as her separate property; nay, if she merely allows her money to be paid into his banking account, or allows him to receive it and spend it on his household or in his business, her intention to give it to him will be presumed, and she cannot after his death claim it against his executor. Nay, even where moneys belonging to the wife's separate estate were due from a person to whom her husband owed money, and she allowed the money to be set off against her husband's debt, this was regarded as a payment to the husband with the wife's consent, and, therefore, a gift by her to him.

12. By section 11, the husband may effect a policy of insurance on his own life for the benefit (1) of his wife, or (2) of his children, or (3) of his wife and children, or any of them; and the wife may effect a policy on her own life for the benefit (1) of her husband, or (2) of her children, or (3) of her husband and her children, or any of them.

Nothing is said in the Act to require the children who are to benefit by the policy to be the children of the marriage, and I presume the husband and wife may each provide for the wife and husband respectively, coupled with the children of the insured by another marriage, or for the latter only. The intention that the policy is for the benefit of the husband, wife, children, or husband and children, or wife and children, must be expressed on the policy itself, and, if the insured desires to confine the benefit to certain children, or to define the shares which each person is to take, it should be expressed on the policy itself.

If the policy is expressed to be "for the benefit of any wife, and also of any children or child who may survive" the insured, it is held that the wife and children will take jointly, that is, will enjoy the property equally among them, the survivors benefiting by the death of any of the number. Both as to policy moneys, and other property, the rule is that a gift to a parent and the children of a parent creates a joint interest. It is true the Act makes the widow's interest separate property; but this makes no difference, for where the gift was to the widow and children, the widow taking for her separate use, she was treated as taking jointly with the children, and the words "separate use" were regarded as applying to her share.

If, therefore, the husband or wife effecting the policy desires that the other parent shall take an unequal share of the fund, or shall have the income of the whole for life, it is important to have this expressed on the policy.

13. Sections 12 and 16 may be taken together. The former gives the wife the right to proceed civilly and to proceed criminally against all persons, including (subject to certain qualifications) her husband, "for the protection of her own separate property." For an injury to her separate property, she may, therefore, bring an action or prefer an indictment, according as the injury is an actionable wrong or a criminal offence. But she must not proceed in either way against her husband *by virtue of this Act*, while they are living together, nor

while they are living together, nor while they are living apart for anything done by him about the property while they were living together, unless it was done in the course of leaving or deserting her. These exceptions only apply to proceedings taken by the wife by virtue of this Act, and so she is free, although living with her husband, to proceed criminally for any assault or graver breach of the peace, though her property may have been injured as well as herself, and also to sue for an injunction against threatened loss or injury, as she might have done before the Act.

The words, "except as aforesaid, no husband or wife shall be entitled to sue the other for a *tort*" (or wrong) are puzzling, because nothing was said before those words as to a husband suing his wife at all. The husband's right to proceed against the wife is not mentioned till afterwards in sec. 16, and the words in question can hardly mean that the wife may sue the husband for a wrong in respect of her separate property, but that the husband must not sue her for any *tort* whatever. I presume the words were intended to mean "save as concerns property, while of the wife or husband, neither may sue the other for a wrong;" but there is no provision for such an action by a husband against a wife.

Section 16 empowers the husband to proceed criminally against the wife for any act done by her to his property which, if done by him to her property, would lay him open to criminal proceedings "under this Act." A wife may now, therefore, be guilty of a larceny of her husband's chattels, and a malicious injury to both his real and his personal property.

Before the statute this could not be, for the criminal courts regarded the husband and wife as being one with regard to property, and so, if the wife took away her husband's property and deprived him of it, it was not larceny, nor was it larceny in the person who assisted her. Where there have been convictions for larceny for assisting her, it has been in cases of adultery where the paramour stole, so to speak, the wife and the husband's property together, and knew that he was doing so. In any such criminal proceeding against a husband or a wife as is authorized by the Married Women's Property Act, 1882, the husband and wife, respectively, are competent and admissible witnesses, and, except when defendant, compellable to give evidence. (M. W. P. Act, 1884, 47 Vict. c. 14, s. 1.)

14. Sections 13, 14, and 15 have to do only with the liability of the wife for debts incurred, contracts entered into, and wrongs committed by her before marriage, and with the husband's liability for the same to the extent of any property of hers which he has acquired or become entitled to through her, after deducting any payments he has made, and any judgments *bonâ fide* recovered against him in respect of such liabilities of his wife.

The liabilities of the wife arising before marriage are all that need to be provided for; because after marriage, she is, by sec. 1, liable as if she were single to the extent of her separate property, for all her debts and contracts, and for all wrongs she may commit.

It is hardly necessary to point out, that separate property, and the restraint on anticipation which may be attached to it, are impossible except during marriage. And the woman's liability for debts incurred before marriage, and for wrongs committed by her before marriage, extends to all her property before marriage, and, after marriage, to all that she can dispose of.

These sections are valuable as exempting the husband from the burden arising from the wife's shares in a joint-stock company which is being wound up; an exemption which the former M. W. P. Acts did not contain. The wife's debts as a contributory, whether before or after she is is put on the list of contributories, are now borne by her separate estate. Under the former Acts, coupled with the Companies' Acts, the husband could not escape iability if the wife was put on the list after marriage.

The proviso at the end of sec. 13 preserves the iabilities of wives married before the 1st of January, 1883, as they stood under the former Acts; but still these wives would be liable to the extent of all their property which by this Act is made their separate property. (See the Table). This, however, is of little importance now as most of these liabilities are either satisfied or barred by lapse of time.

Sec. 14 contains the limitation of the husband's responsibility for the liabilities of his wife arising before marriage, as already mentioned, but the proviso at the end preserves the liabilities of a husband married before the Act, as they stood. This is now of little importance owing to the lapse of time.

The 15th section is only concerned with the action which a person, having a claim against the wife arising before her marriage, whether on contract or for a wrong, brings against the husband and wife, when the plaintiff chooses to sue the two together. He is not bound to sue any one but the wife, who, by sec. 1, is subject to be sued alone, whether for a contract or for a wrong, and whose separate property is responsible. The plaintiff will be very foolish to sue the husband unless there is good ground for supposing that he has become entitled to property of the wife, over and above what he has paid or is liable, under judgment, to pay for her antenuptial liabilities. Whether the wife has or has not sufficient separate property, present or in expectation, to satisfy the debt, the effect of suing the husband unsuccessfully will be to saddle the plaintiff with the husband's costs.

To enable the husband, in estimating his liability, to take credit for a judgment, the Act requires the judgment to have been recovered *bona fide*; but it is easy for the husband to protect himself by a friendly judgment, and hard for the creditor to find out whether the judgment is obtained in good faith or not.

The joint action against the husband and wife may be continued against either after the death of the other, but the husband, unless he is the wife's personal representative, cannot be sued alone after the death of the wife. (See ch. xvii., s. 9).

Sec. 23 of the Act of 1882 says that, for the purposes of the Act, the legal personal representative of the married woman shall, in respect of her separate estate, have the same rights and liabilities as she would have had if living. This representative would be her executor or administrator, but the term is said to include her husband, though he is neither, if by virtue of his marital right he has taken the chattels or the leasehold of his deceased wife; in which case he is liable to the extent of this property of hers for her debts incurred either before or after marriage unless the remedy for them is barred. (1891) 1 Q.B. 491. As to his marital right to chattels, see ch. III., s. 8, and to leases, ch. IV., s. 5.

The action against the wife may, of course, be continued against her executor or administrator, and her separate property made liable in his hands, and, by sec. 23, it would seem if the action be not commenced in the wife's lifetime, her executor or administrator may be sued and be answerable to the extent of the deceased wife's separate property.

15. A special mode is provided by sec. 17 for deciding disputes between husband and wife "as to the title to or possession of property." The disputes are to be decided in a summary way by summons before a judge. The summons is a writing directing the other party to appear before the judge, and show cause why the property should not be handed over to the possession of, or treated as belonging to, the party issuing the summons. Both parties, or their solicitors, or counsel, then attend before the Judge at his chamber, or, if he thinks fit, in his private room, and he hears the evidence, usually on affidavit, adjourns the case if necessary for further evidence, and, when all is before him, makes an order as to the property. The judge may be either a judge of the High Court or of the County Court in England, or of the High Court or of a Civil Bill Court in Ireland, according as the property is in England or Ireland. The order made by any of these judges is subject to appeal, and from the County Court judge or the judge of the Civil Bill Court, the case may be removed by the respondent party where the property in question exceeds the amount over which those courts have jurisdiction.

By sec. 23, the executor or administrator of a deceased wife may obtain such a summons, or may be directed to appear upon one, and enjoys the same rights, and is subject to the same jurisdiction as the wife when alive.

If the dispute relates to any stock, funds, shares, or deposit in any company, etc., the latter may issue the summons requiring the husband and wife to attend for the settlement of the question.

16. Sec. 18 is concerned with a wife being executrix or administratrix; that is, being named in a will and appointed by the Court of Probate as the person to execute the testator's wishes, or being the person appointed by the same Court to administer the estate where the deceased person has died without a will, or where there is no executor. The section also relates to the wife being a trustee, which she may become, either under a will, or a deed, or other writing, or by word of mouth, or by operation of law without a word written or said.

A married woman could always be a trustee and, with the consent of the husband, could always accept the office of executrix or administratrix. And a single woman who had become trustee, would remain so after marriage, and, if she had accepted either of the offices above mentioned, would continue to hold it after marriage.

But the appointment of a married woman as trustee, executrix, or administratrix, was attended with inconvenience, because her husband, being liable for her breaches of trust or duty, had a control over her acts and over personal property vested in her in any of these fiduciary capacities. The personal property in fact passed into his legal ownership, and could not be dealt with without his concurrence. The husband was joined with his wife as defendant in any proceeding for a breach of trust or duty on her part, and was individually liable to make it good.

To avoid both these difficulties, sec. 18 enacts that the wife who is trustee, executrix, or administratrix, alone or jointly with another or others, may sue and be sued in those capacities, and may, without her husband and as if she were single, transfer or join in transferring the annuities, stocks, funds, shares, etc., referred to in the section as "aforesaid," meaning those mentioned in secs. 7, 8, and 9.

Section 18 does not authorise the wife to deal, without her husband's concurrence, with any other personal property, such as leases and chattels, vested in her in a fiduciary crpacity; an omission for which there is the less reason as not only can she be sued alone, and therefore be put to trouble through her husband's refusal to concur, but, by section 24, her husband is exempted from liability for her breaches of trust unless he has acted or intermeddled.

The wife's power to deal with estates of inheritance, and life estates vested in her as trustee, is left wholly untouched by the Act. These she must convey as heretofore by an acknowledged deed (see chap. IV., sec. 12) in which her husband concurs, unless she is a "bare trustee," in which case, by the Vendor's and Purchaser's Act, 1874, sec. 6, she may convey or surrender as if she were single. Lawyers are not quite agreed as to what a "bare trustee" is, but such a person may be roughly described as a trustee with no duty to perform, and who holds the legal estate at the disposal of some person absolutely entitled, who may demand a conveyance. It is true that, by secs. 2 and 5, the wife, whether married before or after the Act, may acquire, hold, and dispose of as her separate property, all real and personal property; but "separate property" means that in which she is beneficially interested, and can hardly be held to apply to trust property, in which she is not beneficially interested.

The Act does not expressly say that a wife may accept the office of executrix or administratrix without her husband's consent.

17. In connection with sec. 18 let us consider sec. 24, which ought not to have been separated from it. Sec. 24 contains what is both puzzling and important. It says the word "contract" in the Act, is to include the acceptance of any trust, or of the office of executrix or administratrix, and the provisions as to the wife's liability are to extend to any breach of trust or waste of trust property committed by her before or after marriage, as trustee, executrix, or administratrix.

Again, the husband is not to be liable for the wife's breaches of trust, whether committed before or *after* marriage, unless he has intermeddled. But, for all particular purchase, in which case the appointment will usually be in writing, and must also be by deed if it is to authorize the execution of a deed.

Where the wife is acting in the management of the domestic affairs usually entrusted to a wife, she will be presumed to be acting as the husband's agent, and, unless there is evidence that she is acting on her own account, a judgment will not be obtained against her on an ordinary housekeeping contract. But the *extent* of her agency may come into question when she orders articles unsuited to her condition in life or to the economy in which her husband makes it his rule to live.

When acting in the ordinary course of housekeeping, the married woman need not proclaim that she is only an agent, but must take care not to say that she is acting on her own account. In dealings beyond this range, especially with persons who are not aware of her extended agency, it will be wise for the married woman to tell the person with whom she is dealing that she is not acting for herself, but as agent for her husband or other principal, and, if writing is employed, she should sign her contracts, letters, or other communications either with her principal's name, adding *per*, followed by her own name, or with her own name, adding, "on behalf of," or "as agent only for," followed by the name of her principal.

If, however, she has contracted in her own name, but really for her husband or some other person, she is, as between herself and that person, only an agent, and that person, as her principal, is bound to indemnify her from liability.

It was proper to say so much here on the subject of agency, but it is treated of more fully in chapters XII. and XIII., in connection with the liabilities incurred by the husband through the wife.

4. Nothing in the Act of 1882 or the Act of 1893 imposes any restriction on the wife's liability for wrongs, independent of contract. If, therefore, a wife is sued for such a wrong committed by her before marriage, and judgment is given against her, any property which

she may have in the present or the future, unless it be subject to the restraint on anticipation, will be liable to answer the judgment. And the like result will follow if judgment is obtained against her for a like wrong committed by her after marriage. For this her husband is also liable, as he was before the Acts, to the extent of all his property; for, it is said, the Acts were not intended for the relief of husbands.

The nature of a liability for a wrong, as distinguished from a liability on contract, may, without attempting a definition, be brought to view by naming as examples such wrongs as defamation of character, assault, trespasses to land and to goods, stopping up another's watercourse, injuring the support to his house, or causing him injury by negligent driving, etc. These are acts which are seldom breaches of any contract, but there are circumstances under which it is hard to say whether an act is a breach of contract, or a wrong independent of it, and there are some acts which may be both.

Before the M. W. P. Acts, the husband could obtain a decree against his wife in respect of her separate estate for breach of a contract made with him by which she intended to bind such estate. The Acts do not deprive him of this right and he may sue his wife for money which he has lent her after marriage, and for money which he has paid for her after marriage, upon a request made by her either before or after marriage.

Returning to the first section of the Act of 1882, subsection 5 says that a wife carrying on a trade separately from her husband, shall, in respect of her separate property, be subject to the bankruptcy laws as if she were a single woman. Before the Act, a wife could not be made bankrupt at all, except where she was carrying on a separate trade according to the custom of London, or where her husband was in exile, or had been transported, or where she lived apart from her husband under a judicial separation or a protection order. And she can only now be made a bankrupt if she carries on a *trade*, and does so separately from her husband. This does not mean her living in a separate breaches of contract committed by a woman *after* marriage, she alone, by sec. 1, is liable. If, therefore, the provisions as to the wife's liability on breaches of trust committed after marriage, are to be the same as those concerning her liability on breaches of contracts committed after marriage, that liability is exclusive, and the husband is wholly exempt from penalty for her misdoings during the only period in which he could have a chance of controlling them.

And for all breaches of contract committed by the wife *before* marriage, the husband is, by sec. 14, only liable to the extent of property of hers which he has got or could have got. So that the only case in which the husband could make himself liable by intermeddling would be where the breach of trust was committed by the wife before marriage, and then his liability would only extend to the property of hers which he had got, or could have got. He would thus be less liable for his wife's ante-nuptial breaches of trust than for her ante-nuptial breaches of other contracts, as to which no absence of intermeddling could save him from liability to the extent mentioned.

As long as trust property is in the hands of a married woman, the Court can make it answerable for the trust as well as when it is in the hands of any other trustee, and it may be followed into the hands of other persons who have taken it with notice of the trust. But this section is concerned, not with the applicability of the trust property to the purposes of the trust, but with the liability of the married woman and her husband to make good her breaches of trust out of their own property, and the language used does not admit of reasonable interpretation

The section will probably be construed to mean that the wife is liable for all her breaches of trust, whether as trustee, executrix, or administratrix, just as she is upon contracts; that her husband is not liable for her ante-nuptial breaches of trust, even to the extent of her property which he has received, unless he has intermeddled, but that if he has intermeddled he is to be liable individually, as he was before the Act, whether the breach was before or after marriage.

18. Section 19 says that nothing in the Act "shall interfere with or affect any settlement or agreement for a settlement *made or to be made*, whether before or after marriage, respecting the property of any married woman." The nature and effect of a settlement has been elsewhere explained (see chap. XI.). A settlement may be by the deed, will, or other gift of a third person giving property to a woman, or to a trustee for her separate use in the event of marriage, or if she is already married. Or the settlement may be made between the parties themselves before marriage, or may be made after marriage in pursuance of an agreement made before marriage. Or the settlement or agreement may be wholly post-nuptial. These words, however, do not make any settlement or agreement for a settlement valid, which would not otherwise have been so. Ante-nuptial settlements or those made in pursuance of an ante-nuptial agreement, being made in consideration of marriage, are equivalent to purchases for value of the settled property, and so are good against creditors; but post-nuptial settlements, not being made on that consideration and being for the most part voluntary, are often subject to be set aside by persons who were creditors when the settlement was made.

The restraint against anticipation may be contained in any of these kinds of settlements. It is a provision that the woman, while married, is not to be able to convey away, sell, encumber, or dispose of the principal or *corpus* of the property or its future income, but can only enjoy the income as it comes due. The restraint applies only to property given to, or settled on, the wife for her separate use (Stogdon *v.* Lee (1891), 1 Q.B. 661 and see 1 Coll. 138) and terminates when the marriage ends and revives on another marriage. This restriction is kept in force by sec. 19, except that if it is contained in a settlement of the woman's own property, made or entered into by herself, it is not to be valid against debts contracted by her before marriage. That is to say, that if, whether before or after marriage, the woman, by a settlement, imposes upon herself a restraint upon anticipation, both the income and the principal will be his business appears to be just in the same position by the section as by the Partnership Act, 1890, a person is placed who lends money to one who is engaged in a trade or undertaking on the footing of being repaid by a share of the profits. In both cases the lender is postponed to other creditors for value. But, inasmuch as in the latter case, the creditor who has taken a mortgage on the terms of receiving a share of profits, is not deprived by the Act of the security of his mortgage, it is presumed that a wife who has taken a mortgage to secure a loan to her husband to be used in his business, may retain a mortgaged property, though she cannot prove along with the other creditors for the debt.

8. Section 4 enacts that, where a married woman by her will exercises a *general* power of appointment, the property so appointed is answerable after her death for her liabilities in the same way as her separate estate is. A general power of appointment is where, under a will, gift, or settlement, the married woman has power given her to appoint the person who is to take the property in question, and to appoint whom she pleases. When she does this, the property is as much under her power to leave by will as what was her own, and so is made answerable for claims on her estate. But property over which she has a general power of appointment to be exercised by deed or will, does not become her separate property on her bankruptcy; so she cannot be compelled to execute the power in favour of the trustee of her bankrupt estate for the benefit of her creditors.

9. As to the stocks, funds, shares, etc., mentioned in sections 6, 7, and 8, it is to be observed that they are presumed to be the separate property of the wife alone, if they stand in her sole name, and to be her property jointly with another person or persons, if they stand in the joint names. The burden of proving that these investments are not the property of the woman lies upon the person who disputes her title. These sections apply to such investments whether made by the woman herself or by a stranger, or by her husband; unless indeed the husband has put the share fund, etc., in the joint names of himself and his wife, when the Courts will regard it

the guardians, if it is of small amount, may deprive her of it, and so drive her into the poor-house, in order to maintain her husband there.

The next section, without relieving the husband from any burden, makes the wife, who has separate property, as liable as he is to maintain her pauper children and grandchildren.

20. Section 24 also contains an interpretation of "property" so as to include, when used in the Act a thing in action or *chose in action* (see chap. iii.). This is important to be borne in mind, especially in reading secs. 1, 2, and 5 of the Act. The wife's *choses in action* being given to her as her separate property, sec. 12 gives her the right to sue for them, even as against her husband, and sec. 13 renders her liable to claims upon *choses in action*, even at the suit of her husband.

largely indebted at the time was liable to be set aside as being void as against creditors under the statute 13 Eliz. c. 5.

11. Apart from the claims of creditors, however, there is nothing to prevent either husband or wife making gifts or conveying property to the other. By the Conveyancing Act of 1881, either may execute conveyances of freehold land and may make assurances of "things in action" to the other, either alone or jointly with another person. A "thing in action" or *chose in action* has already been explained in chap. iii. s. 9. As the same section of the Act empowers a person to convey to himself jointly with any other person —which in some cases he could do before—it is presumed that a husband can convey property direct to himself and his wife, and a wife can convey property direct to herself and her husband.

But money and chattels pass by delivery without any writing at all, and either husband or wife can make a good gift of these to the other, if the rights of creditors do not interfere.

The wife may, without any writing, give to the husband any money or chattels which she is at liberty to dispose of as her separate property; nay, if she merely allows her money to be paid into his banking account, or allows him to receive it and spend it on his household or in his business, her intention to give it to him will be presumed, and she cannot after his death claim it against his executor. Nay, even where moneys belonging to the wife's separate estate were due from a person to whom her husband owed money, and she allowed the money to be set off against her husband's debt, this was regarded as a payment to the husband with the wife's consent, and, therefore, a gift by her to him.

12. By section 11, the husband may effect a policy of insurance on his own life for the benefit (1) of his wife, or (2) of his children, or (3) of his wife and children, or any of them; and the wife may effect a policy on her own life for the benefit (1) of her husband, or (2) of her children, or (3) of her husband and her children, or any of them.

require registration as a bill of sale and that the wife had separate possession. The situation being consistent with the possession of either, the law would attribute the possession to the person who had the legal title. (1894) 2 Q.B. 18—C.A.

2. The Act, while rendering the wife liable for wrongs committed by her, either before or after marriage, has only limited the liability of the husband, if sued jointly with her, for wrongs committed by her before marriage, and has left his liability for wrongs committed by her after marriage entirely unaffected. So that the husband can be sued jointly with his wife for a wrong committed by her after marriage, and he may be made individually liable to the extent of all his property, without being entitled to be re-couped out of her separate property (if any) under sec. 13. The Act, the Judges say, was intended to improve the condition of wives as regards property, and not for the relief of husbands: but the more simple explanation of the defect is that it was an accidental omission.

3. The Act of 1882 has not very much enlarged the wife's power of contracting. Long before the Act the law allowed her to bind by her contracts whatever separate estate she had, if it was free from restraint against anticipation. All that the Act has done in this direction is to enable her to bind her future separate property.

But though judgment may be recovered against her, all her property which she is restrained from anticipating is placed by sec. 19 beyond the reach of her creditor. He cannot take it in execution, nor have a receiver appointed to take the income, nor obtain an order to charge it. Nor can he make it liable though it has fallen due and been received by the woman. During the marriage it is answerable for nothing except under the Act of 1893, where the wife sues and has to pay costs to the other side. (1894) 2 Q.B. 559—C.A. And even if the Court were inclined to regard the payment of her creditor as being "for her benefit" under section 39 of the Conveyancing Act, 1881, her consent, required by the same section, would probably be refused.

4. The form of a judgment against a married woman

Sec. 14 contains the limitation of the husband's responsibility for the liabilities of his wife arising before marriage, as already mentioned, but the proviso at the end preserves the liabilities of a husband married before the Act, as they stood. This is now of little importance owing to the lapse of time.

The 15th section is only concerned with the action which a person, having a claim against the wife arising before her marriage, whether on contract or for a wrong, brings against the husband and wife, when the plaintiff chooses to sue the two together. He is not bound to sue any one but the wife, who, by sec. 1, is subject to be sued alone, whether for a contract or for a wrong, and whose separate property is responsible. The plaintiff will be very foolish to sue the husband unless there is good ground for supposing that he has become entitled to property of the wife, over and above what he has paid or is liable, under judgment, to pay for her antenuptial liabilities. Whether the wife has or has not sufficient separate property, present or in expectation, to satisfy the debt, the effect of suing the husband unsuccessfully will be to saddle the plaintiff with the husband's costs.

To enable the husband, in estimating his liability, to take credit for a judgment, the Act requires the judgment to have been recovered *bona fide*; but it is easy for the husband to protect himself by a friendly judgment, and hard for the creditor to find out whether the judgment is obtained in good faith or not.

The joint action against the husband and wife may be continued against either after the death of the other, but the husband, unless he is the wife's personal representative, cannot be sued alone after the death of the wife. (See ch. xvii., s. 9).

Sec. 23 of the Act of 1882 says that, for the purposes of the Act, the legal personal representative of the married woman shall, in respect of her separate estate, have the same rights and liabilities as she would have had if living. This representative would be her executor or administrator, but the term is said to include her husband, though he is neither, if by virtue of his marital right he has taken the chattels or the leasehold of his deceased wife; in which case he is liable to the extent of this property of hers for her debts incurred either before or after marriage unless the remedy for them is barred. (1891) 1 Q.B. 491. As to his marital right to chattels, see ch. III., s. 8, and to leases, ch. IV., s. 5.

The action against the wife may, of course, be continued against her executor or administrator, and her separate property made liable in his hands, and, by sec. 23, it would seem if the action be not commenced in the wife's lifetime, her executor or administrator may be sued and be answerable to the extent of the deceased wife's separate property.

15. A special mode is provided by sec. 17 for deciding disputes between husband and wife "as to the title to or possession of property." The disputes are to be decided in a summary way by summons before a judge. The summons is a writing directing the other party to appear before the judge, and show cause why the property should not be handed over to the possession of, or treated as belonging to, the party issuing the summons. Both parties, or their solicitors, or counsel, then attend before the Judge at his chamber, or, if he thinks fit, in his private room, and he hears the evidence, usually on affidavit, adjourns the case if necessary for further evidence, and, when all is before him, makes an order as to the property. The judge may be either a judge of the High Court or of the County Court in England, or of the High Court or of a Civil Bill Court in Ireland, according as the property is in England or Ireland. The order made by any of these judges is subject to appeal, and from the County Court judge or the judge of the Civil Bill Court, the case may be removed by the respondent party where the property in question exceeds the amount over which those courts have jurisdiction.

By sec. 23, the executor or administrator of a deceased wife may obtain such a summons, or may be directed to appear upon one, and enjoys the same rights, and is subject to the same jurisdiction as the wife when alive.

If the dispute relates to any stock, funds, shares, or deposit in any company, etc., the latter may issue the summons requiring the husband and wife to attend for the settlement of the question.

16. Sec. 18 is concerned with a wife being executrix or administratrix; that is, being named in a will and appointed by the Court of Probate as the person to execute the testator's wishes, or being the person appointed by the same Court to administer the estate where the deceased person has died without a will, or where there is no executor. The section also relates to the wife being a trustee, which she may become, either under a will, or a deed, or other writing, or by word of mouth, or by operation of law without a word written or said.

A married woman could always be a trustee and, with the consent of the husband, could always accept the office of executrix or administratrix. And a single woman who had become trustee, would remain so after marriage, and, if she had accepted either of the offices above mentioned, would continue to hold it after marriage.

But the appointment of a married woman as trustee, executrix, or administratrix, was attended with inconvenience, because her husband, being liable for her breaches of trust or duty, had a control over her acts and over personal property vested in her in any of these fiduciary capacities. The personal property in fact passed into his legal ownership, and could not be dealt with without his concurrence. The husband was joined with his wife as defendant in any proceeding for a breach of trust or duty on her part, and was individually liable to make it good.

To avoid both these difficulties, sec. 18 enacts that the wife who is trustee, executrix, or administratrix, alone or jointly with another or others, may sue and be sued in those capacities, and may, without her husband and as if she were single, transfer or join in transferring the annuities, stocks, funds, shares, etc., referred to in the section as "aforesaid," meaning those mentioned in secs. 7, 8, and 9.

Section 18 does not authorise the wife to deal, without her husband's concurrence, with any other personal property, such as leases and chattels, vested in her in a fiduciary crpacity; an omission for which there is the less reason as not only can she be sued alone, and therefore be put to trouble through her husband's refusal to concur, but, by section 24, her husband is exempted from liability for her breaches of trust unless he has acted or intermeddled.

The wife's power to deal with estates of inheritance, and life estates vested in her as trustee, is left wholly untouched by the Act. These she must convey as heretofore by an acknowledged deed (see chap. IV., sec. 12) in which her husband concurs, unless she is a "bare trustee," in which case, by the Vendor's and Purchaser's Act, 1874, sec. 6, she may convey or surrender as if she were single. Lawyers are not quite agreed as to what a "bare trustee" is, but such a person may be roughly described as a trustee with no duty to perform, and who holds the legal estate at the disposal of some person absolutely entitled, who may demand a conveyance. It is true that, by secs. 2 and 5, the wife, whether married before or after the Act, may acquire, hold, and dispose of as her separate property, all real and personal property; but "separate property" means that in which she is beneficially interested, and can hardly be held to apply to trust property, in which she is not beneficially interested.

The Act does not expressly say that a wife may accept the office of executrix or administratrix without her husband's consent.

17. In connection with sec. 18 let us consider sec. 24, which ought not to have been separated from it. Sec. 24 contains what is both puzzling and important. It says the word "contract" in the Act, is to include the acceptance of any trust, or of the office of executrix or administratrix, and the provisions as to the wife's liability are to extend to any breach of trust or waste of trust property committed by her before or after marriage, as trustee, executrix, or administratrix.

Again, the husband is not to be liable for the wife's breaches of trust, whether committed before or *after* marriage, unless he has intermeddled. But, for all breaches of contract committed by a woman *after* marriage, she alone, by sec. 1, is liable. If, therefore, the provisions as to the wife's liability on breaches of trust committed after marriage, are to be the same as those concerning her liability on breaches of contracts committed after marriage, that liability is exclusive, and the husband is wholly exempt from penalty for her misdoings during the only period in which he could have a chance of controlling them.

And for all breaches of contract committed by the wife *before* marriage, the husband is, by sec. 14, only liable to the extent of property of hers which he has got or could have got. So that the only case in which the husband could make himself liable by intermeddling would be where the breach of trust was committed by the wife before marriage, and then his liability would only extend to the property of hers which he had got, or could have got. He would thus be less liable for his wife's ante-nuptial breaches of trust than for her ante-nuptial breaches of other contracts, as to which no absence of intermeddling could save him from liability to the extent mentioned.

As long as trust property is in the hands of a married woman, the Court can make it answerable for the trust as well as when it is in the hands of any other trustee, and it may be followed into the hands of other persons who have taken it with notice of the trust. But this section is concerned, not with the applicability of the trust property to the purposes of the trust, but with the liability of the married woman and her husband to make good her breaches of trust out of their own property, and the language used does not admit of reasonable interpretation.

The section will probably be construed to mean that the wife is liable for all her breaches of trust, whether as trustee, executrix, or administratrix, just as she is upon contracts; that her husband is not liable for her ante-nuptial breaches of trust, even to the extent of her property which he has received, unless he has intermeddled, but that if he has intermeddled he is to be liable individually, as he was before the Act, whether the breach was before or after marriage.

18. Section 19 says that nothing in the Act "shall interfere with or affect any settlement or agreement for a settlement *made or to be made*, whether before or after marriage, respecting the property of any married woman." The nature and effect of a settlement has been elsewhere explained (see chap. XI.). A settlement may be by the deed, will, or other gift of a third person giving property to a woman, or to a trustee for her separate use in the event of marriage, or if she is already married. Or the settlement may be made between the parties themselves before marriage, or may be made after marriage in pursuance of an agreement made before marriage. Or the settlement or agreement may be wholly post-nuptial. These words, however, do not make any settlement or agreement for a settlement valid, which would not otherwise have been so. Ante-nuptial settlements or those made in pursuance of an ante-nuptial agreement, being made in consideration of marriage, are equivalent to purchases for value of the settled property, and so are good against creditors; but post-nuptial settlements, not being made on that consideration and being for the most part voluntary, are often subject to be set aside by persons who were creditors when the settlement was made.

The restraint against anticipation may be contained in any of these kinds of settlements. It is a provision that the woman, while married, is not to be able to convey away, sell, encumber, or dispose of the principal or *corpus* of the property or its future income, but can only enjoy the income as it comes due. The restraint applies only to property given to, or settled on, the wife for her separate use (Stogdon *v.* Lee (1891), 1 Q.B. 661 and see 1 Coll. 188) and terminates when the marriage ends and revives on another marriage. This restriction is kept in force by sec. 19, except that if it is contained in a settlement of the woman's own property, made or entered into by herself, it is not to be valid against debts contracted by her before marriage. That is to say, that if, whether before or after marriage, the woman, by a settlement, imposes upon herself a restraint upon anticipation, both the income and the principal will be available to satisfy a judgment obtained by a creditor to whom she had contracted a debt before marriage.

The word "debts' is not usually read so as to include a claim for damages for a wrong, and I presume a plaintiff who recovered against the wife for a wrong (or *tort*) committed by her before marriage, could not make the body of the property, if protected by a restraint on anticipation, available to satisfy his judgment.

It will be observed that the only restraint on anticipation which the Court will set at nought in favour of an ante-nuptial creditor, is a restraint contained in a settlement of the woman's own property made by herself. The Courts will still give effect to such a restraint, if contained in a settlement or gift by a third party, or if contained in a settlement made between the man and woman, before or after marriage, as long as it is not a settlement of her "own property."

It is only in the case of a married woman that the restraint on anticipation has any effect, for, in whatever gift or settlement it is contained, it does not operate until marriage, and it ceases upon widowhood.

The proviso at the end of the section, that no settlement or agreement for a settlement should have greater validity against the creditors of a woman than a like settlement or agreement would have against the creditors of a man, is to be understood by reference to what has already been explained as to what kinds of settlements are invalid as against creditors.

19. By section 20, where the husband of any woman having separate property becomes chargeable to a parish or union in England, the guardians of the poor may make the wife pay, out of her separate property, for her husband's maintenance, and, if the husband receives poor relief in Ireland, the cost price of the relief given to him is made a debt recoverable from the wife.

As I read the section, in order to make the wife liable, she must have the separate property at the time when the husband becomes chargeable; so that, if a friend, seeing her husband a pauper, leaves her, or gives her, money it cannot be touched.

Under this section, where the wife's property is liable,

the guardians, if it is of small amount, may deprive her of it, and so drive her into the poor-house, in order to maintain her husband there.

The next section, without relieving the husband from any burden, makes the wife, who has separate property, as liable as he is to maintain her pauper children and grandchildren.

20. Section 24 also contains an interpretation of "property" so as to include, when used in the Act a thing in action or *chose in action* (see chap. iii.). This is important to be borne in mind, especially in reading secs. 1, 2, and 5 of the Act. The wife's *choses in action* being given to her as her separate property, sec. 12 gives her the right to sue for them, even as against her husband, and sec. 13 renders her liable to claims upon *choses in action*, even at the suit of her husband.

## CHAPTER IX.

### REMARKS ON THE EFFECT OF THE ACT OF 1882.

1. *Husband and wife still one person in law.*
2. *Husband still liable for wrongs committed by wife during marriage.*
3. *What property of wife is beyond creditor's reach.*
4. *Form of judgment against wife.*
5. *Wife cannot be imprisoned or, unless a trader, be made bankrupt.*
6. *Consequences.*
7. *Conflict between separate property and conjugal duty.*

1. The unity of person existing at common law between husband and wife is not destroyed by the Married Woman's Property Act, 1882. A testator in 1887 directed a share of a residue to be divided between his sister M. B., D. B., her husband and H. B., his stepdaughter. It was held that the latter took one half, and the husband and wife took each a quarter; the wife's quarter being her separate property. The husband and wife, it is true, were married before the Act, but this did not make any difference, as the property was acquired after the Act, and so came within s. 5. (39 Ch. D. 148; 42 Ch. D. 306; 1893, 2 Ch. 229; W.N. (1892) 88.)

But the married partners may contract with one another and may, therefore, buy and sell of and to one another. A husband sold his furniture and plate to his wife and gave a receipt for the money, expressing what it was received for. She sent the plate to her banker's, but the rest was used in common in the common dwelling. Part was then taken in execution by a creditor of the husband, and there was an interpleader on the claim of the wife. It was held that the receipt did not require registration as a bill of sale and that the wife had separate possession. The situation being consistent with the possession of either, the law would attribute the possession to the person who had the legal title. (1894) 2 Q.B. 18—C.A.

2. The Act, while rendering the wife liable for wrongs committed by her, either before or after marriage, has only limited the liability of the husband, if sued jointly with her, for wrongs committed by her before marriage, and has left his liability for wrongs committed by her after marriage entirely unaffected. So that the husband can be sued jointly with his wife for a wrong committed by her after marriage, and he may be made individually liable to the extent of all his property, without being entitled to be re-couped out of her separate property (if any) under sec. 13. The Act, the Judges say, was intended to improve the condition of wives as regards property, and not for the relief of husbands: but the more simple explanation of the defect is that it was an accidental omission.

3. The Act of 1882 has not very much enlarged the wife's power of contracting. Long before the Act the law allowed her to bind by her contracts whatever separate estate she had, if it was free from restraint against anticipation. All that the Act has done in this direction is to enable her to bind her future separate property.

But though judgment may be recovered against her, all her property which she is restrained from anticipating is placed by sec. 19 beyond the reach of her creditor. He cannot take it in execution, nor have a receiver appointed to take the income, nor obtain an order to charge it. Nor can he make it liable though it has fallen due and been received by the woman. During the marriage it is answerable for nothing except under the Act of 1893, where the wife sues and has to pay costs to the other side. (1894) 2 Q.B. 559—C.A. And even if the Court were inclined to regard the payment of her creditor as being "for her benefit" under section 39 of the Conveyancing Act, 1881, her consent, required by the same section, would probably be refused.

4. The form of a judgment against a married woman

was settled in Scott *v.* Morley, 20 Q.B.D. 120, as follows:—

It is adjudged that the plaintiff recover £—— and costs to be taxed against the [married woman] defendant, such sum and costs to be payable out of her separate property, as hereinafter mentioned and not otherwise. And it is ordered that execution be limited to the separate property of the said [married woman] not subject to any restraint against anticipation, unless, by reason of sec. 19 of the Married Woman's Property Act, 1882, such property shall be liable to execution notwithstanding such restraint.

The latter words have reference only to the case where the debt was contracted before marriage, and the settlement was made by the woman herself.

But now the Act of 1893 has made all the property which the woman may have after she is "discoverte" (*i.e.*, after the marriage has ended) liable to answer the contracts which she makes otherwise than as agent. And so, when judgment is given against a married woman on a contract made after the 5th December, 1893, this form will have to be altered by saying, "it is ordered that during her present or other marriage," etc., and perhaps there should be added a proviso that when she is discoverte execution shall be unlimited.

I ought to add here that the M.W.P. Acts have not taken away the wife's liability at common law upon contracts made by her *before* marriage. A married woman was sued on a bill of exchange accepted by her before marriage, and it was held that the plaintiff was entitled to judgment against her personally and not in the form used in *Scott* v. *Morley*. See *Robinson, King, & Co.* v. *Lynes* (1894), 2 Q.B., 559—C.A.

5. Not only cannot the property under restraint be taken in execution or charged under such a judgment, but the woman cannot be committed under sec. 5 of the Debtors' Act, 1869, for having had the means to pay, and not having done so. The reason is that the married woman is under no personal liability to pay the money, which cannot, therefore, be said to be "due from her."

A bankruptcy notice cannot be issued by the creditor who has obtained such a judgment, so as to found a petition in default of payment; nor can a married woman who is not a trader be bankrupt at all, nor, if bankrupt, can she be made to exercise a power of appointment in favour of her creditors.

6. So that a married woman against whom there is a judgment may live on the income of the property which she is restrained from anticipating, without paying a farthing in satisfaction of the judgment.

7. In conclusion I may be allowed to point out a confliction between the wife's right to separate property, and the husband's conjugal rights. It is a confliction which existed before the Act, but which is accentuated by the enlargement effected by the Act in the area of separate property. Where the woman's property is separate, she is entitled to keep her husband away from it, and use it herself and let any one else use it. If this property is a house, she may live in it, and let anybody else into it, and keep her husband out of it. Living in the house may be the best or the only way of enjoying that particular article of property, and her husband may be unable or unwilling to live there. In that case, if she enjoys the property she neglects her conjugal duties, and, if she performs her conjugal duties, she does not enjoy the property. This difficulty has already cast its shadow across our Courts.

# CHAPTER X.

## OTHER RECENT ENACTMENTS AS TO MARRIED WOMEN'S STATUS AND PROPERTY.

1. *The Naturalization Act*, 1870.
2. *The Married Women's Property* (*Scotland*) *Acts* 1877 *and* 1881. *The Married Women's Policies of Assurance* (*Scotland*) *Act*, 1880.
3. *The Settled Estates Act*, 1877.
4. *The Settled Land Act*, 1882.
5. *The Conveyancing and Law of Property Act*, 1881.
6. *The Land Transfer Act*, 1875.
7. *The Agricultural Holdings Act*, 1883.
8. *The Intestates Estates Act*, 1890.
9. *The Trustee Acts*, 1888 *and* 1893.

**1. As to the national status of married women and infant children, "The Naturalization Act, 1870," sec. 10 enacts as follows:—**

i. A married woman shall be deemed to be a subject of the state of which her husband is for the time being a subject.

ii. A widow being a natural-born British subject, who has become an alien by or in consequence of her marriage, shall be deemed to be a statutory alien, and may as such at any time during widowhood obtain a certificate of re-admission to British nationality in manner provided by this Act.

iii. Where the father being a British subject, or the mother being a British subject and a widow, becomes an alien in pursuance of this Act, every child of such father or mother who during infancy has become resident in the country where the father or mother is naturalized, and has according to the laws of such country become naturalized therein, shall be deemed to be a subject of the state of which the father or mother has become a subject, and not a British subject.

iv. Where the father, or the mother being a widow, has obtained a certificate of re-admission to British nationality, every child of such father or mother who during infancy has become resident in the British dominions with such father or mother, shall be deemed to have resumed the position of a British subject to all intents.

v. Where the father, or the mother being a widow, has obtained a certificate of naturalization in the United Kingdom, every child of such father or mother, who during infancy has become resident with such father or mother in any part of the United Kingdom, shall be deemed to be a naturalized British subject.

And by sec. 8 of "The Naturalization Act, 1872," it is enacted that

Nothing contained in "The Naturalization Act, 1870," shall deprive any married woman of any estate or interest in real or personal property, to which she may have become entitled previously to the passing of that Act [12th May, 1870], or affect such estate or interest to her prejudice.

2. "The Married Women's Property (Scotland) Act, 1877," which applies only to Scotland, removes from the husband's control the wages and earnings, of any married woman gained by her after the 1st of January, 1878, in any employment, occupation or trade in which she is engaged, or in any business which she carries on under her own name, and also any money or property which she acquires after the same date, through the exercise of any literary, artistic or scientific skill, and all investments thereof, and puts all these interests in the position of property settled to her sole and separate use for which her receipts are a good discharge.

In marriages after the 1st of January, 1878, the Act limits the husband's liabilty for his wife's ante-nuptial debts to the same kinds of property as are mentioned in sec. 14 of the English M. W. P. Act, 1882.

"The Married Women's Property (Scotland) Act 1881" was passed on the 18th of July, 1881, and enacts that, where a marriage is contracted after the passing of the Act, and the husband is at the time domiciled in Scotland, the whole movable estate of the wife acquired during the marriage, shall vest in her as her separate estate. The income is also her separate estate, but she cannot dispose of prospective income or principal without her husband's consent. Her separate estate, if placed in her name or of a sort not susceptible of documentary title is to be exempt from execution for her husband's debts; but if her property is mixed with his, it becomes assets in his estate, and she is postponed to his other creditors.

A wife married after the passing of the Act takes the rents, and produce of her heritable property, free from her husband's control.

Where the woman was married before the Act, the Act is to apply, if the husband has not made an irrevocable provision for her in case she survives, and, is to apply as to her moveable and heritable property acquired after the passing of the Act.

Power is given to parties married before the Act, to come under its provisions by registering a joint deed.

The power to make an ante-nuptial settlement, and the effect of it when made are expressly reserved.

"The Married Women's Policies of Assurance (Scotland) Act, 1880, enables a wife domiciled in Scotland to effect an insurance on her own life or her husband's for her separate use, and gives to Scotch husbands and wives the same powers of insuring for the benefit of the other party to the marriage or the children, or both, as are given by the M. W. P. Act, 1882.

8. "The Settled Estates Act, 1877," was passed to enable leases for fixed terms of years to be granted by the person entitled to a present limited interest in the land so as to be valid after his death against the persons having the succeeding interests. In the case of settled estates, this has to be done on an application to the Chancery Division, and usually with the consent of the other persons having subsequent beneficial interests.

Section 52 of the Act enables a married woman, whether of full age or not, to make, or consent to, any such application, but subject to her being examined apart from her husband, in the mode provided by secs. 50 and 51, as to her being aware of the nature and effect of the application and her consenting thereto.

As regards unsettled estates, the same Act, by secs. 46 and 47, enables a husband who is in receipt of the rents and profits in right of a wife seized in fee-simple or as tenant by the courtesy (see chap. iv, secs. 10, 11,) and a wife who is in possession as a dowager (see chap. iv, sec. 9), to grant leases of all except the principal mansion house, its demesnes and the lands usually occupied therewith, for not more than 21 years where the lands are in England, and not more than 35 years where the lands are in Ireland. And such leases, if otherwise framed, as required by sec. 46, will, by the next section, be good against the persons entitled to the land on the death of the grantor. A husband married since 1882, or whose wife acquired her land since 1882 cannot be in receipt of the rents, and profits in right of his wife; but he can still be tenant by the courtesy when she dies.

4. "The Settled Land Act, 1882" was passed to enable the tenant for life of land under a settlement to sell, lease, and make improvements on the land.

The term "tenant for life" means the person or persons beneficially entitled to the rents and profits of settled land for his or their lives.

If the tenant for life sells the property, the sale moneys form "capital money" under the Act, which may be spent in the discharge of incumbrances, or in improvements, or in the purchase of other lands, or may be handed over to any person who would have been absolutely entitled to the land sold. It is to be treated as land for the purposes of transmission and descent and is not to be distributed like personal property (see chap. iii., s. 6), and, the income arising from it is to go to the person who would have been entitled to the income of the land sold.

If the tenant for life grants a lease of the land, the lease is binding, after his death, on the persons who are to succeed him under the settlement, and the rents are then received by them.

The principal mansion, its demesnes and the lands usually occupied with it, are not to be sold or leased by the tenant for life without the consent of the trustees or an order of the Court.

The husband who is tenant for life by the courtesy of his wife's lands is to be in the same position under this Act as if he were tenant for life under a settlement made by his wife (Settled Land Act, 1884, s. 8), and so he can bind her heirs and those who take after him by selling, or leasing, under the Act of 1882.

The 61st section of the Settled Land Act, 1882, enacts as follows:—

Where a married woman who, if she had not been a married woman, would have been a tenant for life, or would have had the powers of a tenant for life under the foregoing provisions of this Act, is entitled for her separate use, or is entitled under any statute passed, or to be passed, for her separate property or as a femme sole, then she, without her husband, shall have the powers of a tenant for life under this Act. (Sub-sec. 2.)

Where she is entitled otherwise than as aforesaid, then she and her husband together shall have the powers of a tenant for life under this Act. (Sub-sec. 3.)

The provisions of this Act referring to a tenant for life and a settlement and settled land shall extend to the married woman without her husband, or to her and her husband together, as the case may require, and to the instrument under which her estate or interest arises, and to the land therein comprised. (Sub-sec. 4.)

The married woman may execute, make and do all deeds, instruments and things necessary or proper for giving effect to this section. (Sub-sec. 5.)

A restraint on anticipation in the settlement shall not prevent the exercise by her of any power under this Act. (Sub-sec. 6.)

**5.** On the subject mentioned in the last sub-section, "The Conveyancing and Law of Property Act, 1881," gives power to the Court, by sec. 39, for the future to bind by judgment or order a married woman's interest in any property, notwithstanding her being restrained from anticipation, if she consents thereto and it appears to the Court to be for her benefit to do so.

Section 40 of the same Act, says that in future:—

"A married woman, whether an infant or not, shall by virtue of this Act, have power, as if she were unmarried and of full age, by deed to appoint an attorney on her behalf, for the purpose of executing any deed or doing any other act, which she might herself execute or do; and the provisions of this Act relating to powers of attorney shall apply thereto."

This does not empower a wife to appoint an attorney to execute a deed which requires acknowledgment (see chap. iv., s. 12), and of course does not enable her to part with the future income of property which she is restrained from anticipating, by giving the right to receive it to an attorney appointed for that purpose.

Section 50 of the same Act provides that, for the

future "freehold land, or a thing in action, may be conveyed by a person to himself jointly with another person, by the like means by which it might be conveyed by him to another person; and may in like manner, be conveyed by a husband to his wife, and by a wife to her husband, alone or jointly with another person."

6. "The Land Transfer Act, 1875," was passed to enable people with good titles to land to have themselves registered as owners, so that all subsequent conveyances and dealings with the land should be effected by registration in a manner commonly used in some of the colonies, but not yet popular in England. Section 87 says that a married woman entitled for her separate use and not restrained from anticipation, who desires to consent or become party to any proceeding under the Act, is to be deemed to be an unmarried woman, but that any other married woman must be examined apart from her husband, and the Court may appoint a "next friend" to act for her.

7. "The Agricultural Holdings Act, 1883," is to enable tenants to obtain from their landlords, on the expiration of the tenancy, compensation for certain improvements. When the amount is not settled by agreement, as it usually is, the mode provided by the Act is an arbitration, with an appeal to the County Court, where the amount claimed exceeds £100. And sec. 26 enacts that where a married woman requires to have a "next friend" for the purposes of the Act, the County Court may appoint, and may remove, him; that where a wife married before the 1st January, 1883, is entitled, for her separate use, to land, her title to which accrued before that day, and is not restrained from anticipation, she shall be regarded, for the purposes of the Act, as if unmarried; but that if she is not entitled to her separate use or, being so, is restrained from anticipation, her husband must concur in what she does under the Act, and she must also be examined apart from him by a County Court Judge to see that she understands and consents to it.

8. The Intestates Estates Act, 1890, which applies to the property of a man who dies after the 1st Sept.,

1890, intestate, and leaving a widow but no children, gives the widow a charge of £500 upon all the property of the deceased without prejudice to her distributive share of what remains after payment of that sum. See ch. xviii., s. 1 and Appendix.

9. "The Trustee Act, 1893," has to do with the liabilities of executors and administrators, and of trustees, whether the latter be expressly appointed or are deemed trustees by construction or implication of law.

Sec. 45 is framed for the prevention of an injustice suffered by trustees who have been cajoled by a married woman into letting her have the handling of her trust property in breach of the trust, on a promise to hold them harmless. It says:—

"Where a trustee commits a breach of trust at the instigation, or request, or with the consent, in writing, of a beneficiary, the High Court may, if it thinks fit, *and notwithstanding that the beneficiary may be a married woman* entitled for her separate use, and restrained from anticipation, make such order as the Court shall seem just for impounding all or any part of the interest of the beneficiary in the trust estate, by way of indemnity to the trustee or person claiming through him."

And this is to apply not only to future breaches of trust, but to those already committed, unless a proceeding is pending in respect of them, on the 23rd Sept., 1893, and had been commenced before the 24th Dec., 1888.

Section 8 of the Trustee Act, 1888, which is unrepealed, says that where, in proceedings commenced after the 1st January, 1890, the trustee is sued for any fraud or fraudulent breach of trust, to which he was a party, or to recover trust property, or the proceeds thereof, still retained by the trustee, or previously received by him, and converted to his use, the trustee, or any person claiming through him, cannot take advantage of the statutes limiting the time within which proceedings may be taken, and such proceedings are not barred by any lapse of time.

But (by sec. 8) if, after the 1st of January, 1890, the trustee, or any person claiming through him, is subjected to any *other* proceeding for breach of trust, or to recover trust property, by a beneficiary who is entitled to an interest in possession, the defendant may take advantage of the statute of limitations, even though the plaintiff is a married woman entitled in possession for her separate use, and whether with or without a restraint upon anticipation.

## CHAPTER XI.

### OF MARRIAGE SETTLEMENTS.

1. *Settlements as needful as before* M. W. P. Act, 1882.
2. *What property is the subject of settlement.*
3. *Settlement of intended* wife's *future property.*
4. *Covenant to settle such property must be made by* wife.
5. Wife *may subject her property to restraint on anticipation.*
6. *Form of agreement for settlement of all present and future property.*
7. *Requisites of agreement for a settlement.*
8. *Nature of a settlement as regards land.*
9. *Its operation.*
10. *Simpler mode of settling land for children equally.*
11. *Who can enforce execution of settlement.*
12. *Meaning of* "trustee" *and* "beneficial owner."
13. *Settlement of* wife's *personal estate.*
14. *Settlement useless without limitations over or restraint on anticipation.*
15. *Separate use and restraint operate only during marriage.*
16. Husband *or* wife *unable to perform covenant to settle future property.*
17. *Consent of* husband *enables* wife *to sell property acquired before* 1883, *and not separate.*
18. *She may sell it where separate without such consent.*
19. *Power of appointment given to* wife *by settlement.*
20. *Personalty in possession and life estates, whenever acquired, of* wife *whenever married.*
21. *Reversion of personalty belonging to* wife *married before* 1883.
22. *When concurrence of* husband *in deed requiring acknowledgment may be dispensed with.*
23. *Ultimate trust for* "next-of-kin" *or* "personal representatives."
24. *How far settlement a protection against creditors.*
25. *Powers of Divorce Court to re-model settlement.*

1. The position which persons, who married without a settlement, occupied before the Married Women's Property Acts, has been explained in chaps. iii. and iv. and the effects of the chief three of these Acts on the rights of the parties, has been set forth in chaps. vii., viii., and ix. I now proceed to point out the uses and the nature of a marriage settlement.

It is a mistake to suppose that the M. W. P. Act, 1882, has rendered settlements unnecessary. As regards the husband's property, the Act has not affected it, and the security afforded by a settlement against misfortune or extravagance is still desirable as regards him.

As regards the woman, a settlement is no longer needed for giving her the control of her property. The Act of 1882 gives the woman married after 1882 all the rights which she had under the Act of 1870, and all property her title to which accrues after 1882, and gives to the woman married after 1882, all the property which she has at marriage, and all property her title to which accrues afterwards. But the more complete the woman's power of disposing of her property is, the more necessary it becomes to protect her from wasting the capital by extravagance or giving it to her husband. This is especially desirable in the interests of the children of the marriage, and is effected by a marriage settlement, with a clause restraining her from anticipation.

When property is given or settled, subject to this restraint, the wife is enabled to use the income as it accrues, but cannot, during marriage, sell or mortgage the property, or give any one a right to receive the income in future.

Real as well as personal property may be given or settled subject to a restraint on anticipation.

2. All the property which either party possesses, or is entitled to, or during the marriage may acquire, or become entitled to, may be the subject of settlement.

The different sorts of property have been described in chapter iii.

As regards the husband's property he may bring into settlement all he has got, and may bind himself by agreement to settle all he may become entitled to.

The woman about to be married may settle, or bind herself by an agreement to settle, all that she possesses or is entitled to at the time. Though property may have been given to her for her separate use, but subject to the restraint against anticipation which may accompany the separate use, she is still at liberty to settle it; for neither of these qualifications comes into operation until marriage, and they cease on widowhood. Be she widow or spinster, therefore, there are for the intended wife no such things as separate use or separate property or restraint against anticipation. She is quite free to sell or to settle all such property or her interest in it, unless her interest is made to go over to some one else on her attempting to part with it, when of course she has no interest at all to sell or settle.

3. The intended wife may also bind herself to settle all future property which she becomes entitled to during the marriage, which is made her separate property (as all now is) by statute, or is, by will or other gift, given to her as her separate property without restraint against anticipation; for separate property means property which a woman, though married, may dispose of as she pleases.

But the intended wife cannot bind herself by any covenant to settle separate property coming to her during the marriage, if subject to a restraint against anticipation: for that restraint enables her only to receive the income as it accrues, without disposing of the principal or body of the property, or giving anyone the right to receive the future income.

The intended wife's agreement to settle her *future* property, therefore, applies only to such as is free from restraint against anticipation.

4. In agreements for a settlement the husband used formerly to covenant to settle all the wife's after acquired property or such as should come to him in her right; but the Act of 1882 has made such covenants useless, because property coming to the wife after 1882 belongs to her and is not his to settle. The Act pretends not to meddle with any settlements, but it has destroyed the effect of this covenant in all existing settlements as

regards all property coming to the wife after 1882. Such property is not the man's to settle, and the woman cannot be made to perform his covenant.

The covenant to settle the wife's future property must therefore be made by herself, just as much as the covenant to settle her existing property where she does not actually settle it.

5. The intended wife may even in the settlement, or agreement for a settlement, subject her property to a restraint against her own anticipation of it; but that will not be good against those to whom she owed money before marriage.

6. The following will serve as an agreement for a settlement of all present and future property:—

Agreement made this day of , between H, of , and W, of ,

In consideration of an intended marriage between the parties hereto, they each agree to settle in the manner usual on a marriage, according to the nature of the respective properties, all real and personal property of which they are now respectively possessed, or which they may respectively acquire or become entitled to during the marriage, provided they have, respectively, power to dispose of the same.

If there are any exceptions they should be added.

7. Settlements and agreements for settlements must be in writing.

The Statute of Frauds, passed in the 29th year of the reign of Charles II., requires all agreements made in consideration of marriage to be in writing, and signed by the party to be charged therewith or his agent.

The word "agreement," as used in the statute, comprehends not only what is commonly called an agreement *for* a settlement, but the settlement itself, which is a more solemn and technical instrument, and which is always made under seal, and if it conveys land is required by the same statute to be so made.

For the purpose of the mere agreement, however, so that there is a signed writing, it does not much matter what form it assumes, as long as it contains the substance. A letter, for instance, or a short memorandum, will, if only distinct, be a sufficient agreement. No person can be bound by such an agreement unless he

08010

or she sign personally, or by an agent. [The agent need not in strictness be appointed in writing; but it would be very unwise to rely upon an agreement signed by an agent of whose agency there was no written evidence. Being appointed he cannot, without authority, depute his powers to another agent.]

Whether the agreement is a formal document, or merely consists of a letter, or short memorandum, it must be stamped before it can be given in evidence.

I must notice that, whether formal or informal, an agreement, to be binding, must show, either expressly or impliedly, between what parties it is made. and on what consideration. Thus a letter will constitute an agreement binding the writer to the person to whom it is addressed; always supposing that it complies with the other requisites of an agreement. And, as regards consideration, marriage itself is a sufficient consideration, though the settlement of property by the other party to the marriage is not contemplated.

For example, the following letter would be a good agreement for a settlement:

"My dear C.—If you marry my daughter D I will settle £5,000 consols on her and you and the children of the marriage in the usual way.

"Faithfully yours, A. B."

If an estate in land had been mentioned, the agreement would be equally binding. If, however, the father merely said he would do what was proper as regards a settlement, that would not be sufficiently distinct.

Such a document as the above should at once be stamped.

8. I will now state shortly the nature of a marriage settlement as regards land.

But I must first premise, that those people are entirely mistaken who suppose that, on the occasion of a settlement, by means of what they call "the law of entail," they can preserve land in their family for ever. Nothing of the sort can be done, by any direct or indirect process. Land can be tied up till the child of a person now alive comes of age, and very properly so. But no one can tie up property, whether land or money, for a longer period than during a life or lives in being, and twenty-one years after. In other words, all land or other property, however strictly settled, is as thoroughly saleable, at the latest when the child of some person now alive comes of age, as it ever was before; and it is, of course, quite as much at the mercy of creditors as if it had never been settled. Where estates are kept in a family from one generation to another, settlements are made for the purpose every few years.

The usual settlement of the husband's land upon a marriage is, that a life estate merely is given to the husband: the wife has an allowance for pin-money during the marriage, and a rent-charge or annuity by way of jointure for her life, in case she should survive her husband. If the land settled is the wife's, she takes the first life estate, and the husband takes a life estate afterwards if he survives her. Then portions for the daughters and younger sons are charged upon the estate, after which the eldest son who may be born of the marriage is made tenant in tail male. In the event of his dying without issue male the second son is to be tenant in tail male, and so on of the third and other sons. [By "tenant in tail male" is here meant one whose ownership of the property is such that, if he leaves it to take its own course of descent without any further sale or settlement (for which purpose he bars the entail) it will only descend to his issue being males. This is the only difference between a tenancy *in tail* and the ordinary ownership in fee simple. There are other kinds of tenancies in tail which need not here be described.] In the event of all the sons dying without issue, the estate usually goes to the daughters.

9. The operation of the settlement is to give the estate, after the husband's death (subject to the jointure and younger children's portions), to the eldest son as tenant in tail. The eldest son may then dispose of the property; but if he does not sell, or re-settle it, or alter the line of succession, his issue male will take it. If, however, they fail, the estate being still undisposed of, it will go to the other sons and their issue successively,

in like manner. If they all fail, then the daughters take equally, and the share of each daughter goes to her issue in like manner; but if there is a failure of issue of any daughter, her share goes to the other daughters and their issue.

These results cannot be attained without vesting the property in trustees, *i.e.*, persons who are regarded as the legal owners, but on whom the Courts impose the duty of holding only for the benefit of the various parties for whom the settlement provides.

10. When it is desired to settle the land so that the children shall take equally, it is best to convey it to trustees upon trust for sale, to be executed with the consent of the tenants for life, and, after their death, at the discretion of the trustees. The proceeds of the sale are then settled as personal estate, with a proviso that, until sale, the rents and profits shall be applied in the same manner as the proceeds would be applicable if a sale had been made. The trust for sale is mere machinery to convert the land into personal estate, and effect its division without the complications of partition and much conveyancing. The land is not likely to be sold; for the tenants for life will not consent, and, after their death, the trustees will not sell unless the state of the family requires that course.

11. Marriage being considered by the law to be a valuable consideration, the husband, the wife, and the children as they come into existence, are in the position of purchasers for value, as regards all interests created in their favour under a marriage settlement made before marriage, or made after marriage in pursuance of an agreement entered into before marriage. And such interests are, in the absence of fraud, protected accordingly against all creditors of the husband or wife, except such as had judgments at the time of the settlement. See sec. 28, *post*.

When an agreement for a settlement made before marriage (commonly called "marriage articles") has not resulted in the execution of the settlement, the husband, wife, and any of the issue may insist on the execution of the settlement, which a Court of Equity will order to be done. Sometimes the articles have contained provisions in favour of collaterals, such as brothers, sisters, and uncles, and they have been regarded as sufficiently within the consideration to entitle them to have the articles specifically performed by the execution of the settlement. If the agreement or the covenants in the articles are made with trustees, they are of course similarly entitled, and at whosever instance the marriage articles are ordered to be carried out, they will be carried out in their entirety, though some provisions are in favour of persons who could not have applied to have them carried out.

12 Settlements are usually (and in some cases can only be) effected by means of a trust; that is to say the property is conveyed to a person as the legal owner, but only to hold it for the benefit of the persons entitled as equitable owners. The former person is called a trustee, or person trusted, and the other are called "equitables owners," "beneficial owners," "persons beneficially entitled," or *cestuis que trustent.*

The trustee is the person with whom the covenants are made for title, and further assurance and for the settlement of future property.

A trustee may hold property partly in trust for himself and partly for another person.

13 Personal property is capable of being settled on a marriage with much the same effect as real property, and a settlement of it is equally important.

Where the intended wife is possessed of personal property, it is usually vested by the settlement in trustees, upon trust to pay the yearly income to her, "into her own hands, for her sole and separate use, exclusive of the then intended or any future husband, but so that she shall not dispose thereof in any mode of anticipation." These latter words are what are commonly used to create the restraint against anticipation so often mentioned. It is then provided, that after her death the income is to be paid to her husband for life, if he survives her, and, after the death of the survivor, whether husband or wife, if the husband and wife have not in their lifetime made a joint appointment of the fund by deed among their children, then the whole fund can be disposed of to one or more of the children by the deed or will of the survivor, whether husband or wife, subject to such limitations and conditions as may be therein contained, provided they are consistent with the law. If no such deed or will is made, then the property goes to the children equally, on coming of age, or, if daughters, either on coming of age or marrying under age with the consent of their guardians.

In case the husband and wife should die while any of their children are under age and unmarried, the trustees have power to lay out the annual produce of each child's expectant share in his or her education and maintenance. Whatever is not so spent has to be accumulated. A power is also given to the trustees to anticipate the sum to which any child may be entitled, by employing it for his or her advancement in life. There is also power to invest the personal property in freehold or copyhold land, with the consent of the husband and wife, or the survivor. Where there are no children, the wife's property is usually subject to an ultimate trust in favour of persons to be appointed by the wife by deed or will, and in default of that, for her next of kin or some relative. A settlement of real and personal property is often effected by the same deed.

14 The above is merely a statement of the chief provisions in the *usual* settlement of the wife's personal property. It is, of course, possible to give her the beneficial interest in the whole of the property without any limitations to other persons after her death. In that case, though the property is subject to a restraint against anticipation, she can dispose of the whole, by will, to whom she pleases, including her husband, and can dispose of the whole as she pleases, when a widow, and if she makes no will, and her husband survives her, and she has not parted with the property, he will take it either in his marital right or as her administrator, according as it is in possession or not. If it is not subject to a restraint against anticipation, she can dispose of it at any time as if there were no settlement at all, and her husband's rights on her death, if she has

not disposed of it, will be as above stated. In the former case, if she survives her husband (and in the latter case whether she does or not), she is as much mistress over the whole property, principal and income, as if there were no settlement at all.

The same remarks apply to property settled on the wife by the deed or gift of a friend, whether on marriage or not, or of the husband himself. Such gifts, if made upon marriage, will usually reserve an ultimate trust, on failure of issue, in favour of the person making the settlement, or his appointees by deed or will, or his next of kin or some relative, but should otherwise resemble the settlement above set forth.

But any settlement of personalty on a woman, whether made in contemplation of marriage or not, should give the beneficial interest on her death to some other person, so as to prevent her, whether single, or married, or a widow, from parting with the principal, and should restrain her from anticipation so as to prevent her, while married, from disposing of her life interest, or the income thereof in advance.

As the reader will have seen from chapter viii., all gifts to a woman after 1882, whether expressed as being for her separate use or not, will be her separate property on and during marriage, whether vested in a trustee or not, and the Court, on an application under sec. 17 of the M. W. P. Act, 1882, or on an action brought by the wife, will protect her rights to the property as against her husband. And this property, to the extent of her interest in it, she may sell, give away, or bequeath, and unless restrained from anticipation, may do so even during marriage.

15 The separate use and the restraint on anticipation (which applies only to the separate property) only exist during marriage, cease on widowhood, and revive again on second marriage, unless created by words applying only to one marriage. That is to say that the woman, if she still retains the property, will on re-marriage have it again as separate and as subject to the restraint.

16 Where the husband has covenanted, in consideration of the interest which he takes in his wife's property,

to settle something upon her, and becomes unable to do so, then the wife or the children, by applying to the Court, may compel him to use the property which he takes of his wife, towards the performance of his covenant.

But if the husband covenants to settle property on the wife *at a future time*, as, for instance, to leave her so much by his will, then, although he be insolvent, no one can prevent him from taking the interest of his wife's property, which is given him by the settlement, because it may be, when the time comes, he will be able to do what he bargained to do.

These propositions, laid down by the Courts in the case of a defaulting husband, would, I presume, apply equally to the case of a defaulting wife.

17 Where a married woman, married before 1883, is possessed of freehold landed property, to which she became entitled before that date, which is neither included in her settlement, nor held by her to her separate use, by virtue of the deed or will by which it is given, or by an agreement with her husband before marriage, her husband's consent is required to enable her to dispose of such property, and then she can only do so after being examined apart from her husband, to ascertain that she is not acting under his compulsion.

With such consent she may sell the property, reserving, if she pleases, a life interest to herself, her husband, or both. If the property is not disposed of, it will descend to her heir at her death, subject to the husband's right to a life interest by the courtesy, if he has had a child by her, whether still living or not, capable of inheriting the land.

18 Where the circumstances and the property are the same, but the latter is given to the woman's separate use without restraint on anticipation, she may dispose of it as she pleases by deed or will, without her husband's consent or a separate examination, and by doing so she may defeat her husband's courtesy.

19 The wife's power of disposing of her property which attaches to all separate property not subject to the restraint, is modified by the usual form of settlement

by the insertion of the restraining words, and even if they are omitted, by the temporary duration of her interest. And sometimes a power of disposition given to her to be exercised under certain circumstances is restricted to a power to appoint by deed or will, or sometimes only by will. The latter has the advantage of protecting her, so to speak, against her own act; a will being revocable during lifetime.

20 The unlimited powers of disposing of separate estate, not subject to the restraint, which are enjoyed by wives married after 1882, and by wives married before that date as to property acquired after it, have been spoken of often enough. But whenever the wife was married, and whenever the property was acquired, personal estate *in possession*, and life interests in real estate, belonging to the wife to her separate use, without restraint on alienation, and whether vested in a trustee or not, and however the property may have become affected with the character of separate estate, may (where not controlled by a marriage settlement), be sold, charged, or otherwise dealt with by the wife as if she were unmarried, without any power of disposition being given her by the instrument giving her the property—if it were given by an instrument. And this may be done without the husband's concurrence or any separate examination and acknowledgment.

21 But where a wife, married before 1883, has an unsettled reversionary interest in personalty to which she is entitled under any instrument executed before 1858, such interest is absolutely unassignable by her or her husband. That is, the woman cannot assign it at all, and the husband could not reduce it into possession, and if he went through the form of assigning it, the assignee would take nothing as against the wife surviving. But, by Malins' Act (20 & 21 Vic. c. 57) where the wife is entitled to a reversionary interest in personalty under an instrument executed after 1857, but not subject to restraint on alienation (anticipation), or settled on her on her marriage, the interest may be disposed of, with the husband's concurrence, by the wife's deed acknowledged after an examination apart from him.

22. As in the case of other deeds requiring such acknowledgment, the husband's concurrence can only be dispensed with where the parties are separated by consent or by decree, or where his residence is unknown, or he is of unsound mind, or incapable of executing a deed, or is transported, or in prison (3 & 4 Will. 4 c. 74 s. 91).

But a wife married after 1882 has, by the M. W. P. Act of that year, an absolute right to dispose of all her separate property, and can convey or release her reversion in personalty without the concurrence of her husband, or the formalities required by Malins' Act.

23 Sometimes, by the settlement, some portion of the wife's property is to go, in default of her appointment by deed or will, to her "next-of-kin," and sometimes it is directed to go to her "personal representatives." The latter expression gives her the whole property (it is like the words used in giving a fee simple in land "to A. B. and his heirs for ever"), and therefore, at her death, her husband will be entitled either as her administrator, or in his *right* as husband. But he cannot be entitled under a limitation, to her "next of kin," unless, indeed, he happens to be cousin, and there are no nearer relations. Nor can *she* be entitled, under a limitation, to *his* "next of kin," unless she is his cousin.

24 I will now point out how far a marriage settlement preserves property against creditors.

A settlement made *before* marriage, and in consideration of marriage, is, in the absence of fraud, good against all the world, even against those to whom the husband or the wife was at the time indebted, for both the husband and wife are regarded as purchasers for value of all the property comprised in the settlement. The same may be said of a settlement which, though made after marriage, is made in compliance with an agreement for a settlement entered into before marriage. And even though there be fraud, the settlements and agreements will be good in favour of the other party, if ignorant of the fraud.

But a settlement made *after* marriage, not being in pursuance of an agreement made before marriage, is treated by the law as *voluntary*, or made not for value. Both as to realty and personalty such a settlement will be void against all persons to whom the settlor was indebted at the time without possessing adequate means of payment, and also against all *subsequent* creditors if made to defraud them.*

But if a settlement, though made after marriage, is made for a valuable consideration, it will be as binding as if made before marriage; as, for instance, if it were made on condition of the husband's obtaining possession of property to which the wife was equitably entitled, or in consideration of an additional portion paid to him by her friends after marriage.

25. After a decree of dissolution of marriage or nullity of marriage, the Divorce Court has power to enquire into any settlements made on the parties to the marriage, and direct the settled property to be applied for the benefit of one or other of the parties or their children, otherwise than according to the settlement (see chap. xix., s. 26).

* Until the 29th June, 1893, a person who had made a voluntary settlement of *land* might defeat it by afterwards selling for value to another, even though the latter knew of the settlement; but, since that date, the Voluntary Conveyances Act, 1893, prevents a voluntary settlor from so revoking. A settlement of personalty could never be thus revoked. A power of revocation may, of course, be inserted in any voluntary settlement.

## CHAPTER XII.

OF THE HUSBAND'S LIABILITIES BY VIRTUE OF THE MARRIAGE.

1. *Husband's duty to support wife. How enforceable.*
2. *Contracts made and wrongs committed by wife before marriage.*
3. *Contracts made by wife after marriage, by husband's express or implied authority.*
4. *Nature of implied authority.*
5. *Rules for the implication of authority.*
6. *Illustrations of implied authority and how it may be rebutted.*
7. *The like where there is no "course of dealing."*
8. *"Necessaries."*
9. *Tradesman to recover against husband must have looked to him for payment. Examples.*
10. *Allowance to wife during husband's temporary absence.*
11. *Tradesman igornant that a woman is married.*
12. *When husband and wife are separate, no authority to bind husband will be* presumed.
13. *But it must be* proved *by the plaintiff. Evidence.*
14. *Where wife deserts husband, tradesman supplies her at his peril.*
15. *Where she elopes, or husband turns her out for bad conduct.*
16. *Husband has a defence where he pays sufficient on separation by consent; or pays alimony under decree of Court or order of justices; or where the wife has a protection order and he pays nothing.*
17. *Otherwise, if he does not pay alimony or allowance, and she has no sufficient maintenance.*
18. *Liability revives where wife is received back after misconduct.*

19. *Liability of husband who drives wife away by his own misconduct.*

20. *A new class of necessaries may arise when wife is wrongfully turned out of doors or deserted.*

21. *Difference in husband's position as to goods supplied to wife, according as he is or is not living with her. Examples.*

22. *Principles on which a jury should decide what are necessaries.*

23. *Some hints to tradesmen.*

24. *Liability of wife's property on her contracts made otherwise than as agent.*

25. *Liability of husband for wrongs committed by wife during marriage.*

26. *Liability of husband for wife's breaches of trust and devastavits.*

1. The law imposes on the husband the duty of maintaining his wife and any children he may have by her, and, also, up to the age of sixteen, any other children she may have living at the time of the marriage, and whether legitimate or illegitimate.

There are ways by which the wife's right to be supported may be directly enforced, some of which will be treated of in another chapter. Where she is chargeable to the parish, the overseers may apply to a police or stipendiary magistrate or to justices of the peace for an order upon the husband to contribute to her maintenance. When the husband has been guilty of violent assault or desertion, the wife may apply to the same authorities for maintenance, and she may obtain alimony from the Divorce Court in a suit for judicial separation, or for divorce.

But, practically, the husband is, by *indirect* ways, forced to perform the duty of supporting his wife if she is without means; for he knows that, in that case, upon his failing to supply her with necessaries, she can pledge his credit for them while she cohabits with him or is kept away from him by his misconduct.

2. In chapter viii., sec. 11, it has been explained that, under the M.W.P. Act, 1882, secs. 13, 14, and 15,

as regards contracts entered into and wrongs committed by the wife *before* marriage, the husband's liability is confined to the extent of the property of hers which he has acquired or become entitled to, after deducting any payments he has made and the amount of any judgments *boná fide* recovered against him on account of such liabilities of his wife.

3. I will now state the nature and extent of the husband's liability upon the contracts and dealings of his wife *after* marriage.

The wife cannot bind her husband by a contract or bargain she may make unless she has acted on his authority. This authority may be either express (*i.e.*, direct) or implied.

By giving an express authority, a man may make his wife his agent for almost any lawful purpose, just as he may his servant or his friend. Thus if he were to take his wife to a jeweller and tell him he might supply the lady with any jewellery she wanted, or were merely to say to his wife, "You may order what jewellery you want, and I will pay for it," he would give an express authority. If, instead of his wife, he had taken a stranger to the shop, or if the words above quoted had been used to a stranger, the man's liability would have been the same.

And a subsequent sanction or ratification is as good as a previous express authority. So though the purchase of the jewels had been made by the wife without the husband's authority or knowledge, if he afterwards, by speech or conduct, sanctions or approves of it, he will be as liable as if he had given an express authority for it. As if he were to tell the jeweller that he approved of the things, or if his wife, having ordered the jewellery without his leave, had worn it in his presence, he would be presumed to have sanctioned the purchase, unless he were deceived as to the nature of the articles, or had reason to think they were not got upon his credit, but came in some other way, as by a gift or by a purchase with the wife's own moneys.

Where, therefore, an express authority is proved, or

a subsequent ratification, which is its equivalent, the case is simple. It is where the plaintiff founds his claim on an implied authority from the husband that the difficulty arises.

4. An implied authority is a presumed authority; one which the law will presume from the circumstances. These circumstances come under two classes: the one where the wife occupies her natural position as mistress of the household, or if absent from home is so with her husband's consent and without losing his friendship and confidence; the other is where the husband and wife are hostile and he neglects his duty of supporting her.

In the former class of cases the presumption arises from the trust which the husband reposes in the wife; in the latter, from the duty which the law casts upon him.

5. As regards implied authority, the following propositions may be collected from the decisions:—

Where the husband and wife are living together and the latter has the management of the household, without having ready money for the purpose, she has implied authority from the husband to make him liable for such things as she buys in the ordinary course of housekeeping for herself and him and the family.

This is an authority not peculiar to the marriage relation, but is what is enjoyed by a sister, mistress, or any other person entrusted with the housekeeping.

Under these circumstances, the husband is said to "hold the wife out" to the tradespeople as his agent for buying things suited to the style in which he lives. I say "the style in which he lives," and not "his income" or "his rank," because he is the sole judge of the style in which he and his family shall live, and this style may be very much below his income, and much below or much above what is usual in his rank.

Where the husband gives the wife a sufficient allowance for housekeeping, or is ready and willing to give her sufficient money as required, and forbids her to buy on credit, she cannot make him liable by doing so.

Where the husband merely gives the wife the shelter of his roof without food or clothing, she has the right, if she is without means, to pledge his credit for necessary food and clothing for herself.

Where the husband turns his wife out of doors, or so misconducts himself that she is obliged to leave him, she leaves his house with implied authority, if she is without means, to pledge his credit for things necessary to her rank in life.

This, it will be observed, may be a larger authority than she possessed while keeping house; for the husband is the sole judge of the style in which his family is to live, and he may choose to live in a mean style.

6. To illustrate the doctrine of implied authority, a few cases may be put, and, throughout them all, it is to be observed that, as the implication or presumption of authority arises from circumstances, so it may be rebutted by other circumstances. For instance, if a draper sues the husband for the price of clothes sold to the wife, and proves that she was living with him, and that the clothes were suitable to her position, the husband may rebut the presumption thence arising by proving that he gives her a sufficient allowance, and has forbidden her to buy on credit, and that the draper either had notice of these facts or had never dealt with him before.

The head-note of *Debenham* v. *Mellon*, an often-quoted case, is as follows:—

> A husband who is able and willing to supply his wife with necessaries, and who has forbidden her to pledge his credit, cannot be held liable for necessaries bought by her. And a tradesman, without notice of her husband's prohibition, and without having had previous dealings with the wife with his assent, cannot maintain an action against him for the price of articles of female attire suitable to her station in life, and supplied to her upon his credit, but without his knowledge or consent." (5 Q.B.D. 394; 6 App. Ca. 24).

Where an implied authority is relied on to make the husband liable, it is frequently proved by the previous conduct of the parties; as where the wife is in the habit of giving orders to tradesmen, as is usually the case in housekeeping, and the husband is in the habit of paying the bills or sanctioning the purchases, there the husband will be liable for all reasonable purchases made in his name by his wife, until he tells the tradesman that she no longer has his authority to order goods, *i.e.*, tells the tradesman not to trust her any more.

Though the habit of the wife to give orders as her husband's agent is usually confined to housekeeping matters, and necessary clothing for herself and the family, yet the husband might equally become liable by suffering his wife to act habitually as his agent in other matters, as ordering corn for his horses, or selling them and giving warranties for them.

The rule is, that wherever the husband, by previous authority, express or implied, or by subsequent sanction, such as making payments, gives his consent to his wife's establishing a course of dealing with any person, that person may presume that the wife's authority continues as long as the husband does not countermand it, and so the husband will be bound. In fact, having allowed his wife to appear as his agent in a series of matters, he cannot suddenly avoid liability by saying she had no authority. To avoid liability the husband must give notice to the person with whom he has suffered his wife to deal, and must inform him that her authority has ceased, or is restricted to a particular kind of transaction, or to a certain amount of money. With a servant the rule is the same. Sometimes it may be necessary to give such a notice to all tradesmen of a particular class, or to all in the neighbourhood; for the wife may go to a new tradesman who may think she has authority to pledge her husband's credit.

When I say "course of dealing" I do not mean necessarily a large number of transactions; two or three purchases previously authorised, or subsequently sanctioned by the husband, would be sufficient to entitle a tradesman to presume that the wife had a continued authority to deal with him for the same kind of goods, at all events if the goods were of that sort usually purchased by wives.

7. But, apart from any express authority or subsequent sanction of the husband, or any authority implied, as above stated, from a course of dealing, while the husband and wife are living together it will generally be presumed that the wife, if she keep house for him, has authority to pledge his credit for necessaries *suitable to that appearance which the family assumes;* nay, if a man takes a woman to live with him and pass as his wife, whether she takes his name or not, the rule will be the same, even though the person supplying the goods is aware of the real nature of the cohabitation.

The man's actual fortune or prospects do not affect this question, but he is the sole judge of what expenditure is suitable or prudent, for his wife, his mistress, or his family, beyond the mere necessaries of life, for which he will always be liable.

Here no question of a "course of dealing" need arise, for we are not considering the wife's having before acted as the husband's agent to buy, and of the presumption that arises from that habit, but we are treating of the presumed authority which arises from the necessity of the case, the goods ordered being necessaries. Goods may, therefore, be ordered by the wife of any person, whether she has previously dealt with him or not, and if the goods turn out to be necessaries the husband will be liable for them.

8. "Necessaries" means such things and services as are suitable to the style of living, and is not confined, except in the poorest families, to what is needed to preserve life. Whether a thing or a service is a necessary depends on the circumstances of each case, and it is impossible to lay down a rule of universal application.

When I say *turn out* to be necessaries, I mean not only that a woman may happen to deceive the tradesman as to her condition in life so as to induce him to supply a silk dress on her husband's credit when a cotton one would have been the proper thing, but it may turn out that she has already silk dresses enough, and so have all the children, or it may turn out that the husband gives his wife a sufficient money allow ance.

Therefore, though a silk dress may appear on the face of it to be a necessary article of dress for the wife of a solicitor, yet she cannot bind her husband by ordering one silk dress at every shop from St. Paul's Churchyard to Regent Street, any more than she can by ordering two hundred dresses at the same shop.

If the husband were being sued for the price of goods supplied to the wife, and evidence were given of her being already supplied, a jury would be directed, if they believed it, to find a verdict for the defendant.

Speaking of the cases in which a jury may infer that the wife was the husband's agent, Lord Abinger said:—"In the case of orders given by the wife *in those departments which are under her control,* the jury may infer that the wife was the agent of the husband, till the contrary appears. For articles such as clothes which are necessary for the wife if she is living with her husband and nothing appears to the contrary, the jury do right in inferring the agency. But if the order was excessive in extent, or if, when the husband has a small income, she gives extravagant orders, these are circumstances from which a jury would infer that there was no agency."

In another case a suburban stationer sued a husband for the price of a gold pencil case, a seal-skin cigar case, a tobacco pouch, a glove box, a guitar, 10 pieces of music, a Russia purse and a double scent-bottle, —£16 odd in all, supplied to his wife. The husband was a clerk at £400 a year, and the wife had a separate income of £90 a year. The tradesman had usually been paid in ready money and had never sent in bills for more than a few shillings. The wife had eloped after ordering these things, and the husband did not hear of the purchases till she had gone. Two juries found for the plaintiff, but the Court set the second verdict aside; and Mr. Justice Willes said:—"If the husband is liable to pay for the things, it must be because the law infers that his wife had authority to order them. What the law infers is that his wife had authority to order such articles as are reasonably necessary for the position in which the husband chooses to live, and are also within the domestic department which is ordinarily entrusted to the control of the wife."

The burden of proving that the articles come within this class rests on the plaintiff. The same learned judge in the same case said:—"Where the articles are such as may or may not be suitable for the position of the husband, or may or may not be within the domestic department, then the plaintiff must show there is a strong probability for inferring authority. The evidence must be evidence on which the jury can act, and not merely conjecture."

A tradesman, therefore, who has not been in the habit of supplying a married woman with her husband's sanction, and has no other reason for supposing that her husband has given her authority to pledge his credit, supplies her at his peril, even with articles which at first sight appear to be necessaries.

And not only may the presumed authority be rebutted by evidence that the articles were not necessaries according to the mode of living in the family, but the husband may also show (either by cross-examination or by his own evidence, or that of his witnesses) that he told the tradesman, or some person serving in the shop, not to supply his wife any more. Or, what is the same thing, if he had said, "You are not to book anything to me any more; my wife is well supplied, and whatever else she wants she must pay for out of her allowance." Or if he had said, "You may give credit to her, but not to me," or words to that effect. The same defence would apply to an action for eatables as well as clothes, and on the same principle.

9. Throughout the foregoing observations I have been speaking on the supposition that the tradesman who supplies the goods does so *bonâ fide* on the credit of the husband, or at all events presumes that the

husband is going to pay, and debits him with the price of the articles. But where the wife makes a purchase on credit of a tradesman with whom she is not in the habit of dealing, it often happens that he, if he is a prudent man, before sending home the things, makes inquiries as to her respectability, and, perhaps, finds out that she has property of her own, held by trustees, or otherwise to her separate use; and without inquiring of her husband whether the articles in question are bought with his authority, delivers them at his house, and, subsequently, not receiving payment, brings an action against him.

The husband is very likely, under these circumstances, to defend the action successfully, because the facts would lead to the conclusion that the tradesman had supplied the goods on the sole credit of the wife, and having satisfied himself of her *ability to pay*, did not look to the husband for payment. I am, of course, supposing that the husband has done nothing after the purchase to ratify or sanction it (see sec. 3).

If the tradesman debited the wife in his books, that alone would be almost conclusive in the husband's favour.

10. Where a husband who lived with his wife made her an allowance during his *temporary* absence, and a tradesman, knowing this, supplied her with goods upon credit, the husband was held not to be liable. Here the reason why the tradesman failed to recover was, that he could not have supposed, when he supplied the goods, that the wife had the husband's authority to pledge his credit—in other words, he had no right "to look to the husband."

Here it was the plaintiff's knowledge of the allowance which prevented him from recovering the price of the goods, though the sale might be otherwise un-objectionable.

11. After what has been said it is hardly necessary to state that where a tradesman, not knowing that a woman is married, supplies her with goods and afterwards finds out that she has a husband, the husband is in no way liable, for it was not upon his credit that

the tradesman contracted. The husband is only liable when the plaintiff originally looked to him for payment, and very often not even then.

12. The rules above laid down refer to the case of the husband and wife living together; but where, at the time the wife makes the contract or bargain, they are living separate, a totally different principle prevails.

I have stated that, during the cohabitation, the presumption is, *until the contrary is shown*, that the wife has authority to contract for necessaries, and the husband will consequently be liable, unless by his own evidence or by his witnesses, or by cross-examination of those called for the plaintiff, one or other of the defences above mentioned is made out.

But where the wife is not living with her husband the presumption is the other way, and a person supplying her goods must either suppose that she is an unmarried woman, iu which case he will not have looked to the husband, or else must have known that she was married, and must have concluded from the fact of her living apart from him that she was not on such terms of friendship and confidence with him that he should trust her to make purchases as his agent.

13. The law, therefore, shifts upon the plaintiff the burden of showing that the wife either had an actual authority from the husband to pledge his credit, or else that she is living apart from him under such circumstances as that she is enabled by law to bind him by making purchases in his name.

In other words, where the husband and wife are living together, the plaintiff who has supplied her with things, which he shows to be necessaries, has nothing more to do than simply state these facts, and this puts the husband on his defence; but where the wife is living apart from her husband the plaintiff has to give some further evidence as to the circumstances under which they are separated, before he is entitled to recover. This may, of course, be done by calling either the wife as a witness, or the husband himself if no other evidence can be obtained.

14. If a woman, simply from caprice or without sufficient reason, chooses to leave her husband and live away from him while he is willing to give her a home and maintain her, he is no longer bound to supply her with the necessaries of life, and she must get her living as she pleases. A tradesman, therefore, who supplies her with goods, though necessary even to maintain life, cannot charge the husband with them, and must take ready money, or run the risk of getting nothing.

15 The same rule will apply with a still stronger reason where the wife elopes from the husband and lives in adultery, and also though, after such misconduct, she has offered to return to him, and he has refused to receive her.

So also where the wife is guilty of unchastity, or is in the habit of getting drunk and dangerously striking the husband, or is otherwise guilty of cruelty to him, and he is obliged for that reason to have her turned out of doors. If, however, the husband instead of turning out his wife under such circumstances, were to leave her in possession of the house, he might find it difficult to escape liability.

16 So if she leaves her husband with his consent (for whatever reason), and he agrees to give her a sufficient allowance, *and pays* it, that fact will be an answer to an action brought against him for necessaries supplied to her.

If a decree is made for alimony by the Divorce Court for the maintenance of the wife as a party to a suit in that court, the husband will have a defence to an action for necessaries supplied to his wife, if he has paid the alimony but not otherwise.

So if the wife, being deserted or turned out of doors by her husband without reasonable cause, has obtained from the court, or from a police-magistrate, or in the country, from justices of the peace, an order protecting her future acquired earnings and property, and has duly registered the order, she is in the position of a single woman as to her contracts, and the order is a bar to an action against her husband for necessaries supplied to her (see chap. xvi).

So if the wife, after a conviction of her husband for an aggravated assault, obtains an order from a magistrate or justices under the Matrimonial Causes Act, 1878 (see chap. xvi.), for alimony; or if, after being deserted by her husband, she gets an order from the convicting magistrates for separation and maintenance against him, under the Married Women's Maintenance in case of Desertion Act, 1886 (see chap. xvi.), and he pays the maintenance, an action cannot be maintained against him for necessaries supplied to her.

17 If a decree is made for alimony and the husband does not pay the alimony, he will be liable to an action for necessaries; and if the husband and wife separate by mutual consent, and she has no sufficient maintenance from other sources, and he either does not agree to give her any allowance, or any sufficient allowance, or, whether he so agrees or not, does not *pay* an allowance, or lets it fall into arrears, then his liability will be the same as regards necessaries for her station in life as if they were living together, except that when they are living together the question of what are necessaries is regulated by the appearance which he suffers her to assume; but when they are living apart she is entitled to be supplied according to the position of herself and husband as regards rank and fortune.

18 If the wife, having been guilty of misconduct such as above-mentioned, has afterwards returned to her husband, and he, being aware of the misconduct, has received and cohabited with her, his liability for her necessaries will be revived, and will remain if they afterwards separate without a repetition of the misconduct.

19 If the husband drives his wife away from him by his cruelty or other indignities (such as taking a mistress to live with him against his wife's will), he will be liable for necessaries supplied to her wherever she goes, for his duty is to provide her with a home, and if he does not do so, but drives her away, he "turns her out on the world, with implied authority to pledge his credit."

So where the wife committed adultery with her

husband's connivance, and he then turned her out of doors, he was held liable for necessaries supplied to her while living separate.

A reasonable apprehension on the part of the wife that the husband intends to place her under improper restraint, for instance as a lunatic, will warrant her in removing to a separate residence and thereby render him liable for necessaries.

20 A married woman living separate from her husband, and who had obtained the custody of their child from the Court of Chancery under Talfourd's Act, now repealed, but was herself unable to provide for the child, was held entitled to pledge her husband's credit for reasonable expenses incurred by her on behalf of the child.

A wife, deserted without cause and left without means, instituted a suit for restitution, obtained a decree for alimony, took the opinion of counsel on the validity of a verbal promise by her husband of a settlement before marriage, and consulted a solicitor as to a distress under which the landlord had seized furniture which was hers before marriage, but became the husband's by the marriage. These legal expenses were held to be necessaries for which she had rightly pledged her husband's credit, and the person to whom the charges were due was held entitled to recover them against the husband's executor.

The cost of articles of the peace exhibited in the Court of Queen's Bench by the wife against the husband in consequence of his outrageous conduct, were in one case recovered against him, and the same rule would apply to the costs of his being bound over by a police magistrate or justices to keep the peace towards her. And, in an action for these charges by the wife's lawyer, the husband cannot protect himself on the ground that he has paid a sufficient maintenance.

But the costs of a *prosecution* of the husband by the wife for assaulting her cannot be recovered against him as necessaries, for there is no necessity for the wife to punish her husband, but only to protect herself, as she may do by binding him over to keep the peace.

21. Even a person who was prohibited by the husband from supplying the wife, while they lived together, is not prevented by that prohibition from supplying her when separated. And, always supposing there was no misconduct on the wife's part, and no sufficient allowance paid by the husband, the person who has supplied her with necessaries, whether from his own shop or bought for her, or has boarded or lodged her, or procured another to do so, may recover the price from the husband. And though a person who lent money to the wife for necessaries, and which was actually spent in necessaries, could formerly only recover it in equity, he may now do so at law.

In short, when the husband and wife are separated, the wife and the person who supplies her stand upon the same footing, and if she is entitled to maintenance from the husband, that person may recover the price of necessaries supplied to her.

If the husband's defence is that he has given an allowance, the jury who try the case will not only decide whether the allowance was paid, but whether it was sufficient. A fixed maintenance from another source will be equivalent to an allowance by the husband.

A husband may be liable for necessaries supplied to his wife during his lunacy; but only where the wife has no sufficient allowance from him or maintenance from other sources.

A husband was a lunatic under treatment in an asylum, and his wife and children lived in a house of his which he held on a long lease. She ordered repairs to the house, which the tradesman executed after knowing of the lunacy, and for the price of which he sued the lunatic husband. The wife had received an allowance from his estate and from his family sufficient to maintain herself, and the children, and to repair the house, and the court held that the plaintiff could not recover; for the wife had no more power to pledge the husband's credit while he was a lunatic, than she had while he was sane.

Let me further illustrate the difference of the situations in which the tradesman will be placed, according as the wife is or is not living with her husband at the time when the goods are supplied.

Where she was living with her husband, the plaintiff will make a *primâ facie* case by simply stating that he supplied so many yards of silk and linen to the defendant's wife, that the plaintiff's profession and style of living are so and so, and that the articles in question were of the quality usually supplied to people of that class. It would then be incumbent on the husband to make out his defence and to show, either by cross-examination of the plaintiff and his witnesses, or by the testimony of himself and witnesses called by him, that he did not in fact authorise the contract of his wife, nor ought such authority to be presumed. For example, he may show either that he forbad the plaintiff to supply his wife, or that the articles in question were not in fact necessaries, his wife being well supplied, or he may make out any of the other defences above mentioned.

But where the wife was not living with her husband, the plaintiff, after stating as above, must go on to show that the wife was not deprived of her home by her own misconduct, but left it either because of her husband's misconduct or by mutual consent; and, in the latter case, must also show that no allowance is paid her by her husband To prove all this the wife herself will, of course, be the best witness.

Thus, when the husband is living with his wife, there is a presumption that he is liable for necessaries, which presumption he may rebut; and when they are *not* living together, there is a presumption that he is *not* liable, which the person who supplies them may rebut.

Though the tradesman when he supplied the goods may never have known of the existence of any of the above matters of defence (such as the wife being already supplied, having an allowance, or having eloped), nay, even though he may expressly have been told the contrary, yet on proof of any of these defences at the trial he will be non-suited.

The responsibility of the tradesman to ascertain the true position of every married woman with whom he deals, is plainly stated by Lord Tenterden: "If a shopkeeper *will* sell goods to every one who comes into his shop, *without inquiring into their circumstances*, he takes his chance of getting paid; and it lies upon him to make out by full proof his claim against any other person."

If the wife, while living apart, has a sufficient maintenance from any other source, she will have no power to bind her husband, any more than she would if the maintenance were received from him; but then it must not be precarious, and must be actually paid.

When a woman, whose husband is absent, but who thinks he is alive, orders necessaries, and it turns out that he was, in fact, dead at the time, she has been held not to be liable. It is a question whether the husband's executor would be liable in such a case, and whether the tradesman would not be entirely without remedy.

In all the above cases the questions of fact are, of course, for the jury, if the case is tried by a jury; for example, where the wife was living with her husband, the jury will decide whether he expressly authorised the purchase which she made, or whether he afterwards assented to it; whether it is a necessary for the household, so that his authority may be presumed; or whether he had forbidden the plaintiff to trust his wife, &c., &c.

So, also, where the wife was living apart from the husband, the jury would have to decide whether she was living apart under circumstances which justified her in doing so, and whether if it was by mutual consent, she had a sufficient allowance for maintenance.

And whether the wife were living apart or not, the question whether the goods were not supplied in the expectation that they would be paid for out of the wife's *separate property*, is for the jury to decide.

22 The principal question, however, for the jury, usually is, whether the articles in question were or were not necessaries for the wife or family of a person of the husband's rank and fortune. This question is important, because if the goods were not necessaries there

will be no *presumption* that the husband authorised their being purchased, and the plaintiff will have to show some kind of assent on the husband's part or previous authority from him.

Although the question what are necessaries for the wife, while living with her husband, is determined not by his rank or fortune so much as by the appearance which he in his discretion permits her to assume; yet the question, what are the husband's means may sometimes arise as an element for the jury to consider in deciding whether or not he is liable for the goods in question, particularly where the wife is living apart without misconduct, in which case she is entitled to a maintenance suitable to the rank and fortune of herself and her husband. And when the husband's property comes in question, the jury are to be guided not only by how much he had with his wife, but by how much he has altogether.

It is much to be hoped, both for sake of trade and of society in general, that the just and strict views continually impressed by judges upon juries on the question of what are necessaries will be gradually adopted, as being calculated to check extravagance, embarrassment, and distress. But no sufficient rule can here be laid down, except that the test of what are necessaries while the wife is living with her husband is not so much the husband's actual means as the station and appearance which he and his wife assume in society; for the master of the house is the proper judge as to whether the wife shall make a display in dress, furniture, equipage, and hospitalities, or whether the family shall lead a frugal and unostentatious life.

28 From a perusal of this chapter the tradesman will lay down for himself the following rules for his guidance in order to avoid bad debts:

When a wife first begins to deal with you to an amount worth speaking of, or when, having before dealt with you, she gives a more extravagant order than usual, inform the husband personally what the wife has ordered, and ask whether the things are to be put down to him. This course will be more satisfactory than sending the

bill in to the husband or writing to him; for the wife, if she meant to deceive him, would take care that he did not get the bill or the letter.

If you mean to get payment from the husband, do not debit the wife in your books.

If the wife says "debit me" she will probably add that she has property of her own. If she gives particulars of it which she knows to be untrue, and you give her credit on the faith of that statement, she will have obtained the goods by a false pretence and may be criminally prosecuted.

If you mean to rely on the wife's separate estate, and it is vested in a trustee, try to get a guarantee from her trustee, that is, a letter stating that if you will supply her to such and such an amount he will pay you from time to time out of her dividends, &c., as they fall due. (Such letter should generally be stamped.) If you take her bill or note, it will be enforced against her separate property, present and future, but it does not amount to a declaration that she has any separate property.

Remember that if you take such security it will be almost conclusive that you did not look to the husband.

If the wife is living apart, be very sure, before you debit the husband, that she is rightfully living separate, and has no allowance from her husband, or fixed maintenance from any other source.

24. Having now endeavoured to explain in what cases the Court will consider that the wife has contracted as an agent, and in what cases she will be regarded as having contracted "otherwise than as an agent," it is only necessary to refer to the Married Women's Property Act, 1893, as to her property being solely liable on contracts which she makes during marriage "otherwise than as an agent." This statute is given in the Appendix, and its effect is described in chap. viii., ss. 2 and 3. For such contracts she is not personally liable, but all her separate property which she is not restrained from anticipating is liable and, when the marriage is ended by death or divorce and the woman is not married again, all that she has is liable, and then, of course, there is no separate property

and, therefore, no restraint on anticipation. As to the meaning of the wife not being personally liable, see ch. ix., s. 6.

25. The liability of the husband for simple wrongs (*i.e.*, wrongs unconnected with contract) committed by the wife during marriage, has been treated of in chap. ix., s. 2, and chap. xiii., ss. 12—15.

26. Where the wife has become trustee, executrix, or administratrix, either before or after marriage, and before or after marriage (but since 1882) commits any breach of trust or devastavit (which means waste of assets), the husband is liable if he has acted or intermeddled in the trust or administration. But to what extent he is liable is not certain (see chap. viii., sec. 14, and ix., sec. 8).

As to breaches of trust and devastavits committed by the wife before 1883, the husband is still solely liable, and the wife's property is not liable *during the marriage*, except for breach of a trust created by the same instrument as created the separate estate, and not even then if there was a restraint on anticipation.

## CHAPTER XIII.

### OTHER LIABILITIES LIKELY TO BE INCURRED BY THE HUSBAND THROUGH THE WIFE.

1. *Husband's authority to wife is either express or implied. Examples.*

2. *Recognition by husband of wife's dealings. Honouring bills and notes signed by her in his name.*

3. *Authority, whether actual or presumed, may be either general or limited. Examples.*

4. *Husband authorising wife to sign agreement or memorandum.*

5. *Wife unable to bind husband by executing deed unless authorised by deed, or executing in his name and presence and by his command.*

6. *Where wife in doing business for the husband commits a fraud. Example.*

7. *Wife, as trustee, executrix or administratrix.*

8. *Wife as partner.*

9. *Wife as a separate trader.*

10. *Wife trading as husband's agent.*

11. *Wife as surety for husband.*

12. *Husband liable for wrongs unconnected with contract committed by wife during marriage.*

13. *On what events the liability ceases.*

14. *Illustrations of simple wrongs.*

15. *Wrongs done by wife in management of her separate property.*

1. In the last chapter I treated of the wife being the agent of the husband as regards ordering necessaries suitable to her rank and station. It was there stated that, besides the authority there treated of, the husband might confer authority upon his wife so as to make her his agent for almost any lawful purpose.

This authority may be either actual or presumptive, or, what is the same thing, express or implied. The former arises from the acts and sayings of the husband, as if, being an incoming tenant, he were to say to the outgoing tenant, "I cannot attend to you now, but will leave my wife to settle what shall be paid for your fixtures." The latter arises from the appearances held out to the world; as, if the husband kept a shop and the wife served in it, he would be bound to be content with the price at which she sold articles, and would be bound by the warranties which she gave on sale as much as if he gave them himself.

2. If she had been in the habit of ordering goods for his shop of the wholesale dealer, and the husband had recognised the purchases, either by seeing the invoices, receiving the goods, or paying for them, he will then be liable on all similar purchases until he gives notice to the merchant that the wife has no longer any authority to buy for him.

So, also, if the wife has been in the habit of indorsing or accepting bills or making promissory notes in the husband's name, and he has ratified such authority by paying the bills or notes, he will in general be liable upon similar bills or notes *to all persons who believe the wife to be still authorised to sign his name.*

When I say "habit" I do not mean necessarily a great number of such acts spread over a long time, but one or two bills or notes so paid by the husband would be evidence from which a jury might presume an acquiescence on his part in his wife's so acting. The latter examples which I have given are of the husband's liability from custom or acquiescence, which, after all, are only a kind of "appearances held out to the world."

The same rules will apply to any transactions in which the husband constitutes the wife his agent or suffers her to become such, whether or not they relate to matters which are usually within feminine experience.

3. It will be observed, however, that both the express and the implied authority which I have spoken of above may be either general or limited, that is, either

# CHAPTER XIII.

## OTHER LIABILITIES LIKELY TO BE INCURRED BY THE HUSBAND THROUGH THE WIFE.

1. *Husband's authority to wife is either express or implied. Examples.*

2. *Recognition by husband of wife's dealings. Honouring bills and notes signed by her in his name.*

3. *Authority, whether actual or presumed, may be either general or limited. Examples.*

4. *Husband authorising wife to sign agreement or memorandum.*

5. *Wife unable to bind husband by executing deed unless authorised by deed, or executing in his name and presence and by his command.*

6. *Where wife in doing business for the husband commits a fraud. Example.*

7. *Wife, as trustee, executrix or administratrix.*

8. *Wife as partner.*

9. *Wife as a separate trader.*

10. *Wife trading as husband's agent.*

11. *Wife as surety for husband.*

12. *Husband liable for wrongs unconnected with contract committed by wife during marriage.*

13. *On what events the liability ceases.*

14. *Illustrations of simple wrongs.*

15. *Wrongs done by wife in management of her separate property.*

1. In the last chapter I treated of the wife being the agent of the husband as regards ordering necessaries suitable to her rank and station. It was there stated that, besides the authority there treated of, the husband might confer authority upon his wife so as to make her his agent for almost any lawful purpose.

This authority may be either actual or [illegible] or, what is the same thing, express or implied. The former arises from the acts and sayings of the husband as if, being an incoming tenant, he were to say to the outgoing tenant, "I cannot attend to you now, but will leave my wife to settle with you [illegible] your fixtures." The latter arises from the [illegible] held out to the world: as, if the husband [illegible] and the wife served in it, he would be [illegible] tent with the price at which she sold articles, and [illegible] be bound by the warranties which she gave [illegible] much as if he gave them himself.

2. If she had been in the habit of ordering [illegible] his shop of the wholesale dealer, and he [illegible] recognised the purchases, either by [illegible] receiving the goods, or paying for them, [illegible] liable on all similar purchases [illegible] the merchant that the wife had no [illegible] to buy for him.

So, also, if the wife has been [illegible] is or accepting bills or [illegible] husband's name, and he [illegible] his paying the bills or [illegible] the upon similar bills or [illegible] told the *wife to be still authorised* [illegible]

When I say [illegible] a week [illegible] and the great number [illegible] ment, the pur- [illegible] from the hus- [illegible] damages of course [illegible] in value between the [illegible] represented to be.

[illegible] ility where his wife is [illegible] tratrix, I have done my [illegible] 17, to explain that section [illegible] omen's Property Act, 1882, [illegible] with that subject, and will add [illegible]

[illegible] ving now full capacity to contract in [illegible] separate property, may enter into part- [illegible] a stranger or with her husband, and her extending to all kinds of transactions or to all transactions of a certain kind, or else may be confined to a particular time, or a particular act, or a limited amount of money.

For instance, as to express or actual authority, the words addressed by the incoming to the outgoing tenant above mentioned would be evidence of an actual authority to the wife of a limited kind.

Whereas if he had said, as men sometimes do, "My wife does as much of my business as I do; she sees my customers, buys and sells for me, gives orders to my men, and looks after my horses;" it would give rise to a presumption of an authority more extended, and the husband would find it difficult afterwards to repudiate any transaction in which he thought his wife had been cheated in any of the various details of his business which he had enumerated, or in others of the same kind. Again, as to *presumed* authority, it would not by any means follow because the wife was seen attending to business while the husband was ill or absent, that therefore she had authority to act in the same way when he was at home and well.

Nothing more can be done here than to state the principle, with one or two examples to illustrate it, for every case must depend on its own circumstances.

4. If the husband were, verbally or by writing, to authorise the wife to sign his name to a memorandum or agreement in writing, whether for the manufacture of goods, to grant a lease, or to make a sale of land or houses, or for almost any other purpose, the signature by the wife of the husband's name would bind him.

Under a verbal authority, she may sign her husband's name to an agreement under hand only, which if a full rent is reserved, will operate as a lease for three years or less; but if the agreement is to grant a lease or is for the sale of land, then, when it comes actually to granting the lease or executing the conveyance, which have to be under seal, these instruments can only be executed in the husband's name by the wife or any other person, if appointed by power of attorney under seal. The deed will be valid, it is true, if executed by her in his name, in his presence, and by his direction; but such an execution would not satisfy a purchaser.

5. So with *bonds* and other deeds or writings under seal, *i.e.*, documents where a seal or wafer is appended near the signature, and which is affixed, or at least touched, by the party signing, by way of *delivering* the writing as his act and deed. The husband cannot be sued upon any deed or contract under seal, entered into and executed by the wife in his name and on his behalf, unless he has authorised her to do so by another deed, usually called a power of attorney; or unless the deed in question was sealed and delivered by her in his name, in his presence, and by his commandment. When this is done it is considered to be a signing and delivery by him, and it will be as well that the way in which the deed was executed should appear in the attestation.

6. If the wife, acting as agent for her husband, commits a fraud, the husband is considered as having himself committed the fraud through his wife, and is therefore liable upon it.

For example, where a baker, having made up his mind to sell his business, left his wife to arrange the matter with the broker in his absence, and she told the broker that they were doing nearly twelve sacks a week when in truth they were only doing nine, and the broker sold the business upon this statement, the purchaser was entitled to recover damages from the husband for the fraud of his wife, the damages of course being measured by the difference in value between the actual business and what it was represented to be.

7. As to the husband's liability where his wife is trustee, executrix, or administratrix, I have done my best, in chap. viii., secs. 16, 17, to explain that section (24) of the Married Women's Property Act, 1882, which is concerned with that subject, and will add nothing about it here.

8. The wife having now full capacity to contract in respect of her separate property, may enter into partnership with a stranger or with her husband, and her

husband, if partner, will then be as liable on her contracts and dealings made within the scope of the business, and for her wrongs done in the course of it, as in any other case of partnership.*

9. Where a husband permits his wife to carry on a trade separately from him (see chap. viii., sec. 2), he is not liable upon her contracts and dealings in that trade, unless he intermeddles.

Where the married woman, having separate property, carries on business with it in partnership with her husband, it has been held that her trade is *a separate* trade; so she can enjoy the profits of such a trade as her separate property under sec. 2 of the Act of 1882, and under sec. 1 (5) will be liable to the bankruptcy laws as a separate trader.

She may have a right to carry on a separate trade by virtue of an express agreement made before marriage or by her husband's permission after marriage.

Where the wife sets up a separate business with her own capital, or with money which she borrows, she can obtain an injunction to prevent her husband from meddling with the stock or the profits, or even from entering the place of business.

If the husband is sued in respect of the business on the ground that he has intermeddled in it, it will be a question of fact for the jury—if the case is tried by a jury—whether the business was separate or not.

To make the business separate, there is no need for the man and wife to live in separate houses, or for cohabitation to cease. The husband may even be employed in the business as the wife's servant. Where a butcher became incapacitated through drink from following his trade, and got into the workhouse, and his wife borrowed money, carried on the business, and took him out of the workhouse, and employed him as her servant in the shop, the court found as a fact that the trading was separate.

10. But if the husband not only lives with his wife

* See my book on "Private Trading Partnership," published by Effingham Wilson and Co.

but takes the profits of the business, especially if he takes part in ordering or selling goods, he will be liable in respect of the business, although the wife is lessee of the house, and is rated for it, and has her name over the door, and the goods are invoiced to her, and the receipts given by her. The wife will be regarded as the husband's agent for carrying on the business.

Where the wife so acts, the husband as principal, will be responsible for all wrongful acts done by her in the conduct of the business; as, where a wife so acting told a servant to drive a cart which was dangerous, to her knowledge but not to his, from ill-repair, and the cart broke down and injured him, the husband was liable as well as the wife.

11. Where a wife mortgages or charges her property to secure the liabilities of the husband, the Court will usually compel the husband to exonerate her property by means of his own. The ground of this right is that the husband was really the principal debtor, though probably not appearing so on the face of the documents, and the mortgage or charge was by way of suretyship. This right is not lost by the wife committing adultery and being divorced, and may be enforced by her heir or executor.

12. By the common law the wife's personal property in possession was transferred to the husband; he had a right to reduce into possession her *choses in action*, and had a large interest in her real estate. Taking so much of her property, it was only right that he should be liable, not only upon her contracts made, but for wrongs committed by her before and after marriage. But the Married Women's Property Act, 1882, has taken away the husband's right to the wife's property, and, while relieving him (except to the extent of property of hers to which he has become entitled) from liability upon her contracts made and for wrongs committed by her before marriage, has left him liable with her for wrongs committed by her after marriage. This was probably through inadvertence in the preparation of the measure.

But, as the husband is not liable on any contracts

made by the wife after marriage without his authority, express or implied, so he is not liable for any wrongs which consist of a breach of her contract, or are founded on, or spring out of, or are connected with a contract of hers made after marriage, but she is solely answerable for them out of her separate property. He is only liable for simple wrongs.

An assault, a defamation of character, and an injury by negligent riding or driving, are examples of the wrongs which can hardly be connected with contract, and for which the husband is liable if sued together with his wife.

The wife being made liable by the Married Women's Property Act, 1882, s. 1, to be sued for wrongs as if she were single, the plaintiff who has suffered the injury may sue her alone for any wrong committed by her before or after marriage, but then he must in each case rely only on her separate property. If he joins the husband as defendant in an action for a wrong committed by the wife before marriage the plaintiff may make the husband liable only to the extent of property of hers which he has become entitled to; but if he joins the husband in an action for the wife's post-nuptial wrong, the husband is liable as he was before the Act, to the extent of all his property, whether it ever was hers or not. A plaintiff who is thus able to make the wife liable in respect of her separate property, and the husband liable personally, will probably join them both as defendants, and if he gets judgment, that judgment will be against the wife's separate property, and against the husband personally. And the execution, though issued against both, may be levied wholly upon the property of either; so that the husband may have to bear the whole burden.

In the latter case, the husband who has satisfied the judgment will not be able to recover from the wife any part of what he has paid; for the Act has not made the wife's separate property primarily liable as between herself and her husband in respect of wrongs committed by her during marriage.

13. The husband will not be liable for wrongs committed by his wife after a decree for judicial separation or the granting a protection order, at any rate, if duly

registered, either of which makes her a single woman as long as it is in operation; but a resumption of cohabitation will render invalid the decree and the order, and the husband's risks will begin again. After the death of the wife or a decree of divorce, the husband's liability for the wrongs which his wife has committed during marriage ceases.

14. In order to explain the distinction between these simple wrongs for which, when committed by the wife after marriage, the husband, if sued jointly with her, is liable, and those wrongs arising out of, or connected with contracts, for which, if committed by her after marriage, he is not liable, and for which her separate property alone is liable—I will mention two cases.

A married woman represented herself as single, and induced a man to marry her, and he, when he found out the truth, brought an action against her and her husband for the damage and loss occasioned by the wife's false representation; but it was held that the husband was not liable because the fraud was in regard to a contract of the wife not made with his authority. So where a married woman persuaded a man to accept her security for another by pretending to be single. Other examples might easily be imagined, as if the wife, exercising the calling of a surgeon, so negligently performed an operation as to injure her patient, or if she kept a lodging-house and knowingly employed a dishonest servant who stole her lodger's goods.

15. Whether a husband would be liable for a simple tort independent of contract, but done by the wife in the management of her separate property, has not, to my knowledge, been decided. For example, if she digs a gravel pit on her land, and leaves it unfenced so near a highway that the plaintiff, travelling by night, without negligence falls into it; or if, having land near a neighbour's house, which has been standing long enough to acquire a right to support, she quarries or digs foundations so near the house that it falls down; or if she diverts a stream passing over her land to the prejudice of a miller lower down who is entitled to the water. Here the husband can neither take the profit

bill in to the husband or writing to him; for the wife, if she meant to deceive him, would take care that he did not get the bill or the letter.

If you mean to get payment from the husband, do not debit the wife in your books.

If the wife says "debit me" she will probably add that she has property of her own. If she gives particulars of it which she knows to be untrue, and you give her credit on the faith of that statement, she will have obtained the goods by a false pretence and may be criminally prosecuted.

If you mean to rely on the wife's separate estate, and it is vested in a trustee, try to get a guarantee from her trustee, that is, a letter stating that if you will supply her to such and such an amount he will pay you from time to time out of her dividends, &c., as they fall due. (Such letter should generally be stamped.) If you take her bill or note, it will be enforced against her separate property, present and future, but it does not amount to a declaration that she has any separate property.

Remember that if you take such security it will be almost conclusive that you did not look to the husband.

If the wife is living apart, be very sure, before you debit the husband, that she is rightfully living separate, and has no allowance from her husband, or fixed maintenance from any other source.

24. Having now endeavoured to explain in what cases the Court will consider that the wife has contracted as an agent, and in what cases she will be regarded as having contracted "otherwise than as an agent," it is only necessary to refer to the Married Women's Property Act, 1893, as to her property being solely liable on contracts which she makes during marriage "otherwise than as an agent." This statute is given in the Appendix, and its effect is described in chap. viii., ss. 2 and 8. For such contracts she is not personally liable, but all her separate property which [illegible] restrained from anticipating is liable and, [illegible] is ended by death or divorce and [illegible] again, all that she has is [illegible] no separate property

and, therefore, no restraint on anticipation. As to the meaning of the wife not being personally liable, see ch. ix., s. 6.

25. The liability of the husband for simple wrongs (*i.e.*, wrongs unconnected with contract) committed by the wife during marriage, has been treated of in chap. ix., s. 2, and chap. xiii., ss. 12—15.

26. Where the wife has become trustee, executrix, or administratrix, either before or after marriage, and before or after marriage (but since 1882) commits any breach of trust or devastavit (which means waste of assets), the husband is liable if he has acted or intermeddled in the trust or administration. But to what extent he is liable is not certain (see chap. viii., sec. 14, and ix., sec. 8).

As to breaches of trust and devastavits committed by the wife before 1883, the husband is still solely liable, and the wife's property is not liable *during the marriage*, except for breach of a trust created by the same instrument as created the separate estate, and not even then if there was a restraint on anticipation.

## CHAPTER XIII.

### OTHER LIABILITIES LIKELY TO BE INCURRED BY THE HUSBAND THROUGH THE WIFE.

1. *Husband's authority to wife is either express or implied. Examples.*
2. *Recognition by husband of wife's dealings. Honouring bills and notes signed by her in his name.*
3. *Authority, whether actual or presumed, may be either general or limited. Examples.*
4. *Husband authorising wife to sign agreement or memorandum.*
5. *Wife unable to bind husband by executing deed unless authorised by deed, or executing in his name and presence and by his command.*
6. *Where wife in doing business for the husband commits a fraud. Example.*
7. *Wife, as trustee, executrix or administratrix.*
8. *Wife as partner.*
9. *Wife as a separate trader.*
10. *Wife trading as husband's agent.*
11. *Wife as surety for husband.*
12. *Husband liable for wrongs unconnected with contract committed by wife during marriage.*
13. *On what events the liability ceases.*
14. *Illustrations of simple wrongs.*
15. *Wrongs done by wife in management of her separate property.*

1. In the last chapter I treated of the wife being the agent of the husband as regards ordering necessaries suitable to her rank and station. It was there stated that, besides the authority there treated of, the husband might confer authority upon his wife so as to make her his agent for almost any lawful purpose.

This authority may be either actual or presumptive, or, what is the same thing, express or implied. The former arises from the acts and sayings of the husband, as if, being an incoming tenant, he were to say to the outgoing tenant, "I cannot attend to you now, but will leave my wife to settle what shall be paid for your fixtures." The latter arises from the appearances held out to the world; as, if the husband kept a shop and the wife served in it, he would be bound to be content with the price at which she sold articles, and would be bound by the warranties which she gave on sale as much as if he gave them himself.

2. If she had been in the habit of ordering goods for his shop of the wholesale dealer, and the husband had recognised the purchases, either by seeing the invoices, receiving the goods, or paying for them, he will then be liable on all similar purchases until he gives notice to the merchant that the wife has no longer any authority to buy for him.

So, also, if the wife has been in the habit of indorsing or accepting bills or making promissory notes in the husband's name, and he has ratified such authority by paying the bills or notes, he will in general be liable upon similar bills or notes *to all persons who believe the wife to be still authorised to sign his name.*

When I say "habit" I do not mean necessarily a great number of such acts spread over a long time, but one or two bills or notes so paid by the husband would be evidence from which a jury might presume an acquiescence on his part in his wife's so acting. The latter examples which I have given are of the husband's liability from custom or acquiescence, which, after all, are only a kind of "appearances held out to the world."

The same rules will apply to any transactions in which the husband constitutes the wife his agent or suffers her to become such, whether or not they relate to matters which are usually within feminine experience.

3. It will be observed, however, that both the express and the implied authority which I have spoken of above may be either general or limited, that is, either

extending to all kinds of transactions or to all transactions of a certain kind, or else may be confined to a particular time, or a particular act, or a limited amount of money.

For instance, as to express or actual authority, the words addressed by the incoming to the outgoing tenant above mentioned would be evidence of an actual authority to the wife of a limited kind.

Whereas if he had said, as men sometimes do, "My wife does as much of my business as I do; she sees my customers, buys and sells for me, gives orders to my men, and looks after my horses;" it would give rise to a presumption of an authority more extended, and the husband would find it difficult afterwards to repudiate any transaction in which he thought his wife had been cheated in any of the various details of his business which he had enumerated, or in others of the same kind. Again, as to *presumed* authority, it would not by any means follow because the wife was seen attending to business while the husband was ill or absent, that therefore she had authority to act in the same way when he was at home and well.

Nothing more can be done here than to state the principle, with one or two examples to illustrate it, for every case must depend on its own circumstances.

4. If the husband were, verbally or by writing, to authorise the wife to sign his name to a memorandum or agreement in writing, whether for the manufacture of goods, to grant a lease, or to make a sale of land or houses, or for almost any other purpose, the signature by the wife of the husband's name would bind him.

Under a verbal authority, she may sign her husband's name to an agreement under hand only, which if a full rent is reserved, will operate as a lease for three years or less; but if the agreement is to grant a lease or is for the sale of land, then, when it comes actually to granting the lease or executing the conveyance, which have to be under seal, these instruments can only be executed in the husband's name by the wife or any other person, if appointed by power of attorney under seal. The deed will be valid, it is true, if executed by her in his name, in his presence, and by his direction; but such an execution would not satisfy a purchaser.

5. So with *bonds* and other deeds or writings under seal, *i.e.*, documents where a seal or wafer is appended near the signature, and which is affixed, or at least touched, by the party signing, by way of *delivering* the writing as his act and deed. The husband cannot be sued upon any deed or contract under seal, entered into and executed by the wife in his name and on his behalf, unless he has authorised her to do so by another deed, usually called a power of attorney; or unless the deed in question was sealed and delivered by her in his name, in his presence, and by his commandment. When this is done it is considered to be a signing and delivery by him, and it will be as well that the way in which the deed was executed should appear in the attestation.

6. If the wife, acting as agent for her husband, commits a fraud, the husband is considered as having himself committed the fraud through his wife, and is therefore liable upon it.

For example, where a baker, having made up his mind to sell his business, left his wife to arrange the matter with the broker in his absence, and she told the broker that they were doing nearly twelve sacks a week when in truth they were only doing nine, and the broker sold the business upon this statement, the purchaser was entitled to recover damages from the husband for the fraud of his wife, the damages of course being measured by the difference in value between the actual business and what it was represented to be.

7. As to the husband's liability where his wife is trustee, executrix, or administratrix, I have done my best, in chap. viii., secs. 16, 17, to explain that section (24) of the Married Women's Property Act, 1882, which is concerned with that subject, and will add nothing about it here.

8. The wife having now full capacity to contract in respect of her separate property, may enter into partnership with a stranger or with her husband, and her

21. Even a person who was prohibited by the husband from supplying the wife, while they lived together, is not prevented by that prohibition from supplying her when separated. And, always supposing there was no misconduct on the wife's part, and no sufficient allowance paid by the husband, the person who has supplied her with necessaries, whether from his own shop or bought for her, or has boarded or lodged her, or procured another to do so, may recover the price from the husband. And though a person who lent money to the wife for necessaries, and which was actually spent in necessaries, could formerly only recover it in equity, he may now do so at law.

In short, when the husband and wife are separated, the wife and the person who supplies her stand upon the same footing, and if she is entitled to maintenance from the husband, that person may recover the price of necessaries supplied to her.

If the husband's defence is that he has given an allowance, the jury who try the case will not only decide whether the allowance was paid, but whether it was sufficient. A fixed maintenance from another source will be equivalent to an allowance by the husband.

A husband may be liable for necessaries supplied to his wife during his lunacy; but only where the wife has no sufficient allowance from him or maintenance from other sources.

A husband was a lunatic under treatment in an asylum, and his wife and children lived in a house of his which he held on a long lease. She ordered repairs to the house, which the tradesman executed after knowing of the lunacy, and for the price of which he sued the lunatic husband. The wife had received an allowance from his estate and from his family sufficient to maintain herself, and the children, and to repair the house, and the court held that the plaintiff could not recover; for the wife had no more power to pledge the husband's credit while he was a lunatic, than she had while he was sane.

Let me further illustrate the difference of the situations in which the tradesman will be placed, according as the wife is or is not living with her husband at the time when the goods are supplied.

Where she was living with her husband, the plaintiff will make a *primâ facie* case by simply stating that he supplied so many yards of silk and linen to the defendant's wife, that the plaintiff's profession and style of living are so and so, and that the articles in question were of the quality usually supplied to people of that class. It would then be incumbent on the husband to make out his defence and to show, either by cross-examination of the plaintiff and his witnesses, or by the testimony of himself and witnesses called by him, that he did not in fact authorise the contract of his wife, nor ought such authority to be presumed. For example, he may show either that he forbad the plaintiff to supply his wife, or that the articles in question were not in fact necessaries, his wife being well supplied, or he may make out any of the other defences above mentioned.

But where the wife was not living with her husband, the plaintiff, after stating as above, must go on to show that the wife was not deprived of her home by her own misconduct, but left it either because of her husband's misconduct or by mutual consent; and, in the latter case, must also show that no allowance is paid her by her husband To prove all this the wife herself will, of course, be the best witness.

Thus, when the husband is living with his wife, there is a presumption that he is liable for necessaries, which presumption he may rebut; and when they are *not* living together, there is a presumption that he is *not* liable, which the person who supplies them may rebut.

Though the tradesman when he supplied the goods may never have known of the existence of any of the above matters of defence (such as the wife being already supplied, having an allowance, or having eloped), nay, even though he may expressly have been told the contrary, yet on proof of any of these defences at the trial he will be non-suited.

The responsibility of the tradesman to ascertain the true position of every married woman with whom he deals, is plainly stated by Lord Tenterden: "If a shopkeeper *will* sell goods to every one who comes into his shop, *without inquiring into their circumstances*, he takes his chance of getting paid; and it lies upon him to make out by full proof his claim against any other person."

If the wife, while living apart, has a sufficient maintenance from any other source, she will have no power to bind her husband, any more than she would if the maintenance were received from him; but then it must not be precarious, and must be actually paid.

When a woman, whose husband is absent, but who thinks he is alive, orders necessaries, and it turns out that he was, in fact, dead at the time, she has been held not to be liable. It is a question whether the husband's executor would be liable in such a case, and whether the tradesman would not be entirely without remedy.

In all the above cases the questions of fact are, of course, for the jury, if the case is tried by a jury; for example, where the wife was living with her husband, the jury will decide whether he expressly authorised the purchase which she made, or whether he afterwards assented to it; whether it is a necessary for the household, so that his authority may be presumed; or whether he had forbidden the plaintiff to trust his wife, &c., &c.

So, also, where the wife was living apart from the husband, the jury would have to decide whether she was living apart under circumstances which justified her in doing so, and whether if it was by mutual consent, she had a sufficient allowance for maintenance.

And whether the wife were living apart or not, the question whether the goods were not supplied in the expectation that they would be paid for out of the wife's *separate property*, is for the jury to decide.

22. The principal question, however, for the jury, usually is, whether the articles in question were or were not necessaries for the wife or family of a person of the husband's rank and fortune. This question is important, because if the goods were not necessaries there

will be no *presumption* that the husband authorised their being purchased, and the plaintiff will have to show some kind of assent on the husband's part or previous authority from him.

Although the question what are necessaries for the wife, while living with her husband, is determined not by his rank or fortune so much as by the appearance which he in his discretion permits her to assume; yet the question, what are the husband's means may sometimes arise as an element for the jury to consider in deciding whether or not he is liable for the goods in question, particularly where the wife is living apart without misconduct, in which case she is entitled to a maintenance suitable to the rank and fortune of herself and her husband. And when the husband's property comes in question, the jury are to be guided not only by how much he had with his wife, but by how much he has altogether.

It is much to be hoped, both for sake of trade and of society in general, that the just and strict views continually impressed by judges upon juries on the question of what are necessaries will be gradually adopted, as being calculated to check extravagance, embarrassment, and distress. But no sufficient rule can here be laid down, except that the test of what are necessaries while the wife is living with her husband is not so much the husband's actual means as the station and appearance which he and his wife assume in society; for the master of the house is the proper judge as to whether the wife shall make a display in dress, furniture, equipage, and hospitalities, or whether the family shall lead a frugal and unostentatious life.

23 From a perusal of this chapter the tradesman will lay down for himself the following rules for his guidance in order to avoid bad debts:

When a wife first begins to deal with you to an amount worth speaking of, or when, having before dealt with you, she gives a more extravagant order than usual, inform the husband personally what the wife has ordered, and ask whether the things are to be put down to him. This course will be more satisfactory than sending the

bill in to the husband or writing to him; for the wife, if she meant to deceive him, would take care that he did not get the bill or the letter.

If you mean to get payment from the husband, do not debit the wife in your books.

If the wife says "debit me" she will probably add that she has property of her own. If she gives particulars of it which she knows to be untrue, and you give her credit on the faith of that statement, she will have obtained the goods by a false pretence and may be criminally prosecuted.

If you mean to rely on the wife's separate estate, and it is vested in a trustee, try to get a guarantee from her trustee, that is, a letter stating that if you will supply her to such and such an amount he will pay you from time to time out of her dividends, &c., as they fall due. (Such letter should generally be stamped.) If you take her bill or note, it will be enforced against her separate property, present and future, but it does not amount to a declaration that she has any separate property.

Remember that if you take such security it will be almost conclusive that you did not look to the husband.

If the wife is living apart, be very sure, before you debit the husband, that she is rightfully living separate, and has no allowance from her husband, or fixed maintenance from any other source.

24. Having now endeavoured to explain in what cases the Court will consider that the wife has contracted as an agent, and in what cases she will be regarded as having contracted "otherwise than as an agent," it is only necessary to refer to the Married Women's Property Act, 1893, as to her property being solely liable on contracts which she makes during marriage "otherwise than as an agent." This statute is given in the Appendix, and its effect is described in chap. viii., ss. 2 and 3. For such contracts she is not personally liable, but all her separate property which she is not restrained from anticipating is liable and, when the marriage is ended by death or divorce and the woman is not married again, all that she has is liable, and then, of course, there is no separate property

and, therefore, no restraint on anticipation. As to the meaning of the wife not being personally liable, see ch. ix., s. 6.

25. The liability of the husband for simple wrongs (*i.e.*, wrongs unconnected with contract) committed by the wife during marriage, has been treated of in chap. ix., s. 2, and chap. xiii., ss. 12—15.

26. Where the wife has become trustee, executrix, or administratrix, either before or after marriage, and before or after marriage (but since 1882) commits any breach of trust or devastavit (which means waste of assets), the husband is liable if he has acted or intermeddled in the trust or administration. But to what extent he is liable is not certain (see chap. viii., sec. 14, and ix., sec. 8).

As to breaches of trust and devastavits committed by the wife before 1883, the husband is still solely liable, and the wife's property is not liable *during the marriage*, except for breach of a trust created by the same instrument as created the separate estate, and not even then if there was a restraint on anticipation.

diligence have got in, and so the wrongs committed by her after separation will present the only source of risk. Nominal or not, however, the indemnity is a good consideration.

9. Where the marriage was after 1882, or where the wife has no separate property, or what she has needs no provision respecting it, and the husband is to give her an annuity, the following is the ordinary form stripped of needless verbiage:—

**This Indenture** made the day of 18 , between H of of the first part, W, his wife, of the second part, and X [trustee] of of the third part, for the settlement of unhappy differences which have arisen between the said H. and the said W, WITNESSETH as follows:—

1. The said H. covenants with the said W., and (as a separate covenant) with the said X., that during the life of the said H. the said W. may at at all times live separate from him and free from his control as if she were unmarried, and that he will not in any way compel or endeavour to compel her to cohabit with him, or molest her, or interfere with her in her mode of life, or otherwise, and will not sue or prosecute any person for receiving or assisting her. And will, during the joint lives of himself and the said W., pay to the said W. £100 per annum, by equal quarterly payments on the usual quarter days (the first payment being on the day of next), and this annuity shall be apportionable at its beginning and its termination.

2. The said W. and the said X. each of them covenants with the said H. that the said W. shall not at any time molest, or disturb the said H., and shall not in any way compel, or endeavour to compel him to cohabit with her; and that the preceding covenant on the part of the said H. being duly observed, the said W. and the said X., his heirs, executors, and administrators, will at all times hereafter keep indemnified the said H., his heirs, executors, and administrators, against all debts and liabilities, present and future, of the said W., and against all actions and demands, costs, charges, losses, damages, and expenses in respect thereof or any of them.

3. Provided that, if the said H. and W. shall again cohabit together or the marriage shall be dissolved by any competent Court in consequence of anything done or suffered by either party, after the execution hereof, these presents shall be void, except in respect of any will, or disposition, or other act previously done, and proceedings for breaches of the covenants herein contained, previously committed.

In witness whereof the parties hereto have hereto set their hands and seals the day and year first above written.

10. If the wife or the husband is to have the sole custody of any of the children, the other party being entitled to access to them at convenient times and places, a clause naming the children and stating the arrangements should be inserted. Although the husband has the *prima facie* right to the children, yet, as the mother may apply for their custody under the Infants' Custody Act, 1873, or the Guardianship of Infants' Act, 1886 (see chap. xx.), it will not be vain to expressly give to the father the custody of the children whom he is to keep. The Courts will not easily accede to the wife's application for a custody which she has consented to forego.

11. The deed of separation will be voidable if obtained by the fraud of either party. A deed was set aside when procured by the wife's representation that her life had been chaste, and she desired so to continue, when in fact she had been living in adultery and meant to resume it.

The deed, though void on a resumption of cohabitation, will stand unaffected by the adultery of either party after it.

But the deed is not a licence to either party to commit adultery, and the innocent party may petition for judicial separation or for divorce, as the case may be, for the fault of the other. That is, the innocent husband may have the marriage dissolved for the subsequent adultery of the wife, and the innocent wife may have a judicial separation for the subsequent adultery of the husband, or a dissolution, if his adultery is bigamous or incestuous.

After decree of dissolution of marriage (divorce), the separation deed will become void by force of the proviso. If there is no proviso and no qualification in the covenant itself, the husband will still be liable upon it. But the Court, by virtue of its power to remodel settlements, whether ante-nuptial or post-nuptial, may, on a decree for divorce or nullity, remodel the trusts and make a greater or a less provision for the wife, 22 and 23 Vic., c. 61, s. 5, and 41 Vic., c. 19, s. 3 (see chap. xix).

12. It will be observed that the only proceeding against which each of the parties covenants is a petition for restitution of conjugal rights. If either asserts this right after covenanting to forego it, the other may obtain an order in the nature of an injunction to stay the proceeding, or may set up the deed by way of answer to the petition.

13. Sometimes, in consideration of the husband's covenant to pay an annuity, the wife consents to forego her right to dower out of his lands and her distributive share of his personalty on his dying intestate, and sometimes covenants to pay his debts and to grant him an annuity. And she may agree to forego the charge of £500 now created in her favour by the Intestates Estates Act, 1890. (See Appendix). But a wife cannot, by a separation deed, deal with her real and personal estate to a greater extent than if she were contracting with a stranger. For example, if, being married before the first of January, 1883, she had real estate acquired before that date and not settled to her separate use; or a reversionary interest in personalty, though created after 1857, she could deal with neither without an acknowledged deed and her husband's concurrence, as required in the former case, by 3 and 4 W. IV., c. 74; and in the latter, by Malins' Act, 20 and 21 Vic., c. 57 (see chaps. iii., s. 14, and iv. s. 12).

## CHAPTER XVI.

### OF PROTECTION ORDERS, AND ORDERS BY MAGISTRATES FOR MAINTENANCE, SEPARATION, AND CUSTODY OF CHILDREN.

1. *Protection order in case of desertion.*
2. *Equivalent, as regards property, to decree for judicial separation.*
3. *How obtained and how discharged.*
4. *Its operation.*
5. *Registration of certain protection orders.*
6. *Although reversed, valid in favour of persons dealing with wife in reliance on order.*
7. *Court requires husband if within the jurisdiction, to be served with summons to shew cause against order.*
8. *Date of desertion to be stated in order.*
9. *The Summary Jurisdiction (Married Women) Act*, 1895.
10. *Orders for separation, custody of children and maintenance.*
11. *Remarks about the Act.*

**1. The Divorce Court or magistrates may make orders for protecting the wife's property in cases of desertion.**

Orders protecting the property and earnings of a deserted wife, commonly called "protection orders," are not of so much use now as they were before the Married Women's Property Acts. The Acts of 1870 and 1882 both give the married woman, whether deserted or not, all her earnings acquired in any occupation which she follows separately from her husband (and, when she is deserted, all her earnings must come under that description), while, as for future acquired property, the Act of 1882 gives her, whether deserted or not, as much as the order does. The only advantage possessed by the order consists in the power of the wife to inflict a serious penalty for its infraction.

By sec. 21 of the Matrimonial Causes Act, 1857, (20 and 21 Vict., c. 85), a wife, immediately upon being deserted by her husband, may obtain an order "protecting her earnings and property acquired since the commencement of such desertion from her husband, and all creditors and persons claiming under him," and such earnings and property are then to belong to her as if she were a single woman.

The desertion must be continuing at the time when the order is made and a *bonâ fide* offer to return takes away the right to the order.

2. During the continuance of the order *and* of the desertion, the order puts the woman in the same position as regards property and contracts, and suing and being sued, as if she had obtained a decree of judicial separation, that is in the position, in those respects, of a single woman. There is no saving of settlements in this Act, and so no restraint on anticipation contained in any will or gift, under which the woman acquires property after the desertion and under the order will have any effect. The wife is a single woman as to property without any proviso. This is more than the Married Women's Property Act, 1882, does; for it preserves the restraint upon anticipation, if there be one.

But the chief advantage, which the woman has under the order, is that, if the husband, or any creditor, after notice of the order, seizes or continues to hold any property of the wife, she can sue him and make him restore the specific property, and pay damages to double its value.

3. The wife, if living anywhere in England, may obtain the order from the Divorce Court, or its president; and if living in the metropolitan district may obtain it from a police magistrate; and if in the country from justices in petty sessions. The authority granting the order must be satisfied of the marriage,

and that the desertion was without reasonable cause, and that the wife is maintaining herself by her own industry. She must not be a brothel keeper, or living in adultery, or by prostitution. If the order is made by a police magistrate, or in petty sessions, it is to be entered within ten days with the Registrar of the County Court, within the jurisdiction of which the wife is resident.

The same section, 21, provides that the husband and any creditor, or person claiming under him, may apply for the discharge of the order. The application may be made to the court, whether the order was granted by the court or not. It may be made after the death of the wife (*Mudge* v. *Adams*, 6 P.D. 54).

The husband, of course, has an interest in discharging the order, both because it is an imputation upon him and because the acquisitions of his wife, under the order, will not come to him on her dying intestate. But it is hard to see how the husband's creditor can now discharge the order; for what the wife earns and the property which she acquires—order or no order—are hers and not her husband's, and cannot be taken for his debt.

If the order was made by a police magistrate, the application may be made to him or his successor, or the person acting in his place. And, if the order was made at petty sessions, the application may be made to the justices sitting there, whether they are those who made the order or not. (Matrimonial Causes Act, 1857, s. 21, and Matrimonial Causes Act, 1864).

Resumption of cohabitation or the ending of the separation, which is the same thing, puts an end to the protection order, as it does to a decree of judicial separation.

The order not being equivalent to a decree of judicial separation (except in respect of property, suing and being sued), is not conclusive of the fact of desertion as against the husband, and, if he has not really been guilty of desertion, he may resume cohabitation at pleasure, or petition for restitution of conjugal rights.

4. Unlike a decree for judicial separation which operates only from its date, a protection order relates back to the desertion and affects all property which the wife acquires after the desertion. It includes property to which she was entitled for an estate in remainder or reversion at the date of the desertion; but does not apply to property of which she was in possession at that date. Such property may be her separate property or not hers at all; but it is not within the order, because it cannot be said to have been acquired, or to have come to her, since the desertion. If it is hers, she has her ordinary remedy for protecting it, but she cannot get the double value from the person who seizes or holds it. The order covers all that is acquired, or comes to, or devolves upon the woman since the desertion (sec. 25), however much time has elapsed between the desertion and the order. A woman, deserted in 1832, did not apply for an order till 1861, but the order protected all that she had acquired, or that had come to her, during the previous thirty years and it passed under her will, made in 1861, as if she were a single woman. Of course since 1882 it would pass in like manner without any desertion or any order.

The order covers no earnings but such as are lawful.

The order is expressed to be for the protection of the wife's earnings and property generally, and does not specify any particular properties as having been acquired, or come to her, after the desertion, but leaves her to prove the acquisition or devolution of the property, in case she sues for its return and for damages for its seizure or detention.

Property to which the wife becomes entitled since the desertion, as trustee, or as executrix, or administratrix of a person who died after the desertion is included in the order. (Matrimonial Causes Act, 1858, s. 7).

5. The requirement of registration within ten days, where the order is not obtained from the court, is said to be directory and not imperative, at least as regards time; for a married woman made a will

within the ten days but registered her order after the ten days and died, and the will was admitted to probate.

6. The last mentioned Act provides, in sec. 8, that if the order is reversed or discharged, all dealings with the wife while it was valid shall stand good, and, in sec. 10, that, if the order has been discharged or varied, or has been put an end to by the separation ceasing, all persons and corporations, who have dealt with the wife in reliance on the order are protected, and their dealings valid. But these clauses are of little value now, because a wife may contract, as to her separate property, whether living with her husband or not, and all that she earns apart from him, and all that comes to, or devolves on her, since 1882, is her separate property, whether the man lives with her or not.

7. By rule 195 for Divorce and Matrimonial Causes, the wife must state in the affidavit on which she applies for an order, whether she has any knowledge of the residence of her husband, and, if he is known to be residing within the jurisdiction of the Court, he must be served personally with a summons to shew cause why the order should not be made. A husband will prevent the order being made if he shews that he has only left his wife temporarily, or that he did so with her consent, or in consequence of her misconduct. It may be worth his while to do this in order to prevent being charged with the costs of obtaining the order as a "necessary"; which might happen if the woman had no separate property. But otherwise the order hurts him little, for, beyond depriving him of his right to administration on his wife's death, it takes nothing from him, which could otherwise be his, it relieves him from any future claim for necessaries, and will become void on a resumption of cohabitation.

8. By the Matrimonial Causes Act, 1858, s. 9, the order is to state the time at which the desertion on which it is founded commenced, and this date is to be conclusive as regards all persons who deal with the wife in reliance on the order.

But the order is not conclusive against the husband,

nor, unless he had an opportunity of shewing cause against it, is it even evidence against him. If he does not regard himself as having deserted his wife, and, after offering to resume cohabitation, petitions the Court for restitution of conjugal rights, the protection order is no evidence that he deserted his wife, and is not entitled to have her back again.

9. The Summary Jurisdiction (Married Women) Act, 1895 (58 & 59 Vict., c. 39) enables a wife to apply to a court of summary jurisdiction, that is to two magistrates in petty sessions, or a stipendiary magistrate, under any of the following circumstances:—

(1) Where her husband has been convicted by magistrates of an aggravated assault upon her;
(2) Where he has been convicted upon *indictment* of an assault upon her and sentenced to a fine of more than £5 or to imprisonment for more than two months;
(3) Where he has deserted her; and
(4) Where he has been guilty of persistent cruelty to her, *or* of wilful neglect to provide reasonable maintenance for her or for her infant children, whom he is liable to maintain, *and*, by such cruelty or neglect, has caused her to leave him and live separately and apart from him.

The court of summary jurisdiction to which she applies may be either the court by which her husband was convicted, or the court for the district or place where the cause of complaint wholly or partially arose. And, where the husband has been convicted upon *indictment*, as above mentioned, she may apply to the court before which he was convicted, which becomes a court of summary jurisdiction for this purpose.

10. On this application the court may make an order providing as follows:—

(1) That she is no longer bound to cohabit with her husband, (which is to be equivalent to a judicial separation on the ground of cruelty);
(2) That she may have the custody of the children of the marriage while under 16;

(3) That her husband shall pay to her, or to an officer of the court, or some other person for her, a weekly allowance, which is not to exceed £2 a week;

(4) That she or her husband, or both, shall pay costs.

But, if the wife has committed an act of adultery, an order is not to be made in her favour, unless her husband has condoned or connived at it, or has conduced to it by his wilful neglect or misconduct.

On the application of the wife or husband, and upon fresh evidence being brought forward, the court may alter, vary, or discharge the order and may diminish the amount of maintenance or may increase it, but not beyond £2 a week. And, if it is proved that the wife has voluntarily resumed cohabitation, or has committed an act of adultery, the court is bound to discharge the order.

If the court is of opinion that the application would be more conveniently dealt with by the Divorce Court, the former court may refuse to make an order; but the Divorce Court may require the court of summary jurisdiction to hear and determine the case.

An appeal lies from the court of summary jurisdiction to the Divorce Court against any order or against any refusal to make an order, unless the refusal was made because the case was thought more proper for the Divorce Court.

11. In taking advantage of this statute the wife may find a difficulty which does not exist in an application for a protection order or a decree for judicial separation, namely, that the husband has to be within reach of a summons. But, if once the order is obtained, she enjoys during the desertion, by virtue of the Married Women's Property Act, 1882, all the rights to earnings and property which she could have under the protection order and the maintenance order under this statute as well.

Magistrates often blunder about the question of desertion, which means far more than merely leaving a wife; for, without deserting a wife, a man may leave her for a long time with the intention of returning to her, or letting her come to him, or may leave her for ever for a proper reason (see chap. xix.)

Where the complaint is that the husband has wilfully neglected to provide maintenance, whereby he has caused his wife to live separate, the court has to be satisfied of four things: (1) the marriage, (2) the ability to maintain, (3) the wilful neglect to do so, and (4) that this neglect was such as to make it reasonable that the wife should live separate and that she has done so.

Where an order is made that the wife may cease to cohabit, which is made equivalent to a judicial separation, there arises a presumption that access, that is co-habitation, ceased from the date of the order; so that, in the absence of evidence, a child born more than nine months after the order will be regarded as illegitimate.

## CHAPTER XVII.

### OF THE RIGHTS AND LIABILITIES OF THE HUSBAND AFTER THE DEATH OF THE WIFE.

1. *Marriage dissolved by death or divorce.*
2. *Wife may die wholly or partially intestate.*
3. *Her lands of inheritance on intestacy.*
4. *On intestacy her personalty in possession vests in husband.*
5. *On intestacy her choses in action and in reversion vest in him as administrator.*
6. *On intestacy he has exclusive right to administration.*
7. *But not if wife were divorced, judicially separated, or had protection order.*
8. *What property of deceased wife is subject to her debts.*
9. *On wife's death, husband is free from personal liability on her contracts, or for her torts or devastavits.*
10. *Right of wife's executors under Married Women's Property Act*, 1882, s. 23.
11. *Husband takes joint property by survivorship.*
12. *Husband bound to bury deceased wife.*
13. *His curtesy.*
14. *His right to bring an action against the person who has killed the wife.*

1. The marriage may be dissolved by death or by decree of dissolution of marriage.

2. The wife dies either intestate—that is, without a will—or testate; that is, leaving a will. The will, to be valid, must have been made after marriage, unless made in execution of a certain power of appointment (see ch. v.). And, when she leaves a will, it may dispose of the whole or of part only of what she has a

right to dispose of. In the latter case there is a partial intestacy, and the remarks which follow as to intestacy will apply so far as the intestacy extends.

The wife may, without any concurrence of her husband, make a will of all her real and personal separate property, whether it has become so by gift or settlement, or by force of the Married Women's Property Acts, and whether it was subject to restraint against anticipation or not, and she may dispose by will of any property over which she has a power of appointment which may be exercised by will.

3. In case of her intestacy, her freeholds of inheritance, whether her separate property or not, and whether vested in a trustee or not, descend to her heir, subject to her husband's life estate by the curtesy, if he is entitled to it (see ch. iv.); and the like of her copyholds of inheritance, but subject to curtesy, if any, by the custom of the manor.

4. On the death of the wife intestate, the chattels which were her separate property, whether given to her separate use, with or without a trustee, or become her separate property by force of the Married Women's Property Acts, her money, her leaseholds, and the unpaid rents of her leaseholds or freeholds, vest in her husband in his marital right without his obtaining letters of administration.

5. But her *choses in action* and reversionary interests not reduced into possession will only vest in her husband if he becomes her administrator, an office conferred by the Court of Probate, and entitling him to "administer" her estate.

6. All her personal estate will vest in the husband either in his marital right or as administrator, if he becomes administrator.

The husband has an exclusive right to a grant of administration, and all that he takes under it belongs to him absolutely, to the exclusion of the next-of-kin.

Where the intestacy is only partial, the husband will still be administrator, and the executors will only take what is left by the will.

7. Where the marriage has been dissolved, and the

man survives the woman, he is not entitled to administration, for, when she died, she was not his wife.

When the wife has obtained a decree of judicial separation, all the property which she has acquired, or which has come to her since the date of the *decree*, is to go upon her death intestate, as it would have gone if her husband had been then dead (Matrimonial Causes Act, 1857, s. 25), and the wife who has obtained a protection order is in the same position as regards all property which she has acquired, or which has come to her since the date (not of the order, but) of the *desertion*. In these cases, where the wives die separate, their husbands are not entitled to administration.

8. It has already been explained (chaps. viii., s. 2, and ix., s. 5) that by the M.W.P. Act, 1893, all a married woman's property, present and future, and whether she has any or not when contracting, is made liable to answer all the contracts that she makes otherwise than as an agent. From this property is excepted during marriage such property as is subject to a restraint on anticipation but, after the marriage is ended by death or divorce and the woman is without a husband, this restraint ceases and all the property becomes liable.

9. The 23rd section of the Act of 1882 says :—

For the purposes of this Act the legal personal representative of any married woman shall in respect of her separate estate have the same rights and liabilities and be subject to the same jurisdiction as she would be if she were living.

The ordinary meaning of "legal personal representative" is "executor or administrator"; but it has been held (*Surman* v. *Wharton* (1891), 1 Q.B. 491) that a husband who has not been appointed to either of these offices, but has taken *jure mariti* the personal chattels or leaseholds of his deceased wife, is included in the expression, "legal personal representative," and that, therefore, he is as liable for her debts as if he were executor or administrator. That is to say the surviving husband is, in that case, liable to the extent of all his deceased wife's property that comes to his hands for all her debts and breaches of contract, whether arising before or after marriage, unless, of course, the remedy for them is barred by lapse of time.

For the wrongs committed by the deceased wife, whether before or during marriage (see chap. viii., sec. 14), her estate is in general not liable, because, for personal wrongs, the right of action ends with death. There is an exception, however, under the statute 3 and 4 Will. IV., chap. 42, s. 2, which enacts that, where the deceased person, within six months before death, has done an injury to the real or personal property of another, the latter may sue the executor or administrator within six months of his undertaking the office.

The husband, so far as the wife's property coming to his hands does not extend, is under no *personal* liability in respect of her contracts, or of wrongs committed by her. Upon her contracts made during marriage, he never was liable, except they were made by his authority, in which case the contract was his own, and the liability continues until barred by lapse of time. Upon her contracts made before marriage, and upon wrongs committed by her before or during marriage, his liability—limited in case of the former wrongs to certain property—ceases wholly on death as on divorce. To make the man liable, he has to be sued jointly with his wife, which, after death or divorce is impossible.

10. From the words of the 23rd section of the Act of 1882, which says that a wife's personal representative shall have the same rights and liabilities as she would herself have if living, and be subject to the same jurisdiction, a curious result may follow. If the wife left a will and did not appoint her husband executor, the executor would probably be able to avail himself of the jurisdiction under sec. 17, to make the husband give up property included in the will.

11. The husband takes by survivorship all property, real or personal, held or possessed by him and his wife jointly.

12. The husband is bound to bury his deceased wife. Where a wife died during the absence of the husband, a person who had paid the necessary and suitable expenses of her funeral was held entitled to recover them in an action against the husband. And, even if the husband is under age, he may bind himself for the

necessary funeral expenses of his wife and his lawful children, such funerals being, in fact, necessaries for himself. Whether, as administrator, a husband may charge the funeral expenses to the estate, and so leave less for creditors, instead of bearing them himself, is doubtful.

13. The husband's right to a life estate in his wife's estates of inheritance where he has had issue by her capable of inheriting, has already been treated of in chap. iv. All that need here be said is that where the property is separate, she can bar this right by her disposition of the property in her lifetime or by will.*

As for the administration of the wife's estate by a husband who is executor or administrator, it will be guided by the ordinary rules on the subject, which have no place here.

14. The husband has the same right, under Lord Campbell's Act, to bring an action against the person who, by a wrongful act, neglect, or default, has caused the death of the wife as the wife has when the death of the husband has been so caused (see next chap., sec. 15).

---

The husband is still entitled to a tenancy by the curtesy out of his wife's undisposed of real estate. (*Hope* v. *Hope* (1892), 2 Ch. 336.)

# CHAPTER XVIII.

## OF THE RIGHTS AND LIABILITIES OF THE WIFE AFTER THE DEATH OF THE HUSBAND.

1. *General view of widow's rights and liabilities.*
2. *Husband may leave a will or die wholly or partially intestate.*
3. *Administration and distribution on intestacy.*
4. *Paraphernalia.*
5. *What was separate property during marriage remains to widow.*
6. *Widow takes joint property by survivorship.*
7. *Her chattels real.*
8. *Her choses in action and in reversion.*
9. *Dower.*
10. *Rights of widow who has mortgaged or pledged her property as security for her husband's debts.*
11. *Liabilities which revive on widowhood.*
12. *Widow liable to imprisonment for them under sec. 5 of Debtors' Act, 1869.*
13. *Position of widow as to contracts made by her during marriage to bind her separate property.*
14. *Burial of husband.*
15. *Damages under Lord Campbell's Act for death of husband.*

1. Unlike the husband, the wife incurs hardly any liabilities by virtue of the marriage. She never was liable, nor was her estate, upon her husband's contracts or for wrongs committed by him, and she is no more so when a widow. Her liabilities on her husband's death consist chiefly of the revival of her former liabilities or her becoming solely answerable for an existing one. The rights of the widow on the death of her husband without a will consist chiefly of the right to dower, which seldom arises, her right to a distributive share

of his personal estate, and a right by survivorship to any property held jointly with her husband.

And now, by the Intestates Estates Act, 1890 (see Appendix), if he dies intestate and without issue after the 1st Sept., 1890, she is entitled to the whole of his real and personal estate if their value taken together does not exceed £500; while, if it exceeds £500, she is entitled to that sum, to be contributed by the real and personal estates in proportion to the value of each and also to her distributive share out of what is left. So that if the man dies intestate and without issue, leaving £600 clear of debts, funeral expenses and charges, his widow would take £550, and his next of kin £50.

"Without issue" means without children by *any* wife or the descendants of such children. The Act does not apply to a partial intestacy.

2. The husband dies either intestate, that is without leaving a will, or testate, that is leaving a will. The will to be valid must have been made after marriage, unless made in the execution of a certain power of appointment (see c. vi. and s. 18 of the Wills Act, which applies to all wills). And where he leaves a will it may dispose of part only of his property, which is a partial intestacy and, so far as there is an intestacy, the rules as to intestacy apply; but as there is a will, the Intestates Estates Act, 1890, does not apply.

Where the husband leaves a will it regulates the disposition of the property included therein.

3. If the husband leaves no will, or in as far as the will does not apply, the law takes in hand the distribution of his personal property (see chap. iii.), while the real property (see chap. iv.) unless it is the subject of settlement, or is required on intestacy to satisfy the widow's charge of £500, devolves upon his heir; but see section 9.

The law vests the personal property in the person appointed by the Court of Probate to administer the effects of the deceased. The Court usually grants administration to the widow, but may, if it please, give it to the next-of-kin or to both.

Where there are children, the widow takes one third to herself, and the rest goes among the children.

Where there are no children, the widow if her charge of £500 is satisfied, takes one half of the personalty, and the rest is distributed among the next-of-kin, whoever they may be.

Sometimes there are no next-of-kin, as where the husband is a bastard, who can have no next-of-kin, and in this case there being no children, all except the share of the widow, (one half) belongs in strictness to the Crown.

It is very important for the widow to distinguish between what is wholly her own and free from her husband's liabilities, and what forms part of his intestate estate, of which she only gets a share of what remains after all claims upon it are satisfied

4. On the death of the husband, testate or intestate, the widow may claim paraphernalia, that is to say, such articles of personal apparel and personal ornament suitable to her rank and degree but belonging to her husband, as she continued to use by his permission during the marriage. But it will be enough though she used them only upon great public or private occasions, or though they remained in the keeping of her husband. Nor is their value material, so that they are suitable to her rank.

[The articles would belong to the husband if they were the wife's at marriage, before 1883, and were not affeced with the character of a separate estate, just as much as if he had bought them. If they were her separate property, as by purchase out of her separate property, or by gift from a stranger, or from her husband, they are hers, and form no part of his estate, and what is here said about her *claiming* them from his estate does not apply.]

When I say she may *claim* them, I mean she is entitled to them, as against the *legatees* under her husband's will, and as against all the world except his creditors, who have exhausted all the other assets, and even as against them she is entitled to her necessary clothing.

The husband may pawn, sell, or give away these paraphernalia during his lifetime though he cannot leave them by will at his death; a woman has no claim on them, therefore, till she is a widow.

If her husband's creditors take her jewels or other paraphernalia to satisfy their claims, the Court will compel them first to resort to other property.

I have said the husband may pawn the paraphernalia, but if the person who advanced the money has not sold them before the husband dies, the wife will in general be entitled to redeem them.

If the widow dies without claiming paraphernalia, they will fall into the husband's estate, and cannot be claimed by the executor or administrator of the widow. For instance, if her husband were to leave them in his will to her for her life and then to some one else, and her conduct showed that she chose to take them under the will instead of treating them as things over which her husband had no power of disposal, they would, at her death, go to the person mentioned in the will, and the widow's executor or administrator could not claim them.

What has been said above does not apply to personal ornaments given to the wife by a third party, or otherwise forming part of her separate property, nor to wedding gifts to her, which are always separate property; for the husband cannot dispose of such property by will, nor are they assets for his creditors.

5. On the dissolution of the marriage by death or divorce, that which has been separate estate or separate property of the wife ceases to be so, for there is no longer a husband from whom it is to be separate, and the restraint on anticipation, which can only be annexed to separate property, ceases also; so that the widow can dispose of it as if single. It is necessary, however, still to speak of separate estate or property, meaning that which, during the marriage, was affected with the separate character,

On the death of the husband, whether testate or intestate, all the widow's separate property, whether made so by gift or settlement, or by the force by any statute remains hers, freed, until she marries again, from its character of separate and from restraint on anticipation.

6. Whether the husband dies testate or intestate, and whether administration is granted or not, the widow will take by survivorship all property, real or personal, which she held or possessed jointly with him; such as estates of inheritance, in land conveyed to them jointly, or shares standing, or money lodged or deposited in their joint names.

7. Some other sorts of property not separate survive to the wife on the death of the husband, whether with or without a will.

Where a woman possesses chattels real, such as leases or the next presentation to a living (see chap. iv.), though not rendered separate by any gift or settlement, nor—owing to the date of her marriage—rendered separate by either of the Married Women's Property Acts, and not disposed of by her husband in his lifetime, she is entitled to them at his death, for he cannot dispose of them by will.

8. A widow, whether there is a will or not, is also entitled to all her *choses in action*, such as debts and arrears of rent due to her, her reversionary interests in personalty, her legacies, residuary personal estate bequeathed to her, her trust funds, stock, balance at a bank, etc., though not made separate property by gift, settlement, or statute, provided her husband has not, in his lifetime, reduced them into his own possession, or done anything which the law considers tc amount to a getting possession of them (see chap. iii.)

9. As regards the husband's lands, the wife beside her charge of £500 mentioned in sec. 1, may have a claim to a third part for her life, which is called her dower, but this claim seldom arises now. A widow whose marriage took place before January 1st, 1834, may be entitled to dower out of all lands held by her husband whether he left a will or not, where the whole legal fee is vested in him, or he has (whether wholly equitable, or partly legal and partly equitable) what is equivalent to an estate of inheritance.* I am of course

* As to dower and gavelkind lands and copyholds, see note in chap. iv.

supposing that the lands have either not been settled at all or not in a way which precludes the right to dower from arising.

But where the marriage took place since January 1st, 1834, the wife's dower is placed wholly in the power of her husband. His absolute disposition in his life or by his will excludes her altogether. So his contracts and charges in his lifetime or by his will will bind her, and he may, when an estate is conveyed *to* him, cause it to be declared by the deed of conveyance that his widow shall not be entitled to dower out of such land (for it is not necessary that he himself should execute the deed), or he may bar her right by his declaration in any other deed, or in his will, either generally or partially. It is where none of these things are done that the claim arises.

If a man gives any property to his wife by will, he should, where he has land liable to dower, or has contracted for the purchase of such land, state whether he means the gift to be in bar of dower or not. Such a precaution may prevent a lawsuit.†

10. When the husband wishes to borrow money, or to pay off a debt, it often happens that the wife joins in a mortgage of her land, or gives her separate personal estate in pledge by way of security, and the right to redeem is sometimes reserved to the husband. When this is the case the wife has also the right to redeem both before and after the death of her husband, unless indeed the transactions showed that she not only intended to give a security for her husband's debt, but to pass to him the beneficial interest in the property mortgaged, subject only to the mortgage.

So also after his death she is entitled to stand in the place of the person who has advanced the money, and to have her estate *exonerated* out of the other property of her husband. She is in fact a surety for him, and has as great a claim to repayment as the other creditors have to be paid their debts.

---

† These remarks upon dower have been taken nearly word for word from Lord St. Leonards' 'Handy-Book on Property Law.'

11. As the widow's rights survive, so her liabilities revive. Where no judgment has been obtained against her and her husband jointly, the widow, whatever the date of her marriage, is solely liable upon all contracts entered into, or legal obligations incurred, or wrongs committed by her *before* marriage, unless, by lapse of time or otherwise, the remedy is barred. In the absence of such a joint judgment, she is also solely liable for all wrongs committed by her during the marriage, if the remedy is still subsisting.

12. Upon a judgment obtained against her *during widowhood* for any of these causes of action, her property is liable to execution, unprotected of course by any restraint on anticipation, and, if she refuses or neglects to satisfy the judgment, or any instalment of it which is due, and the Court is satisfied that she has, or since the judgment or instalment was due has had, the means of payment, she may be imprisoned under sec. 5. of the Debtors' Act, 1869. The imprisonment is for not more than six weeks, or until payment, but it may be repeated from time to time, and is not a satisfaction of the debt, or a bar to any kind of execution.

13. The woman who during marriage has contracted in respect of, and so as to bind, her separate estate is not personally liable but has only made her property liable for the debt or damages resulting. She therefore cannot be imprisoned under section 5 of the Debtors' Act, 1869, for default in payment of a sum of money as due under any judgment in an action on such a contract, and, when the marriage is ended by death or divorce, she enjoys equal immunity. Until the Act of 1893 was passed, the property which the woman possessed after the marriage was ended would not have been liable; for only separate property was made liable (see *Scott* v. *Morley*, chap. ix., sec. 5), and, when the marriage is ended there can be no separate property. But now, by sec. 2 of the Act of 1893, all that the woman has after divorce or during widowhood is liable.

14. Whether the widow, not being executrix or administratrix of her deceased husband, is bound to bury

him is doubtful; but it is certain that, if she gives orders for the funeral, she may be made to pay for it.

15. Under Lord Campbell's Act, 9 and 10 Vict., c. 93 amended by 27 and 28 Vict., c. 95, where the death of a person is caused by such wrongful act, neglect, or default, as would have entitled him to an action if he had lived, the wrong-doer shall be liable to damages though the act may have amounted to felony. The damages are for the benefit of the wife, husband, parents, grand parents, step parents, children, grand children, and step children of the deceased, in such shares as the jury may direct. Where there are a wife and children, a jury is not likely to give a share to persons more remotely connected. The action must be brought within a year by the executor, but if he does not do so within six months from the death, or if there is no executor or administrator, the action may be brought in the names of the persons who claim the benefit of it.

The rights and duties of the wife as executrix or administratrix of the husband in dealing with his estate are beyond the scope of this book.

The rights of the wife with regard to the children will be treated of in the chapter on children (chap. xx.)

Throughout this chapter it has been assumed that the wife is not judicially separated or living separate under a protection order. The rights of wives so situated are dealt with in the chapters which deal with judicial separation and protection orders.

# CHAPTER XIX.

## Of judicial separation and divorce.

1. *Jurisdiction in divorce belonged to the Ecclesiastical Courts.*
2. *Jurisdiction of the Divorce Court established in* 1857.
3. *Domicil.*
4. *How an objection to the jurisdiction is to be raised.*
5. *Judicial separation, on what ground granted. Adultery, cruelty, desertion for two years.*
6. *Effect of decree of judicial separation.*
7. *Decree obtained in absence of other party.*
8. *Order to protect deserted wife's earnings from husband and his creditors. Effect of such order.*
9. *The Summary Jurisdiction (Married Women) Act*, 1895, *as regards desertion.*
10. *The same Act as regards cruelty.*
11. *Complete divorce or dissolution. How obtained, and on what grounds by husband and wife respectively.*
12. *Proof of adultery by husband or wife. Examples.*
13. *Adultery, incest, bigamy, rape, &c., cruelty, desertion.*
14. *What will be an answer to the petition. Collusion, connivance, condonation.*
15. *Absolute and discretionary defences in suits for divorce.*
16. *Sorts of defences open to co-respondent.*
17. *Defences to suits for judicial separation.*
18. *Dismissal of the co-respondent from the suit.*
19. *Court has power to award alimony. Its nature.*
20. *Alimony* pendente lite, *or pending suit.*
21. *Permanent alimony.*

22. *Principles upon which they are respectively awarded.*

23. *Alimonial provision after marriage dissolved.*

24. *Time for which, and principles on which it is awarded.*

25. *Bankruptcy of husband.*

26. *Court may make orders as to property under marriage settlement, and property of adulterous wife.*

27. *Criminal conversation. Damages against adulterer, how to be applied. Costs.*

28. *Respondent resisting dissolution of marriage on the ground of the misconduct of the other party may have same remedy as if such respondent were petitioner.*

29. *Nullity of marriage.*

30. *Proceedings on petitions for separation and dissolution of marriage. Evidence of husband and wife.*

31. *Custody, education, and maintenance of children.*

32. *Intervention by the Queen's Proctor.*

33. *Final decree, when considered as pronounced.*

34. *When, after marriage dissolved, the parties may marry again.*

35. *Husband's liabilities in respect of wife end with divorce.*

1. Formerly the power of granting divorce was vested in the Ecclesiastical Courts, so called because they administer not the common law of the land, but the Roman and the canon law, which alone were acknowledged by the Church of Rome, and which still form the basis of the jurisprudence of most Roman Catholic countries.

Divorce was of two kinds (1) *a mensâ et thoro*, from bed and board; and (2) *a vinculo matrimonii*, from the marriage bond. The former was merely a separation by the act of the court, and the latter was an entire destruction of the marriage, but did not so operate as to enable the parties to marry again without the assistance of an act of Parliament.

2. The Matrimonial Causes Act, 1857 (20 and 21 Vict., c. 85), created a new court, called "The Court for Divorce and Matrimonial Causes," to ad-

judicate on divorce and matrimonial causes in England. The court has power to decree a judicial separation (which is the new term for what was formerly called a divorce from bed and board), and a "dissolution of marriage," which is the name given to a complete dissolution of the marriage-tie, commonly called a divorce, and often so spoken of in this book.

It is this Court which also makes decrees of nullity of marriage, already mentioned in chap. ii., and decrees of restitution of conjugal rights; as to which see chap. xv.

The Court also has jurisdiction in cases of jactitation of marriage, which is where one falsely boasts of being the husband or wife of another, so that a reputation of marriage may ensue.

The Court is a Court for England only, which means England, Wales, and Berwick-upon-Tweed. It is not a Court for the United Kingdom or for Great Britain; and Ireland, Scotland, and the colonies are, in respect of jurisdiction, as much foreign countries as France or Spain.

The question of the jurisdiction of the court, therefore, depends greatly upon the domicil of the parties.

3. "Domicil" means a man's permanent home, the place in which he settles with the intention of remaining there for ever, and not leaving, except for a temporary purpose, unless something unexpected or uncertain should induce him to do so.

Domicil is of three sorts (i), by origin; (ii), by law; and (iii) by choice. The first is obtained by parentage, as where a man is born, either in England or abroad, of domiciled English parents. The second is where the law assigns to one the domicile of another on whom he is dependent, as where the wife's domicil follows the husbands; and, till judicially separated, she can acquire no other of her own. As to the national status of married women and of children see chap. x., sec. 1. The third is where a man voluntarily abandons his previous domicil, as by leaving his own country, and settling permanently in another, with the intention of never returning except for a temporary purpose. This acquired domicile may be abandoned in favour of another domicil of choice, or by a return to the domicil of origin. For this latter purpose there must be not only an intention to resume the original domicil, but an actual return. An Englishwoman, who had acquired a French domicil, meant to return to England to resume her original domicil, but on arriving at the sea was too sick to make the passage, and died at an inn in France, was held to have retained her acquired French domicil.

Where the parties are domiciled in England, though both the marriage and the adultery took place abroad, the Court will dissolve the marriage. So if only the husband is domiciled in England.

If the husband is permanently and *bonâ fide* resident in England when his wife commits adultery abroad, and when he presents his petition, the Court will dissolve the marriage though both parties are foreigners and the marriage was solemnized in a foreign country.

Two natural-born British subjects married in England and the husband went to the United States, and became domiciled and committed bigamy there. The wife petitioned in England, and the Court dissolved the marriage because the man, though he had acquired a foreign domicil, had not lost his original allegiance to English law. An Englishman it was said, who goes to live in China, owes the same allegiance to the sovereign of his native conntry as if he had remained at home, and as much after twenty years as after the first day of foreign residence.

It is difficult to reconcile the latter case with rule that the wife's domicil follows the husband's; because when the man became domiciled in the States, one would suppose the woman would be domiciled there too and would have to seek her remedy for the matrimonial offence, in the place of her husband's domicil.

It is a principle that a wife can only seek her remedy for such offences in her husband's domicil.

Where an Englishman by race, domiciled in Australia, did not allow conjugal rights to his wife in England, where they were on a visit, and returned to Australia, and the woman petitioned for restitution, the Court told her that she could only seek her remedy in Australia for two reasons—one that the Court has no jurisdiction over a domiciled Australian, and the other that sec. 42 of the Matrimonial Causes Act, 1857, only allowed a citation to be served abroad in the suits mentioned in sec. 41, namely, separation, divorce, nullity and jactitation.

The jurisdiction to enquire into the validity of the marriages celebrated in England between foreigners, and if necessary to decree nullity of marriage (see chap. ii., sec. 8) has nothing to do with the law of domicil, but is exercised on the principle that the validity of a marriage is to be decided by the Courts of the country in which it is solemnised.

4. By rule 22, if a party cited wishes to raise any question as to the jurisdiction of the Court, he or she must enter an appearance under protest, and within eight days file in the registry his or her act on petition in extension of such protest, and on the same day deliver a copy thereof to the petitioner. After the entry of an absolute appearance to the citation a party cited cannot raise any objection as to jurisdiction.

5. Either husband or wife may obtain a judicial separation on the ground of adultery, or of cruelty, or of desertion without cause for two years or upwards.

The presiding judge, with or without any of the other judges, may make a decree of judicial separation on any of the three grounds above mentioned.

With regard to the first ground, nothing need here be said (but see sec. 13).

As to cruelty, it is impossible to give a legal definition of it, but it must usually consist of bodily violence, either by blows, gestures, or threats, and has seldom been established by mere unkindness or causing of mental suffering, however acute.

There must be something which makes it unsafe for the parties to live together; there must usually be actual violence and ill-treatment, endangering or threatening life, person or health, or else such words or actions of menace as should give to a person of ordinary courage a reasonable apprehension of danger. There must be bodily hurt (not trifling or temporary), or a reasonable apprehension of bodily hurt.

Far stronger evidence would of course be required to make out a case of cruelty from mere words or gestures, than from evidence of unmistakable acts of ill-treatment. But where such acts have been few, words and gestures go to make up the measure of cruelty.

A persistent course of harsh, irritating conduct, unaccompanied by actual violence, but carried to such a point as to endanger the petitioner's health, and renewed after the resumption of intermitted cohabitation, was held to constitute legal cruelty.

Where a question of cruelty comes before a jury as a ground for judicial separation, the jury is to determine, not only whether such and such acts were done, but whether they amount to cruelty.

Desertion takes place when one party has left the other *against his or her will*, and without proper cause.

The mere fact, therefore, of the husband and wife being separate does not of itself prove desertion, but is only one element in the proof. Therefore, where the husband was absent upon his ordinary occupation, as a sailor, it was not considered as a desertion, nor would the Court take into consideration a former desertion in past years which had been terminated by a return to cohabitation. If, however, the sailor had taken to the sea in order to get rid of his wife, the decision would have been otherwise.

A wife resided with her husband for four years, the husband then went away in search of employment, and during the first year of his absence he wrote several affecting letters, urging his wife to correspond with him, but the two last were not answered by her. During the sixteen subsequent years he only once communicated with her, and the wife did not at any time during the absence apply to her husband to return to cohabitation. It was held that there was no desertion, and that absence to constitute desertion must be without the consent, direct or indirect, of the party deserted, and in spite of her wish.

The desertion must be against the will of the other party; therefore, where it appears likely that they separated by consent, the judicial separation will not be granted unless the circumstances are explained.

But if a married person takes advantage of a temporary absence, and avoids a resumption of cohabitation with the intention of never renewing it, that will be desertion. (L.R. 1 P. & D. 489; 27 L.J., P. & M. 64; 4 Sw. & T. 242.)

A compulsory absence will not constitute desertion; as where a man suspected of theft left his home with the knowledge and consent of his wife to avoid arrest, and then got caught, convicted, and imprisoned, and then wanted to return to his wife but found her unwilling, and this happened three times, and occupied five years; it was held that there was no desertion, because the separation was involuntary on his part and the wife's refusal, though reasonable, was not founded on any matrimonial offence.

Where a deed of separation has been executed, judicial separation on the ground of desertion will of course be refused, because where there is consent there is no desertion.

To entitle the petitioner to a decree of separation the desertion must not only be of the kind above described, but must have continued, without a *bona fide* offer to return, for two years. But when the two years are once passed without an offer to return, a subsequent offer to return, though made in good faith, will be no answer to the petition.

6. After a judicial separation has been decreed the wife is, from the date of the sentence, and whilst the separation continues, considered as a single woman with respect to property of every kind which may come to or devolve upon her, and she may dispose of such property in every respect as if she were single. She can leave it by will, or if she does not it will go at her death as if her husband were dead. If she again returns to her husband it will be separate estate, unless before returning she has entered into a written agreement that it shall not be so. Independently of the Matrimonial Causes Act, 1857, all the wife's separate earnings, and all property which comes to her after 1882, would be separate property, by the Married Women's Property Act, 1882, whether she rejoined her husband or not, unless on rejoining him she agreed that it should not be so.

From the date of the decree the wife will, while she remains separate, be in the position of a single woman in respect of all buying and selling, and other contracts and bargains of whatever nature which she may make, and for all wrongs and injuries committed by her; and her husband will not be liable either for such contracts or wrongs, or for any law costs she may incur as plaintiff or defendant.

The position of the wife as to power of contracting, and as to future acquired property, will be the same though the separation was decreed for her own misconduct, but she will seldom be allowed alimony except during the suit, and, in pronouncing the decree, the judge will very likely exercise the discretion (given him by the Act of 1857) by which he may order any of her property, either in possession or reversion, to be settled for the benefit of her husband or the children (see sec. 26).

And if either no alimony is decreed, or where it is decreed if the husband pays it, he will incur no liability even for necessaries supplied for her use.

The Court may order the alimony to be paid to the wife, or to a trustee for her, and under any terms or restrictions that may be thought fitting.

7. Where one party to the marriage has obtained a decree of separation against the other in his or her absence (as would often happen where *desertion* was the ground of the application), the latter may at any time thereafter petition the Court for the reversal of such decree, on the ground that it was obtained in his or her absence, *and* (where desertion was relied on) that there was reasonable ground for the alleged desertion. But the wife's liabilities in respect of transactions, of whatever kind, which occurred after the decree of separation, and before its reversal, will be left untouched.

8. I have hitherto spoken of desertion when without cause, and continued for two years, as a ground for a judicial separation on the application of the party deserted. But a wife, the moment she is able to prove that her husband has really deserted her without cause, and against her will, for however a short a time may

obtain from a Judge of the Divorce Court an order to protect against her husband, against his creditors, and against any person claiming under him by way of purchase, or otherwise, any property she may acquire by her own lawful industry, or may become possessed of *after* such desertion.

The order may be obtained in any case from the Court, and where the wife lives in London from a police magistrate, or where she lives in the country, from two magistrates sitting in petty sessions.

As to the effect and advantages of such an order, see chap. xvi.

This order does not prevent the husband from returning to his wife, but only prevents his taking her earnings while the desertion continues. The husband's right to return depends on whether he has really deserted his wife or not. If he has, she is not bound to receive him, whether she has a protection order or not. If he has not, the protection order makes no difference, and he can, moreover, have it discharged.

9. But without applying to the Divorce Court, and, without waiting for the two years, a deserted wife is provided with a cheap and rapid remedy extending beyond a mere protection of her future acquired property, namely, under the Summary Jurisdiction (Married Women) Act, 1875; see chapter xvi., ss. 9-11.

10. A wife who suffers from her husband's violence may resort to a simpler remedy than a petition to the Divorce Court on the ground of cruelty.

By the Act, 24 and 25, Vict. c. 100, s. 43; a person who has committed an aggravated assault upon any male child, under 14, or upon any female, may be charged before two justices [or a police or stipendary magistrate] by the person aggrieved, or by any one else, and may be either imprisoned, with or without hard labour, for not more than six months, or fined not more than £20 including costs and may be imprisoned for six months if it is not sooner paid, and may be bound over to keep the peace for six months, from the expiration of his sentence.

And, by the Summary Jurisdiction (Married Women) Act, 1895, the court by which the husband has been convicted of an aggravated assault upon her as above mentioned, *or* the court before which he has been convicted upon *indictment* and sentenced to a fine of more than £5 or for imprisonment for more than two months, may exercise the jurisdiction set forth in chap. xvi., ss. 9-11.

Where under this Act an order is made which is equivalent to judicial separation, there arises a presumption that access, that is, cohabitation, ceased from the date of the order, so that, in the absence of evidence, a child born more than nine months after the order, will be regarded as illegitimate.

The order is to be wholly annulled on a resumption of cohabitation and the wife cannot claim the maintenance afterwards.

As to protection orders, see chap. xvi.

11. Next, as to dissolution of marriage, *i.e.* the entire breaking asunder of the marriage-tie.

This is obtained by petition, which is heard before the Judge Ordinary, who will hear the evidence in open Court, and give his decision upon the facts as well as the law, but either party is entitled to have the questions of fact decided by a jury.

The grounds on which a dissolution of marriage may be prayed for by the husband and wife respectively are as follows:

By the husband—

On the ground that his wife has since the marriage committed adultery.

By the wife—

1. Where her husband has since the marriage been guilty of incestuous adultery (*i. e.* of adultery with some person whom he could not lawfully marry if his wife were dead).
2. Where he has since the marriage been guilty of

bigamy with adultery, which means, adultery with the person with whom he has committed bigamy.

3. Where he has committed rape or other unmentionable offences.
4. Where he has committed adultery coupled with cruelty, such as, without adultery, would have entitled her to judicial separation as above mentioned.
5. Where he has committed adultery coupled with desertion, without reasonable excuse, for two years.

It will thus be seen that where the *wife* commits adultery the husband is entitled to a divorce; but where the *husband* commits adultery the wife is only entitled to a judicial separation, unless the adultery is coupled with some aggravating circumstance.

I have stated that on any of the above grounds a dissolution of marriage *may be prayed for;* but, though the prayer will usually be granted, it rests in the discretion of the Court, and if it appears that the petitioner, whether husband or wife, has been guilty of gross misconduct, so as to conduce to the commission of the fault by the other party, the Court will often do no more than decree a judicial separation.

Where the petition is filed by the husband the adulterer must, as a matter of course, be made a co-respondent, *i. e.* a co-defendant in the suit along with the wife, unless the Court expressly dispense with his being made a party; but where the wife is the petitioner, the woman with whom the husband is alleged to have committed adultery need not be joined unless the Court so orders. If the petitioner wishes the co-respondent to pay him his costs of the suit, he must ask in the petition for a decree to that effect. But it will not be granted if the co-respondent, at the time of committing the adultery, was ignorant that the respondent was a married woman.

Where the wife's conduct is notoriously depraved, as where she lives in a house of ill-fame, and the husband is unable to fix upon an adulterer, and under other circumstances where the adultery is clear, and efforts to identify the man have been vain, the Court will generally excuse the husband from joining any particular person as co-respondent.

12. Let me make one or two remarks with regard to proof of adultery, whether by husband or wife.

It is not expected that the act of adultery shall be proved by ocular evidence, or be fixed to any particular place or moment of time, but it is sufficient if the Court can infer the conclusion, though the persons who are alleged to have committed adultery are not seen in the same bed or in any situation in itself proving adultery.

Every case must rely on its own circumstances, as to which no rule can be given, except that they must be such as to leave no doubt on the mind of a man of common sense.

Facts which, if isolated, would be mere matter of suspicion, when taken together may be conclusive. Gross indecorum alone is no proof of guilt. Opportunity alone is of course no proof of guilt, but when indecent familiarities have taken place, combined with frequent private meetings, especially if a lengthy correspondence has been kept up between the parties, the conclusion that adultery has been committed has often been irresistible. Where there has been general cohabitation, adultery will always be presumed.

Where a man visits a house of ill-fame, knowing its character, a strong presumption of adultery is raised, which can only be rebutted by the clearest evidence ; but when a woman does so, the proof is conclusive.

Shortly after the marriage the wife renewed her acquaintance with a young man to whom she had been attached, and carried on clandestine correspondence with him. During the absence of her husband he visited her at her lodging during the day, and once during the night, when undue familiarities passed between them ; they also walked and rode out together. It was held that, as the criminal intention existed, and the evidence showed that there had been ample opportunities, it must be presumed that adultery had been committed.

The birth of a child of the wife, with distinct evidence that the husband was absent from her at the time when the child must have been begotten, will alone be conclusive proof of her adultery.

The above remarks have been made to give the reader an idea of the circumstantial character of the evidence by which facts of this nature can be proved. But, in addition to this kind of evidence, admissions of guilt are frequently made by the wife to her husband, or *vice versâ*, or to some friend.

18. The adultery of the wife is of itself sufficient ground for a dissolution of marriage on the petition of the husband (always supposing his own conduct not to have conduced to the offence).

But the mere adultery of the husband is considered, and with great justice, not to be of itself a sufficient ground for the dissolving of the marriage-tie, but one for granting a judicial separation on the petition of the wife. In order to entitle her to have the marriage dissolved the adultery of the husband must be coupled with one or other of the five circumstances of aggravation mentioned above, namely, incest, bigamy, rape, &c., cruelty, or desertion.

An incestuous adultery is an adultery with some person with whom if the wife were dead, the husband could not lawfully marry, such as his aunt or his wife's sister, and *vice versâ* of the wife.

The term *bigamy* applies to a second marriage, whether it takes place within the dominions of her Majesty or elsewhere.

Rape and the other disgusting offences mentioned in the act shall not here be dilated on.

Cruelty has been treated of above in section 8.

And desertion has been defined in the same section.

14. Having enumerated the acts, which, when committed by one party to the marriage, form a ground for a petition for dissolution by the other, I will now state what conduct on the petitioner's part-

will *take away* his or her right to have the marriage dissolved.

In the first place, not only must the petitioner swear by affidavit, but the Court must be satisfied there is no collusion or connivance between the petitioner and the other party to the marriage. If any collusion or connivance appears the decree will not be made.

Collusion is agreement between the parties for one to commit or appear to commit a matrimonial offence in order that the other may present a petition to the Court on that ground.

Connivance is where the one party winks at the adultery of the other from any motive or for any purpose whether from indifference, from a desire to extort money from the adulterer, or with an intention, collusive or not collusive, of presenting a petition to the Court. Thus, *connivance* has reference to the act of adultery, *collusion* to the proceedings before the Court. The same line of conduct may be called by either name, according as it is viewed with reference to the adultery itself or with regard to the proceedings to be founded upon it.

The one is open to objection as a fraud upon the Court, and the other as an attempt to treat as an injury that to which the petitioner has assented.

Connivance and collusion generally go together. They are frauds difficult of proof, since they may be only known to the parties to the cause. But it sometimes happens that the intentions and feelings of the man and his wife can be as clearly collected from their proved conduct as if their thoughts were committed to paper. When the behaviour of a husband shows that he is either insensible to his own dishonour or unwilling to seek redress, it will be as great an obstacle to his obtaining a divorce as if he had actively promoted the adultery.

But the Court must be able to see, in his conduct, an intention, more or less strongly marked, to wink at his wife's guilt; and mere inattention, over-confidence, dulness of apprehension, or indifference, will not debar him from redress.

His witnessing an entire disregard of decorum on her part in her conduct towards men does not constitute connivance; his acquiescence under circumstances pregnant with suspicion of her guilt does not constitute connivance. A man is not bound to proceed against his wife upon suspicion, he must wait for adequate proof; but he must not sleep upon his rights. If he finds that his wife has been committing adultery, and he means to object to it, he must do so at once, and must not wait till he feels attracted by some other woman, and thinks a divorce would be convenient.

A deed of separation is no evidence of connivance by the wife unless it is shown that at the time it was entered into she was aware of the adulterous intercourse of the husband with another woman, and consented to it being continued. If the wife, though unwilling that the husband should commit adultery, yet consents to it in order to obtain a larger allowance, this amounts to connivance.

Connivance at adultery with one person is a good answer to a charge of adultery with another, because it is a sanction of immorality.

The condonation or forgiveness by one party of the conduct of the other will form an insuperable obstacle to a divorce, as also to a judicial separation, but is no answer to a husband's claim for damages against a co-respondent. Condonation, with regard to the grounds of a divorce, is where the one party *with a full knowledge* of a conjugal offence committed by the other, not only forgives it, but completely blots out the offence imputed and restores the offending party to the same position which he or she held before the offence was committed. Mere forgiveness would be consistent with an intention never to see the offending party again. The Court must be satisfied that there has been no condonation.

The person charged with adultery may plead both that no adultery has taken place, and that, though adultery has taken place, it has been condoned. The same with reference to cruelty or any other act which forms part of the ground relied upon.

It is impossible to give any general rule applicable to condonation; every case must rest on its own circumstances. But condonation will be presumed from far slighter testimony than what will be required to prove connivance or collusion, for the latter involves a criminal participation, while the former may only show a kindness of feeling which, especially in a wife, may be highly meritorious.

Of course, if the husband sleep with his wife after her guilt is thoroughly known to him, that will amount to condonation, and if the wife stays in the same house with the husband, though only for one day, after her conduct is known to him, he will be called upon to prove that they have not since slept together; and where she has lived for three weeks in the house, and has dined with him three times, though they did not sleep together, that was considered evidence of condonation.

Where a husband has suspicions of his wife's faithlessness he is in this dilemma, that, if he avoids her he discloses his suspicions, which may prevent discovery, and if he treats her as usual he may be considered to have condoned the offence. He must be prepared to show that he has kept aloof from his wife from the time that he could no longer hope that she was innocent. Where his wife has run away from him, he will, of course, be free from trouble upon that ground.

Condonation, however, on the wife's part is regarded with greater laxity than when coming from the husband, because it may be done from kindness to him and his children, and with a view to reclaiming his affections. Still, though a mere living under the same roof, to give the husband an opportunity of amending, would not amount to condonation, yet a voluntary return by her to cohabitation or a continuance in it would be so viewed.

I have hitherto spoken of condonation as applying exclusively to a case of adultery, but it applies equally to cruelty and other offences. The wife's adultery is a sufficient ground on which a husband can apply for a dissolution of marriage, and indeed is the one ground on which he can do so (If she treats him with cruelty it is merely a ground for a judicial separation.) But when a *wife* petitions, some other ingredient must combine with the adultery of the husband in the four cases in which that may form a ground of complaint (see sec. 11). The husband must have committed incest, bigamy, or cruelty, or must have deserted the wife. These offences are all capable of condonation. Incest and bigamy are usually so mixed up with the adultery that if the one is condoned the other is so too; but it may be otherwise, as where a wife knows that her husband has committed adultery with some woman, and means to forgive him instead of applying for a separation, and she then discovers that his paramour is her own sister, which raises the offence to incest, she may then apply for a dissolution of marriage.

So, also, though a wife, knowing only that her husband has committed adultery, may forgive him, yet, when she finds out that he has gone through the form of marriage with his paramour, she will not be debarred from obtaining a dissolution.

I mention this to point out that incest and bigamy are matters for condonation over and above the accompanying adultery, for a woman may overlook a simple adultery without being ready to pardon it in its aggravated form.

Moreover, condonation, to be a good answer must be, a condonation of the offence charged. If, for instance, the charge is adultery with A, it is useless to prove condonation of an adultery with B. Herein condonation differs from connivance, for connivance at adultery with A is a good answer to a charge of adultery with B.

Cruelty is also a distinct matter for condonation, and when forgiven it will fail as a ground for judicial separation, and it will equally fail when it is relied on by the wife, together with adultery, as a ground for dissolution of marriage.

The wife being the weaker party, the charge of cruelty usually proceeds from her; but several instances have been known of divorce from bed and board, or what is called under the new practice judicial separation, on the ground of cruelty by the wife to the husband.

Either husband or wife may obtain a judicial separation on the ground of cruel treatment by the other, and the wife may obtain a dissolution of the marriage on the ground of the husband's cruelty coupled with adultery.

Cruelty usually consists (see sec. 5) of a repetition of acts or threats, and it does not follow because they are submitted to once that a repetition is not to be complained of; nay, in some cases, even where the wife has cohabited with the husband after the last act of cruelty, it has been held that she has not condoned it, and a decree has been made accordingly.

But in every case condonation is a forgiveness, with an implied condition that the injury shall not be repeated; and if it be repeated, though not in an equal degree, the condonation is done away with, and the former offence stands as if it had never been forgiven. Even in the case of adultery former offences will be opened up again by a repetition after the forgiveness.

A condonation of adultery, however, should be made, especially by the husband, so as carefully to exclude all suspicion of connivance.

The offence condoned and revived, and the subsequent offence which revives it, need not be the same. Thus, if adultery is condoned, subsequent cruelty will revive it, and *vice versâ*. Condoned cruelty is not revived by subsequent desertion, but will be revived by subsequent cruelty of the same nature though less in degree. The revival operates whether the revived offence is used as a ground of petition or as a ground of defence ; as, for instance, to a suit for restitution.

In addition to the implied condition, which attaches to every act of condonation, an express condition may be introduced, as that the husband shall break off a certain partnership, or shall restore his wife to her proper position in the house. In such cases the condition must be performed, or the condonation will be void at the option of the condoning party.

15. In suits for dissolution of marriage there are four grounds of defence which, if successful, take it out of the power of the Court to make the decree.

The first is a denial of the marriage or the matrimonial offence or offences charged. The fact of the ceremony of marriage is seldom denied, but sometimes facts are alleged which shew the marriage to be null and void, such as the incapacity of the other party for sexual intercourse or his or her prior and subsisting marriage.

The other three defences which absolutely bar the suit are connivance, condonation, and collusion, which have already been considered.

In the event of the three latter defences being established, or in case adultery is not proved, the Court is required by the Matrimonial Causes Act, 1857, sec. 30, to dismiss the petition.

And by sec. 31, five other grounds of defence are left to the discretion of the Court. The Court is not bound to pronounce a decree of dissolution of marriage if (1), the petitioner has during the marriage been guilty of adultery, or (2) has been guilty of unreasonable delay in presenting or prosecuting the petition, or (3) of cruelty, or (4) of desertion or wilful separation before the adultery complained of and without reasonable excuse, or (5) of such wilful neglect or misconduct as has conduced to the adultery.

In exercising its discretion under the first of these heads, the Court requires some special circumstances in excuse for or mitigation of the act of adultery. As where the wife had led the husband to believe she was dead, and he had married another woman; where a decree nisi had been pronounced, and the husband thought he was entitled to marry again, and did so; where the wife commits adultery in consequence of the violence and threats of the husband; where the respondent who sets up the adultery as a defence, knew of it long before, and condoned it. But the condonation by the respondent does not bind the Court to look over the adultery as a disqualification of the petitioner.

The fourth defence, namely, desertion or wilful

separation before the adultery complained of, need not have been a desertion or separation for two years.

The defence of misconduct conducing to the adultery is one often resorted to where the husband is petitioner, and many different kinds of facts may be used in aid of it. Under this defence, evidence is often given of the husband spending little of his time with his wife, allowing or encouraging her to go into societies, or to frequent places which presented temptation, shutting his eyes to suspicious circumstances and allowing his wife opportunities of going astray. The petitioner and respondent separated by mutual consent soon after marriage, and only met once afterwards. The petitioner made her a small allowance and, sixteen years after the marriage, discovered that she had committed adultery. It was held that he had conduced to the adultery, and his petition was dismissed.

The nature of the other discretionary defences is sufficiently manifest from what has already been said of the acts of which they consist.

16. The co-respondent may resist the petition by a denial of the adultery, or by an allegation of any facts which would result in the marriage being declared void (see as to nullity, chap. ii.); and if the adultery is not proved, or if any of such facts are proved, he is entitled to be dismissed from the suit and to have his costs.

The co-respondent may also defend himself by showing that the petitioner has been guilty of incestuous adultery, or adultery with bigamy, or simple adultery, such as will result in the dismissal of the petition. The co-respondent will be entitled to the costs of such issues, if he succeeds in them, even though the issue as to the adultery charged against him be found against him, and he is condemned in the costs of proving it.

The husband's connivance at the adultery will also be a complete defence; but his condonation of the adultery will not. He may pardon his wife without pardoning her paramour.

If the wife was living in prostitution, that will be an answer to a claim for damages, and if the co-respondent can satisfy the jury that he did not know that the wife was a married woman it will go largely in mitigation of damages, and so it will if he shews that the husband and wife were living separate when the adultery was committed. And generally, though the co-respondent only answers denying the adultery, he will have the benefit of any circumstances which he can elicit at the trial showing the adultery to have resulted from the petitioner's misconduct or carelessness.

By sec. 34 of the Matrimonial Causes Act, 1857, when the adultery is established the Court may order the adulterer to pay the whole or any part of the costs of the proceedings.

The co-respondent will be ordered to pay all the costs where he was the husband's friend and seduced the wife, and usually when he knew she was a married woman, though the husband was remiss. If the adultery is not established, the statute does not allow the Court to saddle the co-respondent with costs; but it does not follow that he should receive his costs, for he may have indulged in undue familiarities, which led the husband to join him in the suit. The adultery may be proved and yet the petition dismissed. In this case, the co-respondent will not receive costs, and has sometimes been ordered to pay the costs of proving the adultery which he has disputed.

17. In suits for judicial separation, as in all proceedings other than to dissolve a marriage, the Court is required by sec. 22 of the Matrimonial Causes Act, 1857, to act and give relief on principles and rules as nearly as may be conformable to those which guided the old Ecclesiastical Courts.

The chief of these rules is that the Court will not decree judicial separation in favour of a husband or a wife who has been guilty of adultery. The adultery on the petitioner is therefore always an answer to the petition.

A young woman met a foreigner in the streets of London, persuaded him to marry her, spent all his money, and returned to an adulterous connection with a former lover. The husband then assaulted her was bound over to keep the peace, and went to gaol if, default. She petitioned for divorce on the ground of adultery and cruelty, but failed to prove any adultery and the only cruelty she proved was the assault. She then asked for separation on the ground of cruelty, but the Judge Ordinary refused it because she had herself committed adultery. He remarked that the petitioner's adultery had always hitherto been a bar to separation, but he could imagine cases where it ought not to be so, as where the respondent's misconduct had directly led to the adultery. *Grossi* v. *Grossi*. (3 L. R. P. and M, 118).

Cruelty exercised by the petitioner is said to be no answer to a petition for separation on the ground of adultery; though it would be an answer to such a petition founded on desertion.

But in *Lempriere* v. *Lempriere* (1 L. R. P and M, 569) Lord Penzance pointed out that the Divorce Act (Matrimonial Causes Act, 1857), had made desertion a matrimonial offence, which it was not in the Ecclesiastical Courts, where the remedy for desertion was not a separation which would gratify the deserter, but restitution; and then he added:—"It is doubtful whether, since the passing of the Divorce Act, a husband, who has been guilty of cruelty and desertion, can obtain judicial separation on the ground of his wife's adultery."

The connivance by the petitioner at any adultery by the other party, and the condonation by the petitioner of the adultery or other offence *complained* of, are bars to a suit for separation as they are to one for divorce.

But collusion seldom takes place in suits for separation.

By section 11 of the Matrimonial Causes Act, 1858, in petitions for divorce, if, after the close of the evidence on the part of the petitioner, it turns out that there is no sufficient evidence against the co-respondent; or against the woman with whom the husband is charged with having committed adultery, if she is joined as respondent—which is rarely the case—the Court may dismiss the co-respondent, or the woman, from the suit. There are many things which are evidence against the wife which are not evidence against the co-respondent; for instance, the wife's confessions made by word of mouth to her friends or written in her diary. It would be highly unjust that the wife should, by such means, be able to incriminate another, and equally just that the evidence should be strongly condemnatory of herself. In such cases, if there is no evidence against the co-respondent, he is discharged on the ground that he has committed no adultery with the wife, and at the close of the case the jury find the wife guilty of adultery with the co-respondent. This may be an unavoidable contradiction, but it makes the law look silly.

19. Where a petition is presented, either for judicial separation or for dissolution of marriage, the Court has power to order the husband to pay a reasonable allowance for the support of his wife, during the suit. This is called alimony *pendente lite* or during suit.

The Court has also power on decreeing judicial separation, to order a permanent allowance to the wife if she has shewn herself deserving of it, and this is called "permanent alimony."

Where the relation of husband and wife is ended by divorce an allowance is sometimes ordered for the wife under the name of "alimonial provision."

20. When the wife is either petitioner or respondent in a suit, it is considered right, without reference to her prospect of success in the suit, that she should be maintained during the course of it. A wife, therefore, who has no separate property, or no sufficient property of her own or of her husband's in her hands, presents a petition as soon as she pleases after the commencement of the proceedings praying for alimony pending suit. The commencement of the suit is by service of the citation on the respondent, or order to dispense with such service. If the wife is respondent, she must enter an appearance to the citation before filing her petition for alimony.

If the wife has no income at all, the amount allowed is usually one fifth of the husband's nett income, all his property, though producing no income, such as pictures and horses, being treated as capital the interest of which is reckoned as income. The sum awarded is ordered to be paid to the wife, or to some person or persons to be nominated in writing by her, and approved by the Court as a trustee or trustees on her behalf. The wife's solicitor is often so appointed. The sum may be ordered to be paid by weekly, monthly, or quarterly instalments, and continues till a final decree is made in the suit.

If the husband neglects to pay, he may be compelled to do so by attachment, *i. e.*, imprisonment; and may, moreover, be liable in the meantime to be sued by tradesmen and others who may have given credit to his wife (see chap. xii.).

But there are some exceptions to the rule that a wife, whether petitioner or respondent, is entitled to alimony pending suit, as, for instance, where she is leading the life of a prostitute, or is being supported by the co-respondent.

Alimony *pendente lite* is payable from the service of the citation, and down to the final decree in the cause, for it is only after final decree that permanent alimony (if any) begins.

The Court derives its power to award alimony *pendente lite* from the transference to it of the jurisdiction of the Ecclesiastical Courts by the Matrimonial Causes Act, 1857, s. 6.

**21.** Permanent alimony is allowed to the wife who has obtained a judicial separation from her husband on the ground of his misconduct, and where she is without means, it is usually one third of the husband's nett income, reckoned in the mode above mentioned. Where she has an income less than one third of his, the two are added together, and he is directed to pay such a sum as will make up her income to one third of the joint income. It is payable only during the husband's life.

**22.** The wife's right to alimony *pendente lite* does not depend on the nature of the suit, any more than on her prospect of success in it. She is as much entitled to it in suits for nullity as in other suits; and, even in a suit for nullity by reason of bigamy, inasmuch as the *factum* of a marriage is necessarily pleaded, and sworn to by affidavit; and the woman, till she is proved guilty, is to be assumed innocent, and entitled to support.

But permanent alimony was refused to a wife on a sentence of nullity pronounced by reason of her former husband having been alive at the time of the second marriage.

Where judicial separation is sought for on the ground of the cruelty of the wife, the Court, though it cannot award permanent alimony, will withhold its decree until the husband makes some reasonable provision for the wife's maintenance, though he will not be required to give a bond with sureties for the payment of it.

28. Although alimony is strictly a sum paid under the order of the Court to a person who, though separate, continues to be a wife, yet there is a provision in the nature of alimony, usually called an "alimonial provision," which is sometimes ordered to be paid by the former husband to the former wife, or *vice versâ*, after the marriage has been dissolved by decree, and the relation of husband and wife has therefore ceased to exist between them.

The award of this provision is made under sec. 32 of the Divorce Act, and under the Matrimonial Causes Act, 1866 (29 and 30 Vict., c. 32); and, when granted, it is usually embodied in the decree dissolving the marriage, *i.e.*, the decree absolute, which will be hereafter explained.

Sec. 32 says that, in cases of dissolution of marriage the Court may order the husband to secure to the wife such gross sum of money, or such annual sum of money, for any term, not exceeding her own life, as shall be thought fit, considering her fortune, if any, the husband's means, and the conduct of the parties. And the decree may be suspended till the proper deed is executed. The Act of 1866 enables the Court to order weekly or monthly payments instead of a gross sum, and to discharge or modify the order if the husband should be unable to pay.

This alimonial provision must be applied for by a separate petition, as is required in case of an application to remodel settlements (see sec. 26). The petition cannot be filed till a decree *nisi* is pronounced, and may be filed within a month after decree absolute, or such extended time as the judge may allow, and therefore the order for the provision need not form part of the decree absolute, though it usually does so.

24. In awarding this permanent provision under sec. 32 to a woman whose marriage has been dissolved by reason of her husband's misconduct, the court will act on the same principles as those upon which the Ecclesiastical Courts allotted permanent alimony after a decree of divorce, *a mensa et thoro*, and will order him to secure to her about one-third of the joint income.

Permanent alimony on separation is payable only during the husband's life. Alimonial provision on dissolution of marriage is sometimes only while the wife remains chaste and unmarried, and sometimes without such restriction, and, as allowed by sec. 32, for the wife's life.

In awarding alimonial provision the Court will sometimes take into consideration, on settling the amount, that the guilt of one of the parties has now been established, and will make the amount greater or less, according as the wife is innocent or guilty; and it will require special circumstances to induce the Court to grant alimonial provision in favour of a wife whose marriage is dissolved for her own guilt.

25. The Court will not make an order for payment of alimony where the husband is an uncertificated bankrupt; and, when alimony has been already decreed, the husband, if he obtains an order of discharge in bankruptcy, is protected against all proceedings to enforce arrears of alimony.

26. A decree of judicial separation, or of dissolution of marriage, or of nullity, might have the effect of doing a great injustice to the innocent party and the children of the marriage, if the Court had no power to make just arrangements as to property.

By sec. 46 of the Matrimonial Causes Act, 1857, where the Court makes a decree of divorce or judicial separation for adultery of the wife, it may order a reasonable settlement of any of her property either in possession or reversion to be made for the benefit of the innocent party and the children of the marriage or any or either of them. And by the Matrimonial Causes Act, 1860, s. 6, such settlement is not to be affected by the disability of coverture (if any exists), that is by the woman being a married woman; as she would be in case of judicial separation or until decree absolute in divorce.

By sec. 5 of the Matrimonial Causes Act, 1859, the Court *after* a final decree of nullity of marriage or dissolution of marriage, may enquire into any settlements made on the parties and may order the whole or a portion of the settled property to be applied for the benefit of the children or their respective parents.

By the Matrimonial Causes Act, 1878, 41 Vict., c. 19, s. 3, the Court may exercise these powers though there are no children of the marriage.

The Act of 1857, it will be observed, applies only to the property of a guilty wife and has nothing to do with nullity; while the Act of 1859 applies equally to the settled property of either party irrespective of which is to blame and including cases of nullity where neither may be to blame.

The application for the exercise by the Court of its power under the sections above mentioned is required by rule 95 to be made by separate petition, to be filed within a month after decree unless the judge extends the time. A copy of the petition is to be personally served on the opposite party and on persons having any legal *or* beneficial interest in the property and such latter persons must enter an appearance before answering. The opposite party has a fortnight to answer on oath, and the petitioner has the same time to reply. The registrar then examines the parties and reports on the property, and the matter is decided by the Court on motion.

By the Guardianship of Infants Act, 1886, s. 7, the Court on pronouncing a decree of judicial separation or of divorce, may declare the parent for whose misconduct the decree is made, to be for ever unfit to have the custody of the children. See chap. xx., sec. 10, where the section is given.

The other events in which the Court has power to interfere for the benefit of children are summed up in chap. xx.

27. By the Matrimonial Causes Act, 1857, s. 33, a husband can no longer maintain an action before the ordinary tribunals to recover damages from an adulterer for criminal intercourse with his wife. But such action is only transferred to the new Divorce Court, in which the husband may claim damages from the adulterer in a petition for divorce, or a petition for judicial separation, or in a petition *limited to the claim for damages.* Condonation of the wife's adultery is no answer to the claim for damages. The case for damages is to be tried in the same way as the old action, for criminal conversation, and the damages must be assessed by a jury. The Court has power, after verdict, to direct in what manner the damages are to be paid and applied, and may order the whole or any part to be settled for the benefit of the children of the marriage, or for the maintenance of the wife.

A ridiculous result may arise from the proceeding for damages being assimilated to these in the now abolished action. Where the respondent, confident of his innocence, does not appear, the jury must find *some* damages against him as being in default; so that he is saddled with damages for adultery, though the jury find there has been none, and the petition is dismissed.

I should mention that on a petition praying a dissolution of marriage, the Court may decree a judicial separation instead; but if separation only be prayed for, a dissolution cannot be granted. The adulterer may be ordered to pay the whole or any part of the costs.

28. By the Matrimonial Causes Act, 1866 (29 Vict., c. 32, s. 2), it is provided that "in any suit instituted for dissolution of marriage," if the respondent shall oppose the relief sought on the ground (in case of a suit by the husband) of his adultery, cruelty, or desertion, or (in case of a suit instituted by a wife) on the ground of her adultery or cruelty, the Court may in such case give

to the respondent on his or her application the same relief to which he or she would have been entitled in case he or she had filed a petition seeking such relief.

29. The Court has power to decree nullity of marriage, that is, that a marriage was void at its commencement (see chap. ii), and the same powers may then be exercised by the Court concerning children as are mentioned in the case of dissolution of marriage.

30. When a petition is filed, the petitioner must swear to the truth of the petition as far as possible by affidavit, and must also swear that no collusion or connivance exists between the petitioner and the other party to the marriage or alleged marriage.

The respondent, on filing an answer, has also to deny connivance and collusion; and if the answer contains not merely a denial of the facts charged in the petition, but substantive statement of facts, these facts must, as far as possible, be verified, by the respondent's affidavit.

A copy of every petition, together with a writ called a citation, must be personally served on the respondent and co-respondent, unless from their keeping out of the way to avoid service, or for some other good reason, the Court thinks fit to dispense with service or to order a service on some relative or friend of the person in question. This is called a substituted service.

When the proceedings are ripe for trial the case will, in the ordinary course, be tried before one of the judges of the Court, and the evidence of the witnesses will be delivered orally; but the judge will accede to an application of either party to have the cause tried by a jury, and, if damages are claimed against a co-respondent, they can only be awarded by a jury.

An appeal lies to the full court, and thence to the House of Lords.

The rules as to the verification by affidavit of the petition and answer, and the service of the citation and copy of petition, are the same in the case of judicial separation, dissolution of marriage, and nullity.

The Court may direct any matter of fact to be tried by the Court itself, or by a jury, and either on oral or affidavit evidence, the former being more usual, unless either party insists, as he or she may do, on the question of fact being tried by a jury; and no damages can be awarded against the adulterer except by a jury.

The petitioner must, as above stated, have pledged his or her oath by affidavit to the truth of the petition, as far as his or her knowledge will extend, but it is to be observed that by s. 43 of the Matrimonial Causes Act, 1857, the Court itself has power to require any petitioner to attend and be examined or cross-examined on oath, on the hearing of the petition; and the judge will usually put a few questions to a petitioner on oath, even though he or she be not tendered as a witness.

On the hearing of every petition for the purpose of obtaining a decree of nullity of marriage, and of every petition for restitution of conjugal rights, and of every petition for judicial separation on any other ground than that of adultery, both husband and wife have from the first been both competent and compellable to give evidence.

But, by the Act to Amend the Law of Evidence, 1869, the parties to *any proceeding instituted in consequence of adultery*, which, of course, includes all petitions for dissolution of marriage and some for separation, are competent but not compellable to give evidence; that is to say, if the husband (or wife, as the case may be) does not tender himself or herself as a witness, the opposite party cannot compel him (or her) to do so. "Provided that no witness in any proceeding, whether a party to the suit or not shall be liable to be asked or bound to answer any question tending to show that he or she has been guilty of adultery, unless such witness has already given evidence in the same proceeding in disproof of his or her alleged adultery."

Although, as stated in sec. 18, the *admissions* by the respondent wife (as in conversations, letters or diary) are not evidence against the co-respondent, yet it has been held (*Allen* v. *Allen*, 1894, 2 Q.B. 242) that the *testimony* of either, if called as a witness, is evidence against the other, because each is entitled to cross-examine the other.

No husband is compellable to disclose any communication made to him by his wife during the marriage; and no wife is compellable to disclose any communication made to her by her husband during the marriage.—(Evidence Amendment Act, 1853, s. 2.)

81. Upon a petition for a decree of judicial separation, of dissolution of marriage, or of nullity of marriage, the Court has power to make any order that it may deem just as to the custody, maintenance, and education of the infant children of the marriage, and may, if necessary, order them to be made wards in Chancery (see chap. xx.).

82. By the Matrimonial Causes Act, 1860, sec. 7, and the Matrimonial Causes Act, 1873, in suits for dissolution of marriage and in suits for nullity, the Queen's Proctor is enabled to intervene at any stage of the case under the direction of the Attorney General, and with the leave of the Court. Any person may give information to the Queen's Proctor as to the case, and if, from that information or otherwise, he suspects that the parties to the suit are acting in collusion to obtain a decree contrary to the justice of the case, he may, under the direction and with the leave mentioned, allege the collusion, and retain counsel, and subpœna witnesses to prove it. The Court may order the costs of the intervention to be paid by the parties or such of them as it shall think fit, including a wife if she has separate property. And by the Matrimonial Causes Act, 1878, sec. 2, the Court may make an order as to the costs, not only of the Queen's Proctor, but of any other person who intervenes; but if the Queen's Proctor is ordered to pay costs the Treasury may allow him to treat them as expenses of his office.

When the Queen's Proctor thus intervenes during the progress of a suit, he enters an appearance and files a plea in answer to the petition, and delivers a copy of his plea to the petitioner, and then proceeds as if an original party to the suit.

By the Matrimonial Causes Act, 1878, the Court may make an order for costs in favour of or against any person who enters an appearance to shew cause against making a decree absolute.

88. In cases of judicial separation the final decree is pronounced at once, unless the judge takes time to consider, and subject of course to a motion for a new trial. But in cases of dissolution of marriage and of nullity the decree made at the trial of the cause is only a decree *nisi*; that is a decree that, unless cause be shown to the contrary, the marriage is dissolved or declared null and void, as the case may be.

By the Matrimonial Causes Act, 1860 (23 and 24 Vict., c. 144), s. 7, and by the Matrimonial Causes Act, 1866, (29 and 30 Vict. c. 32) s 3, a decree for divorce is required in the first instance to be a decree nisi, and not to be made absolute until after the expiration of six months, unless the Court otherwise directs, and by the Matrimonial Causes Act, 1873, these provisions are extended to suits for nullity of marriage.

During this six months, or other period, the parties continue man and wife and alimony *pendente lite*, if awarded, continues to be payable. Adultery committed during this period is adultery during the marriage, and, if brought to the notice of the Court, may be regarded as a reason for not making the decree absolute.

A decree *nisi* is a "decree unless," and means a decree which does not operate at once but after a certain time can be made absolute on motion, unless sufficient reason is shewn why it should not.

The object of the decree being at first conditional only, is to enable *any* person to shew cause against its being made absolute, such as that material facts were not brought before the Court, or that the decree was obtained by collusion—a course often taken by the Queen's Proctor on receiving information of collusion, or the suppression of material facts.

The intervention by the Queen's Proctor at any stage of the cause has been spoken of above, but in shewing cause against a decree nisi being made absolute he stands in the same position as regards the Court as the rest of the public do, but has to get the directions of the Attorney General, which the rest of the public do not.

The person whether Queen's Proctor or not, who wishes to shew cause, enters an appearance in the cause, and within four days files affidavits of his facts and gives copies to the party in whose favour the decree is. That party has eight days to answer and the person shewing cause has eight days to reply and then the judge on motion directs the matter to be argued, or if necessary that some question shall be tried by a jury.

84. After a decree for dissolution of marriage or a decree of nullity of marriage has been made absolute each of the parties may at once marry again, as if the other were dead, if there is no right of appeal. The decree nisi cannot be made absolute till six months after it has been pronounced unless the Court otherwise directs. Where there is a right of appeal, neither party must marry again till the lapse of one month after the decree is made absolute, which is the time allowed for appeal, and, if an appeal is instituted, he or she must abide its result. Where there is a right of appeal, a marriage within the month will be void, and so will a marriage pending the appeal, if instituted. The appeal is to the House of Lords. In suits for dissolution of marriage, no respondent or co-respondent who has not appeared "and defended the suit on the occasion of the decree nisi being made" has a right of appeal against the decree absolute, unless the Court, upon application made at the time of pronouncing the decree absolute, shall see fit to permit an appeal, (Matrimonial Causes Act, 1868, ss. 3, 4).

No clergyman of the Church of England need solemnise the marriage of such a person, but he must allow his church or chapel to be used by any other clergyman of the diocese for the purpose.

85. On the dissolution of marriage by divorce, as on its dissolution by death, all the husband's responsibilites arising from the marriage are ended. Being incapable of being sued jointly with his wife, the man is no longer liable upon the contracts entered into, or for the torts committed by the woman before marriage, nor for the torts committed by her after marriage, nor has she any longer any implied authority from him by which she can make him liable upon contracts for necessaries or upon any other contracts.

## CHAPTER XX.

### Of children.

1. *Legitimacy. Legitimacy Declaration Act*, 1858.
2. *National status of children.*
3. *Father, and after his death, mother is legal guardian.*
4. *Where both parents die leaving children under age.*
5. *Father may, by deed or will, appoint guardian. Guardian in socage.*
6. *Power given by statute of* 1886 *to mother to appoint guardian.*
7. *Powers of guardians.*
8. *Court may allow mother access to, or custody of, children under* 16.
9. *Court may remove certain guardians.*
10. *Divorce Court may exclude a parent for ever from custody of children.*
11. *To what Courts application for custody, etc., may be made.*
12. *Relative positions of parents as to custody, guardianship, etc.*
13. *Guardian's rights and duties.*
14. *Act of* 1889 *for protection of children.*
15. *Benefit conferred by stranger on condition of guardianship.*
16. *Illegitimate children and children of the wife before marriage.*
17. *Ward of Court not to leave kingdom or to be married without permission of Court.*
18. *Father, when excused from maintaining children.*
19. *Religious education of orphan children.*
20. *Grounds on which children will be taken away from parent.*

21. *Divorce Court may make orders as to custody, maintenance and education.*
22. *Divorce Court may provide for children out of property of either parent and out of damages paid by co-respondent.*
23. *A few examples.*
24. *Parent taking possession of infant's property.*
25. *Powers of Chancery where infant convicted of felony.*
26. *Infant may make marriage-settlement with leave of Court.*
27. *Recent statutory enactments as to infant's property.*
28. *Parents not liable on contracts of infants.*
29. *Necessaries.*
30. *Infants' Relief Act.*
31. *Infant's rights to property and powers of contracting. Gavelkind.*
32. *Infants may sue and be sued.*
33. *Court may withhold Custody of infant from Parent or Guardian.*

1. All children are presumed to be legitimate which are born of the wife during the marriage, even although the wife has committed adultery, unless it be clearly shown that *no* sexual intercourse took place between the mother and her husband, or unless, as in the case of judicial separation, or separation under a magistrate's order (see chap. xvi.), there arises a presumption of non-access.

Any natural-born subject or person whose claim to be a natural-born subject depends on legitimacy, or on the validity of a marriage, may petition the Divorce Court for a decree declaring that he is the legitimate child of his parents, and that the marriages of his grandfather and grandmother, father and mother, and himself and his wife, respectively were legal.

There is an appeal to the House of Lords.

2. The law with regard to the national status of children, as well as of their parents, is given in chap. x.

3. The father is by law the guardian of his legitimate children during their infancy, and after his death the mother, if living, will be their guardian during her life,

as long as they are infants. A mere separation of the father and mother by consent, without any stipulation as to custody of children, will not affect this right.

4. If both parents die before the children are of age, and without a guardian being appointed by either parent, the Chancellor, as exercising the parental authority of the Crown over infants, will, where there is any property, appoint a guardian for them, usually some friend or relative in whom the father or mother placed confidence. This guardian then becomes an officer of the Court, and bound to act under its control, but, subject to such control, he has a parent's authority, and the children are called wards of Court. If the Court does not appoint a guardian, the care of the infant will devolve on the guardian in socage (to be mentioned shortly) or to the corporate officers, or persons entitled by the custom of the city, manor, or place to the guardianship,

5. By the statute of the 12th of Charles II., chap. 24, the father, whether himself of age or not, may, by deed (*i.e.*, by writing under seal), or by will, appoint a guardian, to have the custody and tuition of the father's infant, and unmarried children, until they come of age, or for any lesser time named in the writing. The appointment will not apply to children who, at the father's death, have come of age, or have married, but may include his children born after his death. The guardian so appointed will, after the father's death, have the same rights as the father, as to the custody and maintenance of the child, and, unless other provisions are made by will or settlement, will receive the income of the child's lands, and have the management of his personal estate for his benefit.*

* The powers given by the statute to the guardian appointed by the father are those of a "guardian in socage." This means a guardian of the heir of lands held in socage tenure. This was the tenure of lands not held of the Crown in chief, or by knight service, or copyhold of a manor, and, by the statute, all the latter (except copyhold) were reduced to the tenure of "free and common socage," which is now the ordinary tenure. Where a man died seised of socage lands leaving his heir under fourteen, the nearest male relative, to whom the land could not

Guardians so appointed by will are called testamentary guardians.

6. But, by the Guardianship of Infants' Act, 1886, s. 2, on the death of the father of an infant, and, in case the father shall have died prior to the passing of the Act (25th June, 1886), then, from the passing of the Act, the mother, if surviving, shall be the guardian of the infant, either alone, when no guardian has been appointed by the father, or jointly with any guardian so appointed. Where the father has not appointed a guardian, or that guardian dies or refuses to act, the Court may appoint one or more guardians to act with the mother.

By sec. 3, the mother may, by deed or will, appoint a guardian or guardians to act *after the death of herself and the father*, and, if both parents appoint guardians, they are to act jointly.

The mother may also, by deed or will, appoint a guardian to act *after her death jointly with the father*, but before this guardian can act, the Court has to be satisfied that the father is unfitted to be the sole guardian of his children, and has to confirm the appointment of the guardian who will then act with him.

7. Guardians who disagree about what is best for the child may apply to the Court. By sec. 4, every guardian in England is to have the same powers over the estate and person, or over the estate of the infant, as under the 12 Car. II., c. 24, above mentioned, and every guardian in Ireland is to have the powers conferred in like manner by the Irish Act, 14 and 15 Car. c. II., 19.

8. By sec. 5, the Court, upon the application of the

---

descend, was guardian of the heir's person and estate till fourteen. Before such a guardianship could arise now it would be necessary that both parents should die without either of them appointing a guardian, and leaving the heir, under fourteen, and the Chancellor would then appoint a guardian on petition, so as to avoid a guardianship in socage.

The statute saves the custom of London and other cities, for the mayor and aldermen to be guardians of the infants of their citizens; but these rights only arise where the parents have both died without appointing a guardian.

mother by her "next friend," may make an order as to the custody of an infant, and the access thereto of either parent, having regard to the welfare of the infant and the conduct and wishes of the parents, and may alter the order on the application of either parent, or of the guardian, if both parents be dead.

Independently of the 5th sec. above mentioned, a judge of the Chancery Division has power by the statute 36 Vict., c. 12, the Infants' Custody Act, 1873, to give the mother either the right of access to her infant child or its actual custody up to the age of 16, and, in the latter case, to order that the father shall have access to the child.

The same Act allows the parents to agree in a separation deed that the father shall give up the custody of the infant children, or any of them, to the mother; but the Courts are not to enforce the agreement unless it appears to be for the benefit of the child or children.

9. By sec. 6, the High Court of Justice in England or Ireland and the Court of Session in Scotland, may, if it is for the welfare of the infant, remove a testamentary guardian *appointed or acting by virtue of this Act*, and may also with the same object, appoint another in his place. The words in italics would preclude the Court from removing a guardian appointed by the father under 12 Car. II., c. 24.

10. Sec. 7 is as follows :—

"In any case where a decree for judicial separation, or a decree, either nisi or absolute, for divorce shall be pronounced, the Court pronouncing such decree may thereby declare the parent by reason of whose misconduct such decree is made to be a person unfit to have the custody of the children (if any) of the marriage; and in such case the parent so declared to be unfit shall not, upon the death of the other parent, be entitled as of right to the custody or guardianship of such children.

11. In addition to the Courts already mentioned, the application for custody or access may be made in England or Ireland to the County Court, and in Scotland to the Sheriff's Court; but subject, in England or Ireland, to removal, at the instance of any party, to the Chancery Division, and in Scotland to a removal to the Court of

Session, and subject in all three countries to an appeal to the last mentioned Courts respectively.

12. Both parents are thus placed very nearly on an equality as regards the power of acquiring the guardianship by survivorship and of appointing guardians. The only differences which require noting are (1) that the father may appoint a guardian to act with the mother, but if the mother appoints a guardian to act with the father, the person so appointed has no authority unless confirmed by the Court, on proof of the unfitness of the father, and (2) that the Court can remove a guardian appointed by the mother under the Act, but cannot remove a guardian appointed by the father under the old Act.

These differences, however, are of less importance, because the mother can always apply for the custody of the infant under sec. 5, whether her husband is alive or dead, and, if dead, whether he has appointed a guardian or not. And she can also apply under the Act of 1878. Under former Acts, now repealed, the Court would almost always give the mother the custody of an infant till seven years of age, and the Act of 1878 indicates a longer limit as being reasonable.

The Court also has the general superintendence over the guardian, and will curtail or suspend his authority in case of misbehaviour.

13. The guardian cannot delegate his duty to another, nor upon his death does his office devolve upon his heir or his personal representatives. When more than one are appointed guardians, they have each equal authority during their lives, so that one cannot take the infant away from the others; and upon the death of one the office devolves upon the survivor.

The guardian is entitled to the custody of the infant's person, and to choose the school at which he or she may be placed, and the Courts will order any person who removes or harbours the infant to restore him or her to the guardian. But see sec. 38 of this chapter.

The guardian has all the parent's authority to consent to the marriage of his ward when under age, and whether male or female;* but when a female ward is married she passes under the dominion of her husband, and the guardian's authority over her ceases. With a male, however, it is otherwise, and, though married, he is still under the guardian's authority.

14. Here I ought to mention a statute of 1889 (52 and 53 Vict., c. 44) called "the Prevention of Cruelty to and Protection of Children Act," which imposes certain duties on all persons having the control of children down to a certain age, and enables magistrates, for breach of such duties and for other offences, to deprive such persons of the control of the children.

The first section imposes heavy punishment on every person who, having the control of a boy under 14 or a girl under 16, illtreats, neglects, abandons, or exposes the child, or causes another to do so, in a manner *likely* to cause unnecessary suffering or injury to the health of the child.

Section 2 imposes punishment on the person in control of children, below the ages already mentioned, who causes them to be in any street for the purpose of begging, whether under pretence of singing, performing, selling things, or otherwise; or who causes them to be in any street or public-house singing or performing for profit, or selling things between ten at night and five in the morning; and on the person who is in control of a child under 10, and causes it to be *at any time* in any street, public-house, circus, or place of entertainment where people pay to go in, for the purpose of performing.

Where the person having the control of the child is convicted of an offence under sec. 1, or of any offence involving bodily injury to the child, punishable by penal servitude, or is committed for trial for any such offence, or is bound over to keep the peace towards the child, any person may apply for the control of the child. The petty sessional Court may then make an order giving the person the control of the child till 14, or, in the case of a girl, till 16, or any lesser ages, and may vary the

* If an infant orphan without guardian wishes to marry, the Chancellor, Master of the Rolls, or a Vice-Chancellor will on petition assent to the marriage, if suitable.

order from time to time. If the person in whose favour the order is made is not of the child's religion, the justices must make another order in favour of some one who is of that religion, if willing to take care of the child.

If the person originally in control of the child, and who stood committed for trial is acquitted or not prosecuted, he is to have the child back again at once.

The evidence of the child is not to be acted upon without corroboration, and the accused person, and the husband or wife of the accused person are competent, but not compellable witnesses.

15. Though the parents are the only persons empowered by statute to appoint a guardian, yet they may act in such a manner as to render an appointment by a stranger effectual. Thus, where another person, whether a relative or not, confers a benefit by will, or otherwise, upon the parents or the children, upon the condition that the parents give up the guardianship then, if they accept the benefit, or commit the care of the children to the person appointed by the stranger the parents have no longer a right to interfere with their education, or compel them to be delivered up. But the Court will see that the intercourse between parent and child shall be as frequent as the nature of the case will permit.

16. Although a father has no power to appoint a guardian for his illegitimate children, yet the Court will usually appoint the person of his selection. The mother will be permitted to have access to them, and they will be ordered to have access to the relatives of their deceased parent.

By 4 and 5 Will. IV., c. 76, s. 57, the husband is bound to maintain, as part of his family, any child or children, till the age of sixteen, legitimate or illegitimate, whom his wife may have at the time of marriage.

17. The Court is very jealous of its wards being taken abroad for any lengthened period, and usually requires some security to be given for their return, and for their proper education while absent.

Any man or woman, though under age, who marries

a ward of the Court, without having obtained its leave, as well as those who contrive or assist at such marriage, is guilty of a contempt of Court, and will be subjected to imprisonment. In case of the marriage of a female ward, the imprisonment will last till a proper settlement is executed, to be approved of by the Court.

The proper course, where a ward of Court is to be married, is to obtain the sanction of the Court to the marriage and to a proper settlement. When this is once done another settlement cannot be substituted by waiting till the ward comes of age.

18. The father is bound to maintain his children, and none the less though they have a provision for their maintenance from some other source, and the mother, if she has separate property, is equally bound (see chap. viii., s. 16). But where the parents are unable to maintain and educate their child in a manner suitable to the fortune which the child expects, the Court will order a proper allowance out of the income of the property. But where the children are removed from the husband on account of his misconduct he is no longer bound to support them (except under the order of the Divorce Court) whatever his means may be, and maintenance will be allowed them out of any property they may have from any other quarter.

19. It will be understood that unless some provision has been made for the children these applications to the Court cannot be granted; not because the Court has not jurisdiction over rich and poor alike, but because there is no means of bringing its power to bear.

The father being the lawful custodian of his children is the person who is entitled to regulate their religious education. This right is not interfered with by the Guardianship of Infants' Act, 1886, and the father enjoys it whether he is Protestant, Roman Catholic, Greek Catholic, Mohammedan, Parsee, or Buddhist. After his death the Court will usually direct the children to be brought up in the religion chosen by their father, and will pay great attention to the expression of his wishes, both in the appointment of a guardian and in sanctioning a particular mode of education.

But, further than expressing his wish, a father cannot regulate the religious faith of his children by his will, except indirectly, by appointing a guardian of his own faith. When this is done the Court will uphold the appointment, if otherwise proper.

A Roman Catholic father who had married a Protestant lady, but had entered into no stipulation as to the faith in which his children were to be brought up, appointed a Roman Catholic priest sole testamentary guardian of his children. The Lord Chancellor (Cottenham) said it would be an act of very great injustice to interfere.

A Protestant father married a Roman Catholic mother, and, with his consent, his children, aged respectively ten, nine, and three, were for three years educated as Roman Catholics, and his two elder children were admitted to communion in that faith. The father afterwards became dependent for support on the Protestant clergy, and caused his children to be educated as Protestants, and died the following year without appointing a guardian. The Court held that he had not abandoned his right to have his children brought up in his own faith, and appointed a Protestant guardian to act with the mother.

A pecuniary benefit to the infant will not induce the Court to interfere with the course of religious education to be pursued by the guardian appointed by the father.

But the Court will not make an order to alter the religious education of a child whose mind has for some time received strong impressions adverse to the faith of his father, and who expresses a preference for the faith in which he has been so educated.

A person keeping the child away from the mother will be ordered by the Queen's Bench Division, or the Chancery Division, to restore it to her, although her religion is different from that of her deceased husband, in which the child has been brought up. But the Chancery Division will, on application, make an order that the child's religious education shall continue as before. If, however, no such application is made, and the mother changes the religious education of the child, and firmly indoctrinates its mind with another form of religion, the Court will not order the child to be again instructed in its father's religious belief if, on examination of the child, it appears that it leans strongly to its mother's creed.

20. By the common law the custody of the children, up to sixteen years of age, belongs, as of absolute and exclusive right, to the father. This was upon the natural presumption that the children would be properly cared for and properly educated. But whenever this presumption was removed, and it was proved that the father grossly illtreated his children, or was "in constant habits of drunkenness and blasphemy, or low and gross debauchery, or that he professed atheistical or irreligious principles, or that his domestic associations were such as tended to the corruption and contamination of his children, or that he otherwise acted in a manner injurious to the morals or interests of his children," the Court of Chancery would interfere and appoint a guardian (see Story's Equity Jurisprudence, § 1341). And now, by the Judicature Act, 1873, s. 25, the Courts of Law are to act upon the same rules as to the custody and education of infants as prevailed in the Court of Chancery. And see sec. 33 of this chapter.

The father still enjoys the *primâ facie* right to the custody of the infant children, and all that the statutes do is to enable the wife to apply for the custody or for access. In dealing with such an application, the Courts will be guided by the same considerations as the Court of Chancery was guided by in restoring the children to the husband or removing the custody from him, and the custody will always be refused to a mother who is living in adultery. And see sec. 33 of this chapter.

Sometimes a suit for making children wards of Court is accompanied by a petition for their custody, and both are heard together.

21. The Divorce Court, when a husband or wife petitions for judicial separation, for dissolution of marriage, or for decree of nullity of marriage, may make temporary orders for the custody, maintenance, and education of the children during the suit, and, in pro-

nouncing the final decree, may provide permanently for the same objects, with power, nevertheless, to alter or rescind such orders from time to time to meet the altered circumstances of the parties. And after final decree the Court has the same power of making orders for temporary or for permanent custody.

The Court will usually make a temporary order that *during the suit* the children under seven shall remain in the custody of the father or mother or some other relative, as the case may require, and will even remove older children from the custody of their father, where there is any likelihood of bad example or ill-usage.

The Court may order the children of the dissolved marriage, under age, to be made wards in Chancery.

22. The Divorce Court may exercise the following powers as regards property in favour of the children of the husband and wife whose marriage is in question:

Where a sentence, either of judicial separation or divorce, is given on account of the adultery of the *mother*, it may order a settlement out of her property, whether in possession or reversion, to be made for the benefit of the innocent party, or of the children of the marriage, or any or either of them.

Where damages are recovered by the husband against a co-respondent, the Court may direct the whole or any part thereof to be settled for the benefit of the children (if any) of the marriage, or as a provision for the maintenance of the wife.

Where a final decree of nullity or for dissolution of marriage has been pronounced, the Court may, then or afterwards, inquire into any settlement made on the husband or wife, and may order the whole or any part of the settled property to be applied for the benefit of the children or of the parents, or any or either of them, or of the husband or wife where there are no children.

23. After decree absolute for dissolution of marriage on the ground of the husband's adultery and cruelty, applications were made for the custody of infant children of the marriage by the father and by the mother, and by third persons who had intervened (with leave) for the benefit of the children. The Court being of

opinion that neither the father nor the mother were the proper persons to have the custody of the children, gave them up to the care of the third persons, but directed that the parents should have reasonable access.

In one case, where a marriage was dissolved on the ground of the wife's adultery, the Court would not order her to have the custody of her children or even access to them.

In another case, in which the wife appeared to be the innocent party, although she had elected, on separation, to have the custody of the children, the Court allowed her on her petition, in addition to alimony, a sum of money to be paid by the husband for the past and future maintenance of the children. (Matrimonial Causes Act, 1859; 22 and 23 Vict., c. 61, s. 4).

24. A father or mother entering on land, or taking possession of any other property belonging to a child, does so as *guardian*, and is accountable to the child when he or she comes of age, and cannot charge for personal trouble devoted to the property.

25. By the 3 and 4 Vict., c. 90, where an infant is convicted of felony, a judge of the Chancery Division, on the application of any person wishing to take charge of him, may remove him from the custody of parents or guardians who are unfit to have charge of him, and may assign the custody of him to the applicant, and may revoke such assignment. The infant is to undergo his sentence, and, when the new guardian acquires possession of him, he is not to take him beyond seas or out of the jurisdiction. No fees of Court are taken, and the lawyers may be appointed by the Court to act gratuitously; but the parent may have costs if the appli cation is improper. The Act is not much used.

26. By 18 and 19 Vict., c. 43, a male infant of twenty and a female infant of seventeen years of age may, with the sanction of judge of the Chancery Division, making a binding settlement, or agreement for a settlement, in contemplation of marriage. The settlement may include all or any part of the settlor's property, both in real and in personal estate, and the infant in pursuance of it may execute valid conveyances and

appointments under powers, unless, in the latter case, the words of the power exclude its exercise by an infant. If the infant dies under age, appointments under powers and disentailing deeds executed by him or her in pursuance of the settlement are to be void. The sanction of the Court is to be obtained on petition by the infant or his or her guardian in a summary way, without a suit or action.

27. Where a person entitled in his own right to land in fee-simple, or for any leasehold interest at a rent, is an infant, the land is, by the Conveyancing Act of 1881, s. 41, to be deemed a settled estate within the Settled Estates Act, 1877. This act has already been mentioned (see chap. x., s. 8) and under it (s. 49) an infant may, by his guardian, make an application, or consent to one, or receive notice of one. And by the Settled Land Act, 1882, (see chap. x., s. 4) where a person entitled in his own right to the possession of land is an infant, he is to be deemed for the purposes of the Act, tenant for life, and the land, settled land.

The Conveyancing Act, 1881, contains, in ss. 42 and 43, full directions as to the management by trustees of the property of any infant, who is not a married woman and is beneficially entitled to the possession of any land. Sec. 42 applies to land, and sec. 43 to "any property." Both allow the trustees to apply the income to the infant's "maintenance, education, or benefit," or to pay it to the guardian for that purpose, and the latter section allows them so to apply or pay it, whether the infant is absolutely entitled or only contingently on his attaining twenty-one, or on the happening of some event before he is twenty-one.

28. As to contracts by infants. Young men and women under age are only liable upon contracts and purchases made by them for things necessary to their condition in life, and this whether they have parents or not. Their parents or surviving parent are not liable, except upon bargains to which they themselves are parties, and cannot be sued upon the contracts of their children. The children, however, are often agents so as to bind their parents, and a small amount of participa-

tion by the latter will often involve them in legal liability.

The law concerning infants generally is beyond the scope of this book, but what follows with regard to the legal position of an infant may serve to explain the relation of his parents towards him.

29. What are necessaries for an infant, is a question to be decided by the jury, if the case is tried by a jury, and, if not, by the judge. What is necessary for a young man of large expectations, for an infant invalid, for an infant student, or for an infant officer in the army or navy, would not be necessary for every youth of the same age, whose means were small, and who was not an invalid, or a student, or an officer. Juries of tradesmen will always be liberal and judges will only be a little less liberal in enabling a plaintiff to recover against an infant who is well off, for the supply of any articles necessary for his occupation, health, and proper recreation, or for enabling him to mix in society suited to his position.

In order to avoid the question of whether an article supplied, or a service rendered, was necessary, the tradesman often induced the youth, on coming of age, to make a promise to pay (which had to be in writing), or to agree to an account stated, for articles supplied to him, or money lent to him, by which he was inveigled into a ratification as improvident as was the original acceptance of the goods, money, or service.

30. To put an end to this, "The Infants' Relief Act, 1874," enacted that:—

All contracts, whether by specialty [*i.e.*, by deed] or simple contract, entered into by infants for money lent or to be lent, or for goods supplied or to be supplied (other than contracts for necessaries), and all accounts stated with infants, shall be absolutely void. Provided always that this enactment shall not invalidate any contract into which an infant may, by any existing or future statute, or by the rules of common law or equity, enter, except such as now by law are voidable.

No action shall be brought whereby to charge any person upon any promise made after full age, to pay any debt contracted during infancy, or upon any ratification made after full age of any promise or contract made during infancy, whether there shall or shall not be any new consideration for such promise or ratification after full age.

This statute applies to a ratification of an infant's promise to marry. (See chap. I., s. 8).

81. An infant may acquire and possess personalty, whether money or chattels, and may acquire land by gift or purchase, and may hold it and receive the rent and profits of it, but cannot bind himself by a conveyance of it to another,* nor pass it by will.

Every infant may bind himself by a contract for food, lodging, and clothes, of a sort which are necessary, because these things are required, irrespective of his poverty or rank. If schooling, medical attendance, servants, carriages and horses, are needed by his condition, and within his means, he may bind himself by contracting for them to the extent to which they are needed, or are suitable to his wealth and rank. But he cannot bind himself by a contract which is not for his benefit, such as a bill of exchange or promissory note or a bond or other contract with a penalty. He cannot appoint an attorney even to do what he himself may do, or for legal proceedings, with one exception mentioned below. See *Flower* v. *L. & N.W.R. Co.* (1894), 2 Q.B. 65.

Marriage is not a necessary for an infant, and so he cannot bind himself for the victuals for a marriage feast, nor can he (or she) be made liable for a breach of promise to marry. The other party, however, if adult, is liable to the infant for the breach of a promise to marry, if the guardian has consented.

Marriage when once contracted by an infant is binding, and an infant husband is liable for necessaries which he orders for the wife.

82. Having these rights and liabilities, the infant can sue and be sued during infancy. To protect his property, and obtain what is due to him, he may maintain

---

* Lands subject to the custom of gavelkind, which prevails largely in Kent, descend to all the sons equally, and, in default of nearer heirs, descend in like manner to brothers and other collaterals, and every holder of a freehold estate in gavelkind may dispose of it at the the age of fifteen by feoffment for value. This is done by making public livery (or delivery) of the land (as by giving the door-handle, a twig of a tree, a turf, or the like, in the name of the whole), and the livery should be accompanied by a deed of feoffment, setting out the lands and the estate given.

an action, and he may be sued for wrongs done by him, and upon all contracts by which he can bind himself.

When he sues, he does so by his "next friend." Any body may be a "next friend," but he must sign a written authority to the solicitor to use his name and is liable for costs. When the infant is sued, he defends by guardian *ad litem* (or for the action), who is appointed without an order, on an affidavit by the solicitor, of the guardian's fitness, of his having no interest adverse to the infant, and that he has signed a written consent to act.

But, by the County Courts Act, 1888, s. 96, it shall be lawful for any person under the age of twenty-one years to prosecute any action in the County Court for any sum of money not greater than £50, which may be due to him for wages, or piece work, or for work as a servant, in the same manner as if he were of full age. That is to say, he may sue in person or appoint an attorney; but he must still defend by guardian.

88. By the Custody of Infants Act, 1891, printed in the Appendix, it will be seen that, when a parent or guardian applies to have a child handed over to him or her, the court may refuse to do so if the applicant has abandoned or deserted the child, or if the applicant's conduct has been such that the Court should refuse to grant the application.

# APPENDIX.

## Married Women's Property Act, 1882.
[45 and 46 Vict., chap. 75.]

### ARRANGEMENT OF SECTIONS.

1. *Married woman to be capable of holding property ana of contracting as a feme sole.*
2. *Property of a woman married after the Act to be held by her as a feme sole.*
3. *Loans by wife to husband.*
4. *Execution of general power.*
5. *Property acquired after the Act by a woman married before the Act to be held by her as a feme sole.*
6. *As to stock, &c., to which a married woman is entitled.*
7. *As to stock, &c., to be transferred, &c., to a married woman.*
8. *Investments in joint names of married women and others.*
9. *As to stock, &c., standing in the joint names of a married woman and others.*
10. *Fraudulent investments with money of husband.*
11. *Moneys payable under policy of assurance not to form part of estate of the insured.*
12. *Remedies of married women for protection and security of separate property.*
13. *Wife's ante-nuptial debts and liabilities.*
14. *Husband to be liable for his wife's debts contracted before marriage to a certain extent.*
15. *Suits for ante-nuptial liabilities.*
16. *Act of wife liable to criminal proceedings.*
17. *Questions between husband and wife as to property to be decided in a summary way.*
18. *Married woman as an executrix or trustee.*
19. *Saving of existing settlements, and the power to make future settlements.*
20. *Married woman to be liable to the parish for the maintenance of her husband.*

21. *Married woman to be liable to the parish for the maintenance of her children.*
22. *Repeal of* 33 *and* 34 *Vict., c.* 93, 37 *and* 38 *Vict., c.* 50.
23. *Legal representative of married woman.*
24. *Interpretation of terms.*
25. *Commencement of Act.*
26. *Extent of Act.*
27. *Short title.*

Whereas it is expedient to consolidate and amend the Act of the thirty-third and thirty-fourth Victoria, chapter ninety-three, intituled "The Married Women's Property Act, 1870," and the Act of the thirty-seventh and thirty-eighth Victoria, chapter fifty, intituled "An Act to amend the Married Women's Property Act (1870)":

Be it enacted by the Queen's most Excellent Majesty, by and with the advice and consent of the Lords Spiritual and Temporal, and Commons, in this present Parliament assembled, and by the authority of the same, as follows:—

1. (1.) A married woman shall, in accordance with the provisions of this Act, be capable of acquiring, holding, and disposing by will or otherwise, of any real or personal property as her separate property, in the same manner as if she were a feme sole, without the intervention of any trustee.

(2.) A married woman shall be capable of entering into and rendering herself liable in respect of and to the extent of her separate property on any contract, and of suing and being sued, either in contract or in tort, or otherwise, in all respects as if she were a feme sole, and her husband need not be joined with her as plaintiff or defendant, or be made a party to any action or other legal proceeding brought by or taken against her; and any damages or costs recovered by her in any such action or proceeding shall be her separate property; and any damages or costs recovered against her in any such action or proceeding shall be payable out of her separate property, and not otherwise.

(3.) Every contract entered into by a married woman shall be deemed to be a contract entered into by her with respect to and to bind her separate property, unless the contrary be shown.

(4.) Every contract entered into by a married woman with respect to and to bind her separate property shall bind not only the separate property which she is possessed of or entitled to at the date of the contract, but also all separate property which she may thereafter acquire.

(5.) Every married woman carrying on a trade separately from her husband shall, in respect of her separate property, be subject to the bankruptcy laws in the same way as if she were a feme sole.

**2.** Every woman who marries after the commencement of this Act shall be entitled to have and to hold as her separate property and to dispose of in manner aforesaid all real and personal property which shall belong to her at the time of marriage, or shall be acquired by or devolve upon her after marriage, including any wages, earnings, money, and property gained or acquired by her in any employment, trade, or occupation, in which she is engaged, or which she carries on separately from her husband, or by the exercise of any literary, artistic, or scientific skill.

**3.** Any money or other estate of the wife lent or entrusted by her to her husband for the purpose of any trade or business carried on by him, or otherwise, shall be treated as assets of her husband's estate in case of his bankruptcy, under reservation of the wife's claim to a dividend as a creditor for the amount or value of such money or other estate after, but not before, all claims of the other creditors of the husband for valuable consideration in money or money's worth have been satisfied.

**4.** The execution of a general power by will by a married woman shall have the effect of making the property appointed liable for her debts and other liabilities in the same manner as her separate estate is made liable under this Act.

**5.** Every woman married before the commencement of this Act shall be entitled to have and to hold and to dispose of in manner aforesaid as her separate property all real and personal property, her title to whish, whether vested or contingent, and whether in possession, reversion, or remainder, shall accrue after the commencement of this Act, including any wages, earnings, money, and property so gained or acquired by her as aforesaid.

**6.** All deposits in any post office or other savings bank, or in any other bank, all annuities granted by the Commissioners for the Reduction of the National Debt or by any other person, and all sums forming part of the public stocks or funds, or of any other stocks or funds transferable in the books of the Governor and Company of the Bank of England, or of any other bank, which at the commencement of this Act are standing in the sole name of a married woman, and all shares, stock, debentures debenture stock, or other interests of or in any corporation, company, or public body, municipal, commercial, or otherwise, or of or in any industrial, provident, friendly, benefit, building, or loan society, which at the commencement of this Act are standing in her name, shall be deemed, unless and until the contrary be shown, to be the separate property of such married woman; and the fact that any such deposit, annuity, sum forming part of the public stocks or funds, or of any other stocks or funds transferable in the books of the Governor and Company of the Bank of England or of any other bank, share, stock, debenture, debenture stock, or other interest as aforesaid, is standing in the sole name of a married woman, shall be sufficient primâ facie evidence that she is beneficially entitled thereto for her separate use, so as to authorise and empower her to receive or transfer the same, and to receive the dividends, interest, and profits thereof, without the concurrence of her husband, and to indemnify the Postmaster General, the Commissioners for the Reduction of the National Debt, the Governor and Company of the Bank of England, the Governor and Company of the Bank of Ireland, and all directors, managers, and trustees of every such bank, corporation, company, public body, or society as aforesaid, in respect thereof.

**7.** All sums forming part of the public stocks or funds, or of any other stocks or funds transferable in the books of the Bank of England or of any other bank, and all such deposits and annuities respectively as are mentioned in the last preceding section, and all shares, stock, debentures, debenture stock, and other interests of or in any such corporation, company, public body, or society as aforesaid, which after the commencement of this Act shall be allotted to or placed, registered, or transferred in or into or made to stand in the sole name of any married woman shall be deemed, unless and until the contrary be shown, to be her separate property, in respect of which so far as any liability may be incident thereto her separate estate shall alone be liable, whether the same shall be so expressed in the document whereby her title to the same is created or certified, or in the books or register wherein her title is entered or recorded, or not.

Provided always, that nothing in this Act shall require or authorise any corporation or joint stock company to admit any married woman to be a holder of any shares or stock therein to which any liability may be incident, contrary to the provisions of any Act of Parliament, charter, byelaw, articles of association, or deed of settlement regulating such corporation or company.

**8.** All the provisions herein-before contained as to deposits in any post office or other savings bank, or in any other bank, annuities granted by the Commissioners for the

Reduction of the National Debt or by any other person, sums forming part of the public stocks or funds, or of any other stocks or funds transferable in the books of the Bank of England or of any other bank, shares, stock, debentures, debenture stock, or other interests of or in any such corporation, company, public body, or society as aforesaid respectively, which at the commencement of this Act shall be standing in the sole name of a married woman, or which, after that time, shall be allotted to, or placed, registered, or transferred to or into, or made to stand in, the sole name of a married woman, shall respectively extend and apply, so far as relates to the estate, right, title, or interest of the married woman, to any of the particulars aforesaid which, at the commencement of this Act, or at any time afterwards, shall be standing in, or shall be allotted to, placed, registered, or transferred to or into, or made to stand in, the name of any married woman jointly with any persons or person other than her husband.

**9.** It shall not be necessary for the husband of any married woman, in respect of her interest, to join in the transfer of any such annuity or deposit as aforesaid, or any sum forming part of the public stocks or funds, or of any other stocks or funds transferable as aforesaid, or any share, stock, debenture, debenture stock, or other benefit, right, claim, or other interest of or in any such corporation, company, public body, or society as aforesaid, which is now or shall at any time hereafter be standing in the sole name of any married woman, or in the joint names of such married woman and any other person or persons not being her husband.

**10.** If any investment in any such deposit or annuity as aforesaid, or in any of the public stocks or funds, or in any other stocks or funds transferable as aforesaid, or in any share, stock, debenture, or debenture stock of any corporation, company, or public body, municipal, commercial, or otherwise, or in any share, debenture, benefit, right, or claim whatsoever in, to, or upon the funds of any industrial, provident, friendly, benefit, building, or loan society, shall have been made by a married woman by means of moneys of her husband, without his consent, the Court may, upon an application under section seventeen of this Act, order such investment, and the dividends thereof, or any part thereof, to be transferred and paid respectively to the husband; and nothing in this Act contained shall give validity as against creditors of the husband to any gift, by a husband to his wife, of any property, which, after such gift shall continue to be in the order and disposition or reputed ownership of the husband, or to any deposit or other investment of moneys of the husband made by or in the name of his wife in fraud of his creditors; but any moneys so deposited or invested may be followed as if this Act had not passed.

**11.** A married woman may by virtue of the power of making contracts herein-before contained effect a policy upon her own life or the life of her husband for her separate use; and the same and all benefit thereof shall enure accordingly.

A policy of assurance effected by any man on his own life, and expressed to be for the benefit of his wife, or of his children, or of his wife and children, or any of them, or by any woman on her own life, and expressed to be for the benefit of her husband, or of her children, or of her husband and children, or any of them, shall create a trust in favour of the objects therein named, and the moneys payable under any such policy shall not, so long as any object of the trust remains unperformed, form part of the estate of the insured, or be subject to his or her debts: Provided, that if it shall be proved that the policy was effected and the premiums paid with intent to defraud the creditors of the insured, they shall be entitled to receive, out of the moneys payable under the policy, a sum equal to the premiums so paid. The insured may by the policy, or by any memorandum under his or her hand, appoint a trustee or trustees of the moneys payable under the policy, and from time to time appoint a new trustee or new trustees thereof, and may make provision for the appointment of a new trustee or new trustees thereof, and for the investment of the moneys payable under any such policy. In default of any such appointment of a trustee, such policy, immediately on its being effected, shall vest in the insured and his or her legal personal representatives, in trust for the purposes aforesaid. If, at the time of the death of the insured, or at any time afterwards, there shall be no trustee, or it shall be expedient to appoint a new trustee or new trustees, a trustee or trustees or a new trustee or new trustees may be appointed by any Court having jurisdiction under the provisions of the Trustee Act, 1850, or the Acts amending and extending the same. The receipt of a trustee or trustees duly appointed, or, in default of any such appointment, or in default of notice to the insurance office, the receipt of the legal personal representative of the insured shall be a discharge to the office for the sum secured by the policy, or for the value thereof, in whole or in part.

**12.** Every woman, whether married before or after this

Act, shall have in her own name against all persons whomsoever, including her husband, the same civil remedies, and also (subject, as regards her husband, to the proviso hereinafter contained) the same remedies and redress by way of criminal proceedings, for the protection and security of her own separate property, as if such property belonged to her as a feme sole, but, except as aforesaid, no husband or wife shall be entitled to sue the other for a tort. In any indictment or other proceeding under this section it shall be sufficient to allege such property to be her property; and in any proceeding under this section a husband or wife shall be competent to give evidence against each other, any statute or rule of law to the contrary notwithstanding: Provided always, that no criminal proceeding shall be taken by any wife against her husband by virtue of this Act while they are living together, as to or concerning any property claimed by her, nor while they are living apart, as to or concerning any act done by the husband while they were living together, concerning property claimed by the wife, unless such property shall have been wrongfully taken by the husband when leaving or deserting, or about to leave or desert, his wife.

**13.** A woman after her marriage shall continue to be liable in respect and to the extent of her separate property for all debts contracted, and all contracts entered into or wrongs committed by her before her marriage, including any sums for which she may be liable as a contributory, either before or after she has been placed on the list of contributories, under and by virtue of the Acts relating to joint stock companies; and she may be sued for any such debt and for any liability in damages or otherwise under any such contract, or in respect of any such wrong; and all sums recovered against her in respect thereof, or for any costs relating thereto, shall be payable out of her separate property; and, as between her and her husband, unless there be any contract between them to the contrary, her separate property shall be deemed to be primarily liable for all such debts, contracts, or wrongs, and for all damages or costs recovered in respect thereof: Provided always, that nothing in this Act shall operate to increase or diminish the liability of any woman married before the commencement of this Act for any such debt, contract, or wrong, as aforesaid, except as to any separate property to which she may become entitled by virtue of this Act, and to which she would not have been entitled for her separate use under the Acts hereby repealed or otherwise, if this Act had not passed.

**14.** A husband shall be liable for the debts of his wife contracted, and for all contracts entered into and wrongs committed by her, before marriage, including any liabilities to which she may be so subject under the Acts relating to joint stock companies as aforesaid, to the extent of all property whatsoever belonging to his wife which he shall have acquired or become entitled to from or through his wife, after deducting therefrom any payments made by him, and any sums for which judgment may have been *bonâ fide* recovered against him in any proceeding at law, in respect of any such debts, contracts, or wrongs for or in respect of which his wife was liable before her marriage as aforesaid; but he shall not be liable for the same any further or otherwise; and any court in which a husband shall be sued for any such debt shall have power to direct any inquiry or proceedings which it may think proper for the purpose of ascertaining the nature, amount, or value of such property: Provided always, that nothing in this Act contained shall operate to increase or diminish the liability of any husband married before the commencement of this Act for or in respect of any such debt or other liability of his wife as aforesaid.

**15.** A husband and wife may be jointly sued in respect of any such debt or other liability (whether by contract or for any wrong) contracted or incurred by the wife before marriage as aforesaid, if the plaintiff in the action shall seek to establish his claim, either wholly or in part, against both of them; and if in any such action, or in any action brought in respect of any such debt or liability against the husband alone, it is not found that the husband is liable in respect of any property of the wife so acquired by him or to which he shall have become so entitled as aforesaid, he shall have judgment for his costs of defence, whatever may be the result of the action against the wife if jointly sued with him; and in any such action against husband and wife jointly, if it appears that the husband is liable for the debt or damages recovered, or any part thereof, the judgment to the extent of the amount for which the husband is liable shall be a joint judgment against the husband personally and against the wife as to her separate property; and as to the residue, if any, of such debt and damages, the judgment shall be a separate judgment against the wife as to her separate property only.

**16.** A wife doing any act with respect to any property of her husband, which, if done by the husband with respect to property of the wife, would make the husband liable to criminal proceedings by the wife under this Act, shall in like manner be liable to criminal proceedings by her husband.

17. In any question between husband and wife as to the title to or possession of property, either party, or any such bank, corporation, company, public body, or society as aforesaid in whose books any stocks, funds, or shares of either party are standing, may apply by summons or otherwise in a summary way to any judge of the High Court of Justice in England or in Ireland, according as such property is in England or Ireland, or (at the option of the applicant irrespectively of the value of the property in dispute) in England to the judge of the county court of the district, or in Ireland to the chairman of the civil bill court of the division in which either party resides, and the judge of the High Court of Justice or of the county court, or the chairman of the civil bill court (as the case may be) may make such order with respect to the property in dispute, and as to the costs of and consequent on the application as he thinks fit, or may direct such application to stand over from time to time, and any inquiry touching the matters in question to be made in such manner as he shall think fit: Provided always, that any order of a judge of the High Court of Justice to be made under the provisions of this section shall be subject to appeal in the same way as an order made by the same judge in a suit pending or on an equitable plaint in the said court would be; and any order of a county or civil bill court under the provisions of this section shall be subject to appeal in the same way as any other order made by the same court would be, and all proceedings in a county court or civil bill court under this section in which, by reason of the value of the property in dispute, such court would not have had jurisdiction if this Act or the Married Women's Property Act, 1870, had not passed, may, at the option of the defendant or respondent to such proceedings, be removed as of right into the High Court of Justice in England or Ireland (as the case may be), by writ of certiorari or otherwise as may be prescribed by any rule of such High Court; but any order made or act done in the course of such proceedings prior to such removal shall be valid, unless order shall be made to the contrary by such High Court: Provided also, that the judge of the High Court of Justice or of the county court, or the chairman of the civil bill court, if either party so require, may hear any such application in his private room; Provided also, that any such bank, corporation, company, public body, or society as aforesaid, shall, in the matter of any such application for the purposes of costs or otherwise, be treated as a stakeholder only.

**18.** A married woman who is an executrix or administratrix alone or jointly with any other person or persons of the estate of any deceased person, or a trustee alone or jointly as aforesaid of property subject to any trust, may sue or be sued, and may transfer or join in transferring any such annuity or deposit as aforesaid, or any sum forming part of the public stocks or funds, or of any other stocks or funds transferable as aforesaid, or any share, stock, debenture, debenture stock, or other benefit, right, claim, or other interest of or in any such corporation, company, public body, or society in that character, without her husband, as if she were a feme sole.

**19.** Nothing in this Act contained shall interfere with or affect any settlement or agreement for a settlement made or to be made, whether before or after marriage, respecting the property of any married woman, or shall interfere with or render inoperative any restriction against anticipation at present attached or to be hereafter attached to the enjoyment of any property or income by a woman under any settlement, agreement for a settlement, will, or other instrument; but no restriction against anticipation contained in any settlement or agreement for settlement of a woman's own property to be made or entered into by herself shall have any validity against debts contracted by her before marriage, and no settlement or agreement for a settlement shall have any greater force or validity against creditors of such woman than a like settlement or agreement for a settlement made or entered into by a man would have against his creditors.

**20.** Where in England the husband of any woman having separate property becomes chargeable to any union or parish, the justices having jurisdiction in such union or parish may, in petty sessions assembled, upon application of the guardians of the poor, issue a summons against the wife, and make and enforce such order against her for the maintenance of her husband out of such separate property as by the thirty-third section of the Poor Law Amendment Act, 1868, they may now make and enforce against a husband for the maintenance of his wife if she become chargeable to any union or parish. Where in Ireland relief is given under the provisions of the Acts relating to the relief of the destitute poor to the husband of any woman having separate property, the cost price of such relief is hereby declared to be a loan from the guardians of the union in which the same shall be given, and shall be recoverable from such woman as if she were a feme sole by the same actions and proceedings as money lent.

21. A married woman having separate property shall be subject to all such liability for the maintenance of her children and grandchildren as the husband is now by law subject to for the maintenance of her children and grandchildren: Provided always that nothing in this Act shall relieve her husband from any liability imposed upon him by law to maintain her children or grandchildren.

22. The Married Women's Property Act, 1870, and the Married Women's Property Act, 1870, Amendment Act, 1874, are hereby repealed: Provided that such repeal shall not affect any act done or right acquired while either of such Acts was in force, or any right or liability of any husband or wife, married before the commencement of this Act, to sue or be sued under the provisions of the said repealed Acts or either of them, for or in respect of any debt, contract, wrong, or other matter or thing whatsoever, for or in respect of which any such right or liability shall have accrued to or against such husband or wife before the commencement of this Act.

23. For the purposes of this Act the legal personal representative of any married woman shall in respect of her separate estate have the same rights and liabilities and be subject to the same jurisdiction as she would be if she were living.

24. The word "contract" in this Act shall include the acceptance of any trust, or of the office of executrix or administratrix, and the provisions of this Act as to liabilities of married women shall extend to all liabilities by reason of any breach of trust or devastavit committed by any married woman being a trustee or executrix or administratrix either before or after her marriage, and her husband shall not be subject to such liabilities unless he has acted or intermeddled in the trust or administration. The word "property" in this Act includes a thing in action.

25. The date of the commencement of this Act shall be the first of January, one thousand eight hundred and eighty-three.

26. This Act shall not extend to Scotland.

27. This Act may be cited as the Married Women's Property Act, 1882.

## An Act to Amend the Law by Making Better Provision for the Widows of Certain Intestates in the Distribution of such Intestates' Property.

[25th July 1890.]



BE it enacted by the Queen's most Excellent Majesty, by and with the advice and consent of the Lords Spiritual and Temporal, and Commons, in this present Parliament assembled, and by the authority of the same, as follows:

**1.** The real and personal estates of every man who shall die intestate after the first day of September one thousand eight hundred and ninety leaving a widow but no issue shall, in all cases where the net value of such real and personal estates shall not exceed five hundred pounds, belong to his widow absolutely and exclusively.

**2.** Where the net value of the real and personal estates in the preceding section mentioned shall exceed the sum of five hundred pounds the widow of such intestate shall be entitled to five hundred pounds part thereof absolutely and exclusively, and shall have a charge upon the whole of such real and personal estates for such five hundred pounds, with interest thereon from the date of the death of the intestate at four per cent. per annum until payment.

**3.** As between the real and personal representatives of such intestate, such charge shall be borne and paid in proportion to the values of the real and personal estates respectively.

**4.** The provision for the widow intended to be made by this Act shall be in addition and without prejudice to her interest and share in the residue of the real and personal estates of such intestate remaining after payment of the sum of five hundred pounds, in the same way as if such residue had been the whole of such intestate's real and personal estates and this Act had not been passed.

**5.** The net value of such real estates as aforesaid shall for the purposes of this Act be estimated in the case of a fee simple upon the basis of twenty years purchase of the annual value by the year at the date of the death of the intestate as determined by law for the purposes of property tax* less the gross amount of any mortgage or other principal sum charged thereon, and less the value of any annuity or other periodical payment chargeable thereon, to be valued according to the tables and rules in the Schedule annexed to the Statute 16 & 17 Vict., c. 51, and in the case of an estate for a life or lives according to the said tables and rules.

**6.** The net value of such personal estate as aforesaid shall be ascertained by deducting from the gross value thereof all debts, funeral and testamentary expenses of the intestate, and all other lawful liabilities and charges to which the said personal estate shall be subject.

**7.** This Act may be cited as the Intestates' Estates Act, 1890.

**8.** This Act shall not extend to Scotland.

---

* By 5 & 6 Vic., c. 35, s. 60 (the Property Tax Act), the annual value of lands, tenements and hereditaments is the amount at which they have been let at a rack rent where the rent has been fixed by agreement commencing within seven years, counting from the 5th of April preceding the assessment, otherwise the annual value is the rack rent which the lands are worth by the year.

## Custody of Children Act, 1891.

[54 *Vic. cap* 3.]

Passed 26th March, 1891.

Be it enacted, etc.

1. *Power of Court as to production of child.* Where the parent of a child applies to the High Court or the Court of Session for a writ or order for the production of the child, and the Court is of opinion that the parent has abandoned or deserted the child, or that he has otherwise so conducted himself that the Court should refuse to enforce his right to the custody of the child, the Court may in its discretion decline to issue the writ or make the order.

2. *Power of Court to order repayment of costs of bringing up child.* If at the time of the application for a writ or order for the production of the child the child is being brought up by another person, or is boarded out by the guardians of a poor law union, or by a parochial board in Scotland, the Court may, in its descretion, if it orders the child to be given up to the parent, further order that the parent shall pay to such person, or to the guardians of such poor law union, or to such parochial board, the whole of the costs properly incurred in bringing up the child, or such portion thereof as shall seem to the Court to be just and reasonable, having regard to all the circumstances of the case.

3. *Court in making order to have regard to conduct of parent.* Where a parent has

(*a*) abandoned or deserted his child; or

(*b*) allowed his child to be brought up by another person at that person's expense, or by the guardians of a poor law union, for such a length of time and under such circumstances as to satisfy the Court that the parent was unmindful of his parental duties;

the Court shall not make an order for the delivery of the child to the parent, unless the parent has satisfied the Court that, having regard to the welfare of the child, he is a fit person to have the custody of the child.

4. *Power to Court as to child's religious education.* Upon any application by the parent for the production or custody of a child, if the Court is of opinion that the parent ought not to have the custody of the child, and that the child is being brought up in a different religion to that in which the parent has, a legal right to require that the child should be brought up, the Court shall have power to make such

order as it may think fit to secure that the child be brought up in the religion in which the parent has a legal right to require that the child should be brought up. Nothing in this act contained shall interfere with or affect the power of the Court to consult the wishes of the child in considering what order ought to be made, or diminish the right which any child now possesses to the exercise of its own free choice.

5. *Definitions of "parent" and "person."* For the purposes of this act the expression "parent" of a child includes any person at law liable to maintain such child or entitled to his custody, and "person" includes any school or institution.

6. (*Short title.*)

## The Married Women's Property Act, 1893.

[56 *and* 57 *Vict. chap.* 63.]

Passed 5th December, 1893.

Be it enacted, etc.

1. *Effect of contracts by married women.* Every contract hereafter entered into by a married woman, otherwise than as an agent,

(a) shall be deemed to be a contract entered into by her with respect to and to bind her separate property whether she is or is not in fact possessed of or entitled to any separate property at the time when she entered into such contract;

(b) shall bind all separate property which she may at that time or thereafter be possessed of or entitled to, and

(c) shall also be enforceable by process of law against all property which she may thereafter while discount be possessed of or entitled to;

provided that nothing in this section contained shall render available to satisfy any liability or obligation arising out of such contract, any separate property which at that time or thereafter she is restrained from anticipating.

2. *Costs may be ordered to be paid out of the property subject to restraint or anticipation.* In any action or proceeding now or hereafter instituted by a woman or by a next friend on her behalf, the court before which such action or proceeding is pending shall have jurisdiction by judgment or order from time to time to order payment of the costs of the opposite party out of property which is subject to a restraint on anticipation, and may enforce such payment by the appointment of a receiver and the sale of the property or otherwise as may be just.

3. *Will of married woman.* Section 24 of the Wills Act, 1837, shall apply to the will of a married woman made during coverture, whether she is or is not possessed of or entitled to any separate property at the time of making it, and such will shall not require to be re-executed or republished after the death of her husband.

4. *Repeal.* Subsections (3) and (4) of section (1) of the Married Women's Property Act, 1882, are hereby repealed.

5. *Short title.*

6. *Extent.* This Act shall not apply to Scotland.

# INDEX.

*The Roman numerals stand for the chapters, and the Arabic numerals stand for the sections of the chapters. The letter "h." stands for "husband" and the letter "w." for "wife."*

Stop filming —

THE

# LAW GUARANTEE AND TRUST SOCIETY,

LIMITED.

**Subscribed Capital - £1,000,000**
**Paid up - - - £100,000**

**TRUSTEES.**

The Right Hon. LORD JUSTICE KAY. | The Hon. Mr. JUSTICE DAY.
The Hon. BARON POLLOCK. | The Hon. Mr. JUSTICE GRANTHAM.

**BANKERS.**

Messrs. CHILD & Co., 1, Fleet Street, E.C.
BANK OF ENGLAND (Law Courts Branch).
NATIONAL PROVINCIAL BANK OF ENGLAND, LIMITED (Lincoln's Inn Branch).

General Manager and Secretary—THOS. R. RONALD.
Assistant Secretary—WALTER S. BATES.

## FIDELITY GUARANTEES.

POLICIES are granted on favourable terms guaranteeing to Employers the fidelity of Managers, Secretaries, Clerks, Cashiers, Travellers, Collectors, and other Employees holding situations of trust or confidence. Either separate Policies on individual employees or one Policy to cover an entire staff are issued, as may be preferred.

**RECEIVERS', BANKRUPTCY TRUSTEES', ADMINISTRATORS', and LUNACY COMMITTEES' BONDS.**

## MORTGAGE INSURANCE.
## DEBENTURE INSURANCE.
## LICENSE INSURANCE.
## CONTINGENCY INSURANCE.

## TRUSTEESHIPS.

THE Society is prepared to be appointed Executor or Trustee under Wills, Marriage Settlements, or other Instruments. Absolute security for the corpus of trust funds is provided, while the duties of the Family Solicitor will continue as heretofore.

**TRUSTEESHIPS for DEBENTURE-HOLDERS.**

**Head Office: 49, CHANCERY LANE, LONDON, W.C.**
**City Office: 56, MOORGATE STREET, E.C.**

DUBLIN ...... [illegible], [illegible] Street.
BIRMINGHAM, 104, Colmore Row.
GLASGOW ...... 141, St. Vincent Street.
HUDDERSFIELD, 23, John William Street.
LIVERPOOL...Union Buildings, [illegible], [illegible] Street.
MANCHESTER, 40, King Street.
NEWCASTLE-ON-TYNE ...... Union Chambers, Grainger Street West.

LIEBER'S

# Standard Telegraphic Code.

By B. FRANKIN LIEBER.

**Price TWO GUINEAS net.**

The Code is of 800 pages, and contains over 75,000 code words, 25,000 consisting of tables. There are 10,000 extra ciphers, giving ample opportunity for special phrases. The code words employed are from the "Official Vocabulary." The compilers having only used ciphers from "A" to "F," an opportunity is left to cablers to construct a large private and separate code for their own particular and individual use.

Points about the Code:—

1. The arrangement of the sentences is strictly alphabetical.
2. There are extra ciphers on every other page.
3. The omission of "I" or "we" in the beginning of a sentence, *e.g.*, "botsing" would mean the party signing the message intends to sell; by "Smith botsing" it would signify that "Smith" intends to sell.
4. The double and sometimes sextuple indexing of the subjects, *e.g.*, "Business Credit," "Character," "Credit," "Financial Standing," "Firm's Standing," "Standing of firms." *Also* "Pounds (£)"; "Sterling (£)." *Also* "Express Shipping"; "Shipping by Express."
5. The paper is stout linen paper, firm and strong, and yet thin, that the volume is handy.

From the large number of sentences on all subjects the Code may be used as a Mining and General business code. There is a complete list of United States Stocks, Bonds, and other Securities, together with some International Stocks, with code words, rendering the Code extremely useful to all firms having international dealings. The Code may be used by Bankers, Brokers, Manufacturers, Merchants, Stockbrokers, &c.

# LIEBER'S MANUAL,

*Published bi-monthly.*

**Subscription 12s. 6d. per Annum.**

The names of holders of the Code are inserted free of charge in the above Manual, and care should be taken that the name is sent for insertion at once on purchase. **A subscription to this Manual cannot be too strongly advised.**

LONDON:

**EFFINGHAM WILSON, 11, Royal Exchange, E.C.**

# IMPORTANT COMMERCIAL PUBLICATIONS.

**Australian Mining Manual;** a Handy Guide to the West Australian Market. By G. B. BERMAN and FREDC. C. MATHIESON & SONS. Price 1s. net.

**A Money Market Primer and Key to the Exchanges.** Second Edition, revised. Recommended by the Council of the Institute of Bankers. By GEORGE CLARE. Price 5s.

**Handy Guide to Patent Law and Practice.** By G. F. EMERY, LL.M. Price 6s. net.

**Theory of Foreign Exchanges.** Sixteenth Edition. One Volume, 8vo. By the Right Hon. GEO. J. GOSCHEN, M.P. Price 6s.

**Tables of Interest, &c.** Interest and Discount Tables, computed at 2½, 3, 3½, 4, 4½, and 5 per cent., from 1 to 365 days. By GUMERSALL. Price 10s. 6d.

**African Market Manual,** giving particulars of all Companies (African or otherwise) dealt in the African Market of the Stock Exchange. By [illegible]. Price 5s.

**The Statutory Trust Investment Guide.** By RICHARD MARRACK, M.A. The particulars as to Investments eligible, compiled and arranged by FREDC. C. MATHIESON AND SONS. Second Edition, revised and enlarged. Price 6s. net.

**Home Railways as Investments.** By W. J. STEVENS. Price 2s. 6d. net.

**American Railroads and British Investors.** By S. F. VAN OSS. Price 2s. 6d. net.

**Modern Cambist.** A Manual of Foreign Exchanges. The Modern Cambist, forming a Manual of Foreign Exchanges in the various operations of Bills of Exchange and Bullion, according to the practice of all Trading Nations; with Tables of Foreign Weights and Measures, and their Equivalents in English and French. By TATE. Price 10s. 6d.

**The Business Man's County Court Guide.** A Practical Manual, specially with reference to the Recovery of Trade Debts. By CHARLES JONES. Price 2s. 6d. net.

**The Put and Call.** By L. HIGGINS. Price 2s. 6d. net.

---

London: EFFINGHAM WILSON, ROYAL EXCHANGE.

# BRITISH EMPIRE MUTUAL

## LIFE ASSURANCE COMPANY,

**4 & 5, King William Street, London, E.C.**

FOUNDED 1847.

**Directors.**

THE RIGHT HON. SIR JOHN GORST, M.P., *Chairman.*
THE RIGHT HON. SIR FRANCIS JEUNE, } *Deputy-Chairmen.*
J. H. TROUNCER, ESQ., M.D. }

HENRY MASON BOMPAS, ESQ., Q.C.
HUGH CAMPBELL, ESQ., M.D.
THE RIGHT HON. VISCOUNT DILLON.
PEARSON HILL, ESQ.
THE HON. HENRY NOEL.
GEORGE PHILLIPS, ESQ.
SIR WM. HY. WILLS, BART., M.P.
SIDNEY YOUNG, ESQ.

**Assets (1896) - - £2,400,000.**
**Premium Income - £250,000.**

**No Shareholders. All the Profits belong to the Members.**

LIFE ASSURANCES of all kinds on the most modern and liberal conditions. Immediate Annuities on favourable terms. SPECIAL ADVANTAGES TO TOTAL ABSTAINERS. Six per cent. Investment Policies, guaranteeing a fixed Income for ten years. LEASEHOLD and SINKING FUND Assurances. LONG-TERM Assurances at VERY LOW PREMIUMS with option of continuance.

REVERSIONS and LIFE INTERESTS } PURCHASED, LENT UPON, PROTECTED from all CONTINGENCIES and DEFECTS of TITLE.

**ISSUE RISKS AND GUARANTEES OF SECURITIES UNDERTAKEN.**

Full Prospectus, Report, and Accounts on application to

G. H. RYAN, F.I.A., *General Manager.*

# CATALOGUE

OF

# COMMERCIAL AND OTHER WORKS

PUBLISHED AND SOLD BY

## EFFINGHAM WILSON,

Publisher, Printer, Bookseller, Binder, Engraver and Stationer,

ROYAL EXCHANGE, LONDON.

TO WHICH IS ADDED A LIST OF

## TELEGRAPH CODES,

AND SOME

*Valuable Books of Reference essential to Commercial Establishments and Public Companies.*

**EFFINGHAM WILSON undertakes the printing and publishing of Pamphlets and Books of every description upon Commission, Estimates given, and Conditions of Publication may be had on application.**

September, 1896.

# INDEX.

## WILSON'S LEGAL AND USEFUL HANDY BOOKS.

By JAMES WALTER SMITH, Esq., LL.D., of the Inner Temple, Barrister-at-Law.

**Law of Bills, Cheques, Notes, and I O U's.**
Fifty-ninth Thousand. Price 1s. 6d.

**Joint-Stock Companies Law, 1862—1890.**
New and Revised Edition. Twenty-third Thousand. Price 1s. 6d.

**The Law of Private Trading Partnership.**
Twenty-sixth Thousand. New and Revised Edition. Price 1s. 6d.

**Master and Servant, Employer and Employed.**
New and Revised Edition. Sixteenth Thousand. Price 1s. 6d.

**Husband and Wife.**
Engagements to Marry, Divorce and Separation, Children, &c. Price 2s. 6d.

**Owner, Builder, and Architect.** Price 1s.

**Law of Trustees under the Act 1893.**
Their Duties and Liabilities. New and Revised Edition. By R. DENNY URLIN, Esq., of the Middle Temple, Barrister-at-Law. Price 1s.

**The Investment of Trust Funds under the Trustee Act 1893.**
By R. DENNY URLIN, Esq. Price 1s.

**Law of Wills.**
A Practical Handbook for Testators and Executors, including the new Death Duties. By C. E. STEWART, Esq., Barrister-at-Law. Price 1s. 6d.

**Lunacy Law.**
An Explanatory Treatise on the Lunacy Acts, 1890 and 1891, for all who have the charge of or are brought into contact with persons of unsound mind. By D. CHAMIER, Esq. Price 1s. 6d.

**How to Appeal against your Rates (in the Metropolis).**
By A. D. LAWRIE, Esq., M.A. Second and Enlarged Edition. Price 2s.

**How to Appeal against your Rates (outside the Metropolis).**
By A. D. LAWRIE, Esq., M.A., Barrister-at-Law. Fifth and Enlarged Edition. Price 1s. 6d.

**The Stockbrokers' Handbook.**
A Practical Manual for the Broker, his Clerk, and his Client. New Edition, with Chapter on Options. Price 1s.

**The Broker's Correspondent;**
Being a Letter Writer for Stock-Exchange Business. By JAMES MARTIN. Price 1s.

**Law of Water and Gas.**
By C. E. STEWART, Esq., Barrister-at-Law. Price 1s. 6d.

**The Law of Bankruptcy.**
Showing the Proceedings from Bankruptcy to Discharge. By C. E. STEWART, Esq., Barrister-at-Law. Price 2s.

**Income Tax; and how to get it Refunded.**
By ALFRED CHAPMAN, Esq. Twelfth Edition. Price 1s. 6d.

**Inhabited House Duty: How and when to Appeal.**
By ALFRED CHAPMAN, Esq. Price 1s.

**The Juryman's Handbook.**
By SPENCER L. HOLLAND. Price 1s.

**The Shop Hours Acts, 1892 and 1893.**
With Notes and a Form. By J. R. V. MARCHANT, Esq., Barrister-at-Law. Price 1s.

**Pawnbrokers' Legal Handy Book.**
Based upon the Act of 1872. By CHAN. TOON and JOHN BRUCE, Esquires, Barristers. Price 1s.

## WILSON'S LEGAL AND USEFUL HANDY BOOKS.

**How to obtain a Divorce.** By NAPOLEON ARGLES. Price 1s. 6d.

**Hoare's Mensuration for the Million;**
Or, the Decimal System and its Application to the Daily Employment of the Artizan and Mechanic. By CHARLES HOARE. Price 1s.

**Ferguson's Buyers' and Sellers' Guide; or, Profit on Return.**
Showing at one view the Net Cost and Return Prices, with a Table of Discount. Price 1s. Bound in Leather price 2s.

**House-owners, Householders, and Lodgers;**
Their Rights and Liabilities as such. By J. A. DE MORGAN, Esq., Barrister-at-Law Price 2s.

**Bills of Sale.** By THOMAS W. HAYCRAFT, Esq., Barrister-at-Law. Price 2s. 6d.

**The Law relating to the Sale and Purchase of Goods.**
By C. E. STEWART, Esq., Barrister-at-Law. Price 1s. 6d.

**Houses and Lands as Investments.**
With Chapters on Mortgages, Leases, and Building Societies. By R. DENNY URLIN, Esq., Barrister-at-Law. Price 1s.

**From School to Office.** Written for Boys. By F. B. CROUCH. Price 1s.

**Pearce's Merchant's Clerk.**
An Exposition of the Law regulating the Operations of the Counting House. Twentieth Edition. Price 2s.

**Investor's Book-keeping.** By EBENEZER CARR. Price 1s.

**How to Invest Money.** Revised Edition. By E. R. GABBOTT. Price 1s.

**Double Entry; or, the Principles of Perfect Book-keeping.**
By ERNEST HOLAH, M.I.C.A. Third Edition. Price 2s.

**Theory of Book-keeping.** By BENJAMIN SEEBOHM. Price 1s.

**Book-keeping for Weekly Newspapers.**
A Manual for Newspaper Managers and Clerks. By GEORGE HENRY RICHARDSON. Price 1s.

**The Solicitor's Clerk.**
The ordinary Practical Work of a Solicitor's Office. By CHARLES JONES. Third and Revised Edition. Price 2s. 6d.

**Companion to the Solicitor's Clerk.**
A continuation of the "Solicitor's Clerk," embracing Magisterial and Criminal Law, Licensing, Bankruptcy Accounts, Bookkeeping, Trust Accounts, &c. By CHARLES JONES. Price 2s. 6d.

**Schonberg's Chain Rule:**
A Manual of Brief Commercial Arithmetic. Price 1s.

**The Local Government Act and County Council Guide.**
By R. DENNY URLIN, Esq., Barrister-at-Law. New Edition. Price 1s. 6d.

**Directors' Powers, Duties, and Liabilities under the Companies Acts, 1862—1890.**
By T. W. HAYCRAFT, Esq., Barrister-at-Law. Price 1s. 6d.

**The Law of Innkeepers and the Licensing Acts.**
By T. W. HAYCRAFT, Esq., Barrister-at-Law. Price 1s. 6d.

**The Commercial Handbook and Office Assistant.**
By MICHAEL CROWLEY, Chartered Accountant. Price 1s.

**Validity of Contracts in Restraint of Trade.**
By WILLIAM ARNOLD JOLLY, Barrister. Price 1s.

**The Law of Residential and Business Flats.**
By GEO. BLACKWELL. Price 1s. 6d.

**Copyhold Enfranchisement, with reference to the Copyhold Act, 1894.**
By ARTHUR DRAYCOTT, Barrister. Price 1s. net.

# NEW PUBLICATIONS.

## A HISTORY OF THE BANKING OF ALL NATIONS.

In Four Royal 8vo. volumes, price £5 complete.

VOLS. I, II AND III NOW READY.

VOL. I contains the History of Banking in the United States. By WILLIAM G. SUMNER.

VOL. II contains History of Banking in Great Britain. By HENRY DUNNING MACLEOD. History of Banking in Russia. By ANT. E. HORN. History of Savings Banks in the United States. By JOHN P. TOWNSEND.

VOL. III contains a History of Banking in the Latin Nations, by PIERRE DES ESSARS; of the Banks of Alsace-Lorraine, by ARTHUR RAFFALOVICH, and in Canada, by BYRON E. WALKER.

VOL. IV (in preparation) will contain History of Banking in Germany and Austria-Hungary, Scandinavian Nations, Holland, Canada, China, Japan, &c.

## THE STATUTORY TRUST INVESTMENT GUIDE.

By RICHARD MARRACK, M.A. The particulars as to Investments eligible, compiled and arranged by Fredc. C. Mathieson and Sons. Second Edition, revised and enlarged. Price 6s. net.

"We think the authors have executed their task well, and that their book will be found useful. We have often thought that a lawyer and a practical man writing in concert might produce a very excellent book."—*Law Quarterly Review.*

## IMPERIAL CUSTOMS UNION.

A Practical Scheme of Fiscal Union for the purposes of Defence and Preferential Trade, from a Colonist's standpoint. By K. N. MACFEE, M.A. Price 2s. 6d.

## THE PUT-AND-CALL.

By LEONARD R. HIGGINS. Price 3s. 6d. net.

## AUSTRALIAN MINING MANUAL,

A Handy Guide to the West Australian Market. Compiled by G. B. BEEMAN and FREDC. C. MATHIESON and SONS. Price 4s. net.

Three vols. Imperial 8vo. Price £3 3s. net.

## SOUTH AFRICAN MINES.

By C. S. GOLDMANN, F.R.G.S., and JOSEPH KITCHIN. Giving the Position, Results, and Developments of all South African Mines, including Diamond, Land, Finance. 100 Maps and Plans of Mining Properties, including a Large Scale Map of the Rand in Seventeen Sections, together with dip, tonnage, and other charts.

**BANKS AND BANKING.**
By H. T. Easton. Price 3s. 6d.

**THE MARITIME CODES OF SPAIN AND PORTUGAL.**
Translated and Annotated by F. W. Raikes, Q.C., LL.D. Price 7s. 6d.

**A BIMETALLIC PRIMER.**
By Hon. Herbert Gibbs. Third and revised edition. Price 1s.

**INVESTORS' TABLES,**
For ascertaining the true return of interest on Investments in either Permanent or Redeemable Stocks or Bonds, at any rate per cent. and price from 75 to 140. By T. M. P. Hughes. Price 6s. 6d. net.

**DIAGRAM FOR CALCULATING THE YIELD ON REDEEMABLE STOCKS.**
By A. A. Booth and M. A. Grainger, Price 10s. 6d. net.

**THE RAPID SHARE CALCULATOR.**
By E. de Segundo. Price 10s. 6d. net.

**THE DUTIES OF AUDITORS AND ACCOUNTANTS.**
By V. de S. Fowke, Barrister-at-Law. [In the Press.]

**HISTORY OF THE MONETARY SYSTEMS IN THE VARIOUS STATES.**
By Alex. Del Mar. Containing Chapters on the Moneys used in both Ancient and Modern States, that of the Argentine Republic being subjected to an exhaustive treatment. Price 15s. net.

**HOME RAILWAYS AS INVESTMENTS.**
By. W. J. Stevens. Price 2s. 6d. net.

**LAW RELATING TO LITERARY COPYRIGHT AND THE AUTHORSHIP AND PUBLICATION OF BOOKS.**
By Daniel Chamier, Barrister-at-Law. Price 5s. net.

**STAMP DUTIES ON BILLS OF EXCHANGE ALL OVER THE WORLD.**
By Alfred Kölkenbeck. Price 1s. net.

**MANUAL PRATIQUE DE LA CORRESPONDANCE ET DES OPERATIONS DE COMMERCE.**
By Prof. A. Beaure.

Part I. Éléments de la Correspondance. Price 1s. 6d.
Part II. Partie Appliquée, avec traité pratique des Opérations de Bourse. Price 3s. 3d. net.

## AGER'S TELEGRAM CODES.

**AGER'S SIMPLEX STANDARD TELEGRAM CODE.**
Consisting of 205,500 Code Words. Carefully compiled in accordance with latest Convention rules. Arranged in completed hundreds. Printed on hand-made paper; strongly bound. Price £7 10s.

**AGER'S DUPLEX COMBINATION STANDARD CODE.**
Consisting of 150,000 Words. With a DOUBLE set of figures for every word, thus affording opportunity for each Figure System of Telegraphing to be used. Price £4 4s. net.

The extension of these words to about 45,000 more. Price 21s.

**AGER'S COMPLETE DUPLEX CODE OF 195,000 WORDS.**
In Alphabetical and Double Numerical Order, *i. e.* the above two Codes bound together. Price £5 5s. net.

**AGER'S STANDARD TELEGRAM CODE OF 100,000 WORDS.**
Compiled from the Languages sanctioned at the London Telegraph Convention, 1879. Price £3 3s. net.

**AGER'S 10,250 EXTRA CODE WORDS.**
Following in Alphabetical and Numerical Sequence those in the Standard Code. Price 10s. 6d. net.

**AGER'S STANDARD SUPPLEMENTARY CODE FOR GENERAL MERCHANTS.**
In connection with Dr. Ager's Standard Code. Price 21s.

**AGER'S TELEGRAM CODE.**
Consisting of nearly 56,000 good Telegraphic Words, 45,000 of which do not exceed eight letters. Compiled from the languages sanctioned by the Telegraph Convention. Third Edition. Price £2 15s.

**AGER'S ALPHABETICAL PHRASE TELEGRAM CODE**
Of 50,000 Sentences, Code Words, and Cyphers, in Sequence to the 150,000 Words above mentioned. Price 25s. Two or more copies 21s. each.

**AGER'S TELEGRAPHIC PRIMER, WITH APPENDIX**
or Skeleton Telegram Code, consisting of 19,000 Good English and Dutch Telegraphic Words, compiled from the Dictionaries of Webster and Picard. Some 12,000 of these words have sentences. Price 12s. 6d.

**AGER'S GENERAL AND SOCIAL CODE.** Price 10s. 6d.

# TELEGRAPH CODES.

**AGER'S A Y Z TELEGRAPHIC CODE.**
Nearly 30,000 Sentences and a liberal supply of Spare Words. The words taken from the "Official Vocabulary." 16s. net.

**CLAUSON-THUE'S A. B. C. UNIVERSAL COMMERCIAL ELECTRIC TELEGRAPHIC CODE.**
Fourth Edition. Price 15s. net.

**CLAUSEN-THUE'S A1 UNIVERSAL ELECTRIC TELEGRAPH CODE.** Price 25s. net.

**LAURIE'S UNIVERSAL CODE OF NEARLY 12,000 SENTENCES,**
for Private and Business Telegrams and Mining, Shipping, Stockdealing, Banking, and Mercantile Cablegrams. 2s. 6d.

**LIEBER'S STANDARD TELEGRAPHIC CODE.**
The Code is of 800 pages, and contains over 75,000 code-words, 25,000 consisting of tables. There are 10,000 extra ciphers, giving ample opportunity for special phrases. The code words employed are from the "Official Vocabulary." The Compilers having only used ciphers from "A" to "F," an opportunity is left to cablers to construct a large private and separate code for their own particular and individual use.

The arrangement of the sentences is strictly alphabetical.

For Bankers, Brokers, Manufacturers, Merchants, Stockbrokers, and the Legal Profession. Price 42s.

**MINING AND GENERAL TELEGRAPHIC CODE.**
By Bedford McNeill. Price 21s. net.

**SCOTT'S SHIPOWNERS' TELEGRAPHIC CODE.**
New Edition in the press.

**STOCKBROKERS' TELEGRAPH CODE.** Price 5s. net.

**THE GENERAL AND MINING CODE.**
For the use of Mining Companies, Mining Engineers, Stockbrokers, Financial Agents, and Trust and Finance Companies. By C. Algernon Moreing and Thomas Neale. Price 21s.

**"UNICODE,"**
The Universal Telegraphic Phrase-Book for Commercial and Domestic Use. Price 2s. 6d.

**WATKINS' SHIPBROKERS' TELEGRAPHIC CODE.**
Price £4 net. Two Copies, £7.

**WHITELAW'S TELEGRAPH CYPHERS.** 310,200 in all.

| | |
|---|---|
| 200,000 Words, French, Spanish, Portuguese, Italian, and Latin. Price | 150s. each net. |
| 53,000 English Words | 50s. ,, ,, |
| 42,600 German Words | 50s. ,, ,, |
| 40,000 Dutch Words | 50s. ,, ,, |

§

## RECENT PAMPHLETS.

**Imperial Commercial Federation of the United Kingdom and the Colonies.**
By W. J. Harris. Price 1s.

**A History of Messrs. Backhouse and Co., Bankers, Darlington.**
By Maberly Phillips, F.S.A. Price 1s.

**Gibbs's Address on International Bimetallism.**
Delivered before the London Institution, May, 1895. Price 6d.

**Monometallism Unmasked;** or the Gold Mania of the Nineteenth Century. By A Senior Optime. Price 6d.

**Norman's Science of Money.** Price 1s.

**Norman's Prices and Monetary and Currency Exchanges of the World.** Price 6d.

**The Gold Bug and the Working Man.** Price 6d.

**Excesses of the Witwatersrand Gold Shares Speculation in 1894.**
By Felix Abraham. Price 1s.

**The Currency of China (a Short Enquiry).**
By James K. Morrison. Price 1s.

**What are the Annual Profits of a Company?**
Or, What is the Capital of a Company within the meaning of the legal rule that dividends may not be paid out of capital? By Bernard Dale. Price 1s.

**The Silver and Indian Currency Question.**
By E. Monson George. Price 1s. 3d.

**The Case for Monetary Reform.** By Henry R. Beeton. Price 6d.

**Seyd's (Ernest) Silver Question in 1893.** Price 2s., cloth.

**Costless Life Assurance.** By T. G. Rose. Price 6d.

## TATE'S MODERN CAMBIST: A MANUAL OF FOREIGN EXCHANGES.

THE MODERN CAMBIST: forming a Manual of Foreign Exchanges in the various operations of Bills of Exchange and Bullion, according to the practice of all Trading Nations; with Tables of Foreign Weights and Measures, and their Equivalents in English and French. Twenty-third Edition. By Hermann Schmidt. Price 12s.

## FENN'S COMPENDIUM OF THE ENGLISH AND FOREIGN FUNDS, DEBTS AND REVENUES OF ALL NATIONS.

Together with Statistics relating to State Finance and Liabilities, Imports, Exports, Population, Area, Railway Guarantees, Municipal Finance and Indebtedness, Banks of all Nations, and all descriptions of Government, Provincial and Corporate, Securities held and dealt in by investors at Home and Abroad; the Laws and Regulations of the Stock Exchange, &c., the work being so arranged as to render it alike useful to the Capitalist, the Banker, the Merchant, or the Private Individual. Fifteenth Edition. Thoroughly revised. With Addenda, giving Information to Date of Publication. By Robert Lucas Nash. Price 25s.

"So much useful matter in any one volume is seldom to be met with."—*The Times.*

**RULES AND USAGES OF THE STOCK EXCHANGE.**
Containing the Text of the Rules and an explanation of the general course of business, with Practical Notes and Comments. By G. HERBERT STUTFIELD, and HENRY STROTHER CAUTLEY, Barristers. Second and Revised Edition. Price 5s.

**A GUIDE TO THE BUSINESS OF PUBLIC MEETINGS:**
the Duties and Powers of Chairman, with the Modes of Procedure and Rules of Debate. By JAMES TAYLER. Price 2s. 6d.

**THE AMERICAN RAILROADS AS INVESTMENTS.**
By S. F. VAN OSS. About 800 pages. Containing a brief history with description of the leading American Railroads, the country they traverse, the conditions under which they exist, the influences they are subject to. Cheap Edition. Price 5s.

**THE MONETARY QUESTION IN 1892.**
By OTTOMAR HAUPT. Price 5s.

**GUMERSALL'S TABLES OF INTEREST, &c.**
Interest and Discount Tables, computed at 2½, 3, 3½, 4, 4½, and 5 per cent., from 1 to 365 days, and from £1 to £20,000; so that the interest or discount on any sum, for any number of days, at any of the above rates, may be obtained by inspection of one page only. By T. B. GUMERSALL, Accountant.

Seventeenth Edition. 1 vol., 8vo (pp. 500), price 10s. 6d., cloth; or strongly bound in calf, with the Rates per Cent. cut in at the foredge, price 16s. 6d.

**JACKSON'S BOOK-KEEPING.**
A Check-Journal; combining the advantages of the Day-Book, Journal, and Cash-Book; forming a complete System of Book-keeping by Double-Entry; with copious illustrations of Interest Accounts, and Joint Adventures; and a method of Book-keeping, or Double-Entry by Single. By GEORGE JACKSON, Accountant.

Twenty-first Edition, with the most effectual means of preventing Fraud, Error, and Embezzlement, in Cash Transactions, and in the Receipt and Delivery of Goods, &c. Price 5s., cloth.

**THREADNEEDLE STREET, A REPLY TO "LOMBARD STREET,"**
And an alternative proposal to the One pound note scheme sketched by Mr. Goschen at Leeds. By ARTHUR STANLEY COBB. Price 5s.

Mr. Goschen said at the London Chamber of Commerce, "Mr. Stanley Cobb proposes an alternative to my plan, and I recommend the choice between the two."

**ENGLISH AND FOREIGN BANKS: A COMPARISON.**
I. Constitution of Banks. II. The Branch System. III. Banks and their Functions. By JAMES B. ATTFIELD. Member of the Inst. of Bankers. Price 3s. 6d. net.

**BURDETT'S OFFICIAL INTELLIGENCE;**
Being a carefully compiled *précis* of information regarding British, American, and Foreign Stocks, Corporation, Colonial, and Government Securities, Railways, Banks, Canals, Docks, Gas, Insurance, Land, Mines, Shipping, Telegraphs, Tramways, Waterworks, and other Companies. By HENRY C. BURDETT, Secretary of the Share and Loan Department, Stock Exchange. Published annually under the sanction of the Committee. Price 42s.

**REDRESS BY ARBITRATION;**
A Digest of the Law relating to Arbitrations and Awards. By H. F. LYNCH, Esq., Solicitor. Second and Revised Edition. Price 5s.

**ROBINSON'S SHARE AND STOCK TABLES;**
Comprising a set of Tables for Calculating the Cost of any number of Shares, at any price from 1-16th of a pound sterling, or 1s. 3d. per share, to £310 per share in value; and from 1 to 500 shares, or from £100 to £50,000 stock. Seventh Edition, price 5s., cloth.

**BURGON'S LIFE & TIMES OF SIR THOMAS GRESHAM.**
Including notices of many of his contemporaries. By JOHN WM. BURGON, Esq. 2 vols. Offered at the reduced price of 10s. Published at £1 10s.

**DOLLAR (EASTERN) & STERLING EXCHANGE TABLES.**
At different rates from 1s. 9d. to 3s. 4d., advancing by one sixteenth of a penny. Price 7s. 6d.

**ROYLE'S LAWS RELATING TO ENGLISH AND FOREIGN FUNDS, SHARES, AND SECURITIES. THE STOCK EXCHANGE: ITS USAGES AND THE RIGHTS OF VENDORS AND PURCHASERS.**
With 400 References to Acts of Parliament and Decided Cases, and an Analytical Index. By WILLIAM ROYLE, Solicitor. Price 6s.

**POOR'S MANUAL OF THE RAILROADS AND OTHER INVESTMENT SECURITIES OF THE UNITED STATES.**
An incorporation of the Railroad Manual, the Handbook of Investment Securities, and the Directory of Railway Officials. There are 50 new Maps, bringing the total number to 70. The bonded indebtedness of State, County, and Town is included, together with the status of Industrial Corporations. Published Annually. Price 42s.

A GUIDE TO THE LAW AND PRACTICE OF THE LONDON CHAMBER OF ARBITRATION.
Second and Revised Edition. By MONTAGUE SHEARMAN and THOS. W. HAYCRAFT, Barristers-at-Law. Price 2s. 6d.

CARISS'S BOOK-KEEPING BY DOUBLE ENTRY:
Explaining the Science and Teaching the Art. By ASTRUP CARISS. Second Edition. Price 6s.

CUMMINS' FORMATION OF THE ACCOUNTS OF LIMITED LIABILITY COMPANIES. Price 5s.

BANKRUPTCY ACCOUNTS:
A Handy Guide and instruction for the preparation of a Debtor's Statement of Affairs in Bankruptcy. A Practical Treatise with Schedules filled up, showing a complete set of Accounts, balanced and the deficiency explained. By D. MCEWEN. Price 2s. 6d.

STOCK EXCHANGE BOOK-KEEPING.
By ROBERT WARNER, Stock Exchange Accountant. Price 2s. 6d.

ELLIS'S RATIONALE OF MARKET FLUCTUATIONS.
Third Edition, revised. By ARTHUR ELLIS. Price 7s. 6d.

INGRAM'S IMPROVED CALCULATOR,
Showing instantly the value of any quantity from One Sixteenth of a Yard or Pound to Five Hundred Yards or Pounds at from One Farthing to Twenty Shillings per Yard or Pound. Price 7s. 6d.

THE INVESTOR'S LEDGER,
With a few hints on keeping it. Third Edition. Price 1s. 6d.

INVESTMENT TABLE,
Showing the actual Interest or Profit per cent. per annum derived from any Purchase or Investment, at Rates of Interest from 2½ to 10 per cent. Price 2s.

BOSANQUET'S SIMPLE INTEREST TABLES
For Facilitating the Calculation of Interest at all rates, from one thirty-second upwards. By BERNARD TINDAL BOSANQUET. Price 5s., cloth.

**BOSANQUET'S UNIVERSAL SIMPLE INTEREST TABLES,**
Showing the Interest of any sum for any number of days at 100 different rates, from ⅛ to 12½ per cent. inclusive; also the Interest of any sum for one day at each of the above rates, by single pounds up to one hundred, by hundreds up to forty thousand, and thence by longer intervals up to fifty million pounds. By BERNARD TINDAL BOSANQUET. 8vo, pp. 480. Price 21s., cloth.

---

**THE SILVER QUESTION AND THE GOLD QUESTION.**
Fourth Edition. By ROBERT BARCLAY. Price 2s. 6d.

---

**THE DISTURBANCE IN THE STANDARD OF VALUE.**
By ROBERT BARCLAY. Enlarged Edition. Price 2s.

---

**A COLLOQUY ON CURRENCY.**
By ALDENHAM, Lord (HENRY HUCKS GIBBS). Third Edition. Price 3s. 6d. net.

---

**SCHMIDT'S SILVER QUESTION IN ITS SOCIAL ASPECT.**
An Enquiry into the Existing Depression of Trade and the present position of the Bimetallic Controversy. By HERMANN SCHMIDT. Price 3s.

---

**SMITH'S BIMETALLIC QUESTION.**
By SAMUEL SMITH, Esq., M.P. Price 2s. 6d.

---

**BULL'S CURRENCY PROBLEM AND ITS SOLUTION.**
Price 2s. 6d.

---

**JOURNAL OF THE INSTITUTE OF BANKERS.**
Published Monthly. Price 1s. 6d.

---

**INTEREST TABLES, 2¾ PER CENT. ON £1 TO £20,000 FOR 1 TO 365 DAYS.**
By CHARLES CUMMINS. Price 5s.

---

**LE STOCK EXCHANGE. LES USAGES DE LA PLACE DE LONDRES ET LES FONDS ANGLAIS.**
Par G. CHEVILLIARD. Price 10s. 6d.

---

**HAUPT'S ARBITRAGES ET PARITÉS.**
Traité des Opérations de Banque, contenant les usages commerciaux, la théorie des changes et monnaies, et la statistique monétaire de tous les pays du globe. Par OTTOMAR HAUPT. Huitième édition, complètement refondue et augmentée. Price 12s. 6d.

GOSCHEN'S (THE RT. HON. GEORGE J., M.P.) THEORY OF THE FOREIGN EXCHANGES.

Sixteenth Edition. One Volume, 8vo. 6s.

---

MINER'S HANDBOOK AND INVESTOR'S GUIDE TO WESTERN AUSTRALIA.

By Francis Hart. Latest Maps and Illustrations. Price 1s.

---

LEWIS'S TABLES FOR FINDING THE NUMBER OF DAYS,

From one day to any other day in the same or the following year. By William Lewis. Price 12s. 6d.

---

HOWARTH'S OUR CLEARING SYSTEM AND CLEARING-HOUSES.

By W. Howarth, F.R.Hist.S. New edition in the press.

---

HUTCHISON'S PRACTICE OF BANKING;

Embracing the Cases at Law and in Equity bearing upon all branches of the subject. Vols. II and III. Price 21s. each. Vol. IV. Price 15s.

---

HANKEY'S PRINCIPLES OF BANKING:

Its Utility and Economy. With Remarks on the Working and Management of the Bank of England. By Thomson Hankey, Esq., formerly Governor of the Bank of England. Fourth Edition. Revised as regards the Working and Management of the Bank by Clifford Wigram, Esq., a Director of the Bank. Price 2s. 6d., cloth.

---

BOOK-KEEPING.

By Gérard Van de Linde, F.C.A., F.S.S. Part I.—Journal, Cash Book, and Ledger. Part II.—Balance-sheet, and Profit and Loss Accounts, Companies' Accounts, Fundamental distinction between Capital and Revenue. Part III.—In connection with General Banking. Part IV.—In connection with Colonial and Foreign Banking. Price 3s. 6d.

---

LEGAL FORMS FOR COMMON USE,

Being 300 Precedents and Notes. Twelfth Thousand. New and Re-written Edition. By James Walter Smith, Esq., Barrister-at-Law. Price 5s.

**QUESTIONS ON BANKING PRACTICE.**
Revised by, and issued under the sanction of, the Council of the Institute of Bankers. Fourth Edition. Price 5s.

**EXAMINATION QUESTIONS IN BOOK-KEEPING.**
By Edward Harlow. Price 2s. 6d.

**COMPREHENSIVE TABLES OF COMPOUND INTEREST**
on £1, £5, £25, £50, £75, and £100; showing accumulations year by year for fifty years, at Rates of Interest from 1 (progressing ¼) to 5 per cent.; also Tables of Interest, Rebate, Discount, Brokerage, and Commission. By John Wilhelm. Price 2s. 6d. net.

**ELLISON'S COTTON TRADE OF GREAT BRITAIN.**
Including a History of the Liverpool Cotton Market and the Liverpool Cotton Brokers' Association. By Arthur Ellison. Price 15s.

**PIXLEY'S AUDITORS.**
Their Duties and Responsibilities under the Joint-Stock Companies and other Acts. Seventh edition, revised. Price 21s.

**SCHULTZ'S UNIVERSAL DOLLAR TABLES.**
Complete United States Edition. Covering all Exchanges between the United States and Great Britain, France, Belgium, Switzerland, Italy, Spain, and Germany.

From $4·50 Cents to $5·50 per Pound Sterling, or from 4 Francs 50 Centimes to 5 Francs 50 Centimes per Dollar, or from 4 Pesetas 50 Cents to 5 Pesetas 50 Cents per Dollar, or from $4·50 to $5·50 per 20 Gold Marcs. Price 21s.

**AMERICAN RAILROADS AND BRITISH INVESTORS**
By S. F. Van Oss. Price 3s. 6d.

**THE LAW OF BANKER AND CUSTOMER.**
By James Walter Smith, B.A.Oxon., Barrister-at-Law. Second and Revised Edition. Price 5s.

**A MONEY MARKET PRIMER AND KEY TO THE EXCHANGES.**
With Eighteen Full-page Diagrams. By Geo. Clare. Recommended by the Council of the Institute of Bankers. Second Edition, revised. 5s.

**HOW TO INVEST IN MINES.**
A Review of the Mine, the Company, and the Market. By E. R. Gabbott. Price 2s. 6d. net.

**A HISTORY OF BANKS, BANKERS, AND BANKING,**
In Northumberland, Durham, and North Yorkshire, illustrating the commercial development of the North of England from 1755 to 1894. With numerous Portraits, Fac-similes of Notes, Signatures, Documents, &c. By MABERLY PHILLIPS. Price 31s. 6d.

**DUNCAN ON INVESTMENT AND SPECULATION IN STOCKS AND SHARES.**
Price 2s. 6d.

**PRACTICAL BOOKKEEPING.**
Suitable for all Businesses. By JOHN SAWYER. Price 2s. 6d.

**RAILWAYS IN INDIA, THEIR ECONOMICAL CONSTRUCTION AND WORKING.**
By E. MONSON GEORGE, M. Inst. C.E. Price 2s. 6d.

**SCHULTZ'S UNIVERSAL INTEREST TABLES AND GENERAL PERCENTAGE TABLES.** 7s. 6d.

**SCHULTZ'S ENGLISH-GERMAN EXCHANGE TABLES.**
From 20 Marks to 21 Marks per £, by ·025 Marks per £ progressively. Price 5s.

**SCHULTZ'S UNIVERSAL AMERICAN DOLLAR EXCHANGE TABLES.**
Epitome of Rates from $4·80 to $4·90 per £, and from 3s. 10d. to 4s. 6d. per $, with an Introductory Chapter on the Coinages and Exchanges of the World. Price 10s. 6d.

**CROSBIE AND LAW'S TABLES.**
For the Immediate Conversion of Products into Interest, at Twenty-Nine Rates, viz.: From One to Eight per cent. inclusive, proceeding by Quarter Rates, each Rate occupying a single Opening, Hundreds of Products being represented by Units. By ANDREW CROSBIE and WILLIAM C. LAW, Lloyds, Barnetts, and Bosanquets Bank, Limited. Second Edition, improved and enlarged. Price 12s. 6d.

**DUNSFORD'S HANDBOOK OF PRICES AND DIVIDENDS OF RAILWAYS AND OTHER SECURITIES FOR FIFTEEN YEARS.**
Price 1s.

**WILLDEY'S PARITIES OF AMERICAN STOCKS IN LONDON, NEW YORK, AND AMSTERDAM, AT ALL RATES OF EXCHANGE OF THE DAY.**
Price 2s.

**SILVER TABLES,**

Showing relative equivalents of Bar Silver in London and New York. Vol. I. From 47 to 67 cents. Vol. II. From 67 to 87 cents. By W. H. GASKELL. Price 15s. 2 vols., or if sold separately price 10s. each.

---

**SHAW'S FIRE SURVEYS;**

A Summary of the Principles to be Observed in Estimating the Risks of Building. By SIR EYRE M. SHAW, C.B., late Chief of the London Fire Brigade. Third Edition. Price 2s. 6d.

---

**STOCK EXCHANGE VALUES: A DECADE OF FINANCE, 1885—1895.**

Containing Original Chapters with Diagrams and Tables giving Reviews of each of the last Ten Years. By F. S. VAN OSS, author of 'American Railroads and British Investors,' &c., together with Charts showing at a glance prices of principal securities for past ten years, and Highest and Lowest Prices year by year (1885 to 1894 inclusive) of every security officially quoted on the Stock Exchange, with dates and extreme fluctuations, compiled by Fredc. C. Mathieson & Sons. Price 15s. net.

---

**TAYLER'S RED PALMER.**

A Practical Treatise on Fly Fishing. Third Edition. Price 1s. 6d.

---

**THE BUSINESS MAN'S COUNTY COURT GUIDE.**

A Practical Manual of the ordinary procedure, especially with reference to the recovery of Trade Debts; including Practical Information upon Evidence, Special Defences, &c., and with an Appendix of useful Forms and Table of Fees. By CHAS. JONES. Price 2s. 6d. net.

---

**THE REGISTRATION OF TRANSFERS OF TRANSFERABLE STOCKS, SHARES, AND SECURITIES.**

With a Chapter on the Forged Transfers Acts, and an Appendix of Forms. By GEORGE ENNIS and GEORGE FRANCIS MACDANIEL ENNIS, both of the Middle Temple, Esqs., Barristers-at-Law. Price 7s. 6d.

---

**A SKETCH OF THE CURRENCY QUESTION.**

By CLIVE CUTHBERTSON. Price 2s. net.

---

**THE SCIENCE OF MONEY.**

By ALEX. DEL MAR. Second revised edition. Price 6s. net.

**A HANDY GUIDE TO THE PATENT LAW.**
By G. F. EMERY, LL.M. Price 6s. net.

---

**THE CORN TRADE INVOICE CLERK.**
By HENRY RICHTER. Price 1s. net.

---

**THE LAW OF DISTRICT AND PARISH COUNCILS,**
Being the Local Government Act, 1894, with an Appendix containing numerous Statutes referred to in, or incorporated with, the Act itself, including the Agricultural Gangs Act; the Agricultural Holdings Act; the Allotments Acts; Baths and Washhouses Acts; Burial Acts; Fairs Acts; Infant Life Protection Act; Knackers Acts; Lighting and Watching Act; Public Improvements Act; Public Libraries Acts; and numerous Extracts from the Public Health Act, 1875, and other Statutes. Also the Orders and Circulars of the Local Government Board, together with copious Notes and a full Index. By JOHN LITHIBY, LL.B.(Lond.), of the Middle Temple, Barrister-at-Law. Price 12s. 6d.

---

# MISCELLANEOUS LIST.

---

## VALUABLE WORKS OF REFERENCE, COMMERCIAL, LEGAL, GEOGRAPHICAL, AND STATISTICAL.

---

**ALPE'S LAW OF STAMP DUTIES ON DEEDS AND OTHER INSTRUMENTS.**
Price 6s. net.

---

**ANDERSON'S PRACTICAL MERCANTILE CORRESPONDENCE.**
Thirtieth Edition. By WILLIAM ANDERSON. 3s. 6d.

---

**ART OF INVESTING.** By a New York Stockbroker. 3s.

---

**BANKER'S CLERK (THE).**
Comprising the Principles and Practices of Banking Sixth Edition, revised. Price 2s.

**BRADSHAW'S RAILWAY SHAREHOLDERS' MANUAL.**
Published Annually. Price 12s.

---

**BUCKLEY'S LAW AND PRACTICE UNDER THE COMPANIES ACTS, 1862—1890.**
Containing Statutes and Rules, Orders, and Forms to regulate Proceedings in the Chancery Division of the High Court of Justice. Sixth Edition. Price 34s.

---

**BLEWERT'S TABLES**
For Calculating the Value of the Public Stocks and Annuities, and Investments in all Companies and Adventures where the Capital is converted into Stock. Seventh Edition. Price 7s. 6d

---

**BARTLETT-ARMATI'S TABLES OF WEIGHTS, MEASURES, AND MONEYS.** Price 3s. 6d.

---

**CASTELLI'S THEORY OF "OPTIONS" IN STOCKS AND SHARES.** Price 2s.

---

**CHALMERS' DIGEST OF THE LAW OF BILLS OF EXCHANGE, PROMISSORY NOTES AND CHEQUES.**
By His Honour Judge Chalmers. 4th edition. Price 18s.

---

**FITZPATRICK AND FOWKE'S SECRETARY'S MANUAL OF JOINT-STOCK COMPANIES, WITH FORMS AND PRECEDENTS.** Price 5s. net.

---

**FOWKE'S COMPANIES ACTS, 1862—1890, AND OTHER STATUTES AFFECTING JOINT-STOCK COMPANIES.** Price 5s. net.

---

**GIBSON'S STOCK EXCHANGES OF LONDON, PARIS, AND NEW YORK.** A Comparison. Price 4s.

---

**GILBART'S HISTORY, PRINCIPLES, AND PRACTICE OF BANKING.**
Thoroughly revised and adapted to the Practice of the present day. By A. S. Michie, Deputy Manager of the Royal Bank of Scotland, London. 2 Vols. Price 10s.

---

**GILBERT'S TABLES OF INTEREST,**
From ¼ to 5 per cent., advancing by eighths. From 1 to 60 days, and from £1 to £100,000. Price 21s. net.

**GILBERT'S INTEREST AND CONTANGO TABLES.**
Price 10s. net.

**GOODFELLOW'S MERCHANTS' AND SHIPMASTERS' READY CALCULATOR.**
Exhibiting at one View the *solid contents* of all kinds of Packages and Casks. By J. Goodfellow. Price 7s. 6d.

**HARDWICK'S TRADER'S CHECK BOOK.**
For Buying and Selling by the Hundredweight, Ton, or by Measure, &c. Price 2s. 6d.

**HAMILTON AND BALL'S BOOK-KEEPING.**
New and Enlarged Edition. Price 2s.

**INVESTOR'S REVIEW (MONTHLY)**
Edited by A. J. Wilson. Price 1s. net, post free 14s. per annum.

**INWOOD'S TABLES**
For the Purchasing of Estates, Freehold, Copyhold, or Leasehold, Annuities, Advowsons, &c., and for the Renewing of Leases, held under Cathedral Churches, Colleges, or other corporate bodies, for terms of Years; also for Valuing Reversionary Estates, &c. Twenty-third Edition. Price 8s.

**JEVONS'S INVESTIGATIONS IN CURRENCY AND FINANCE.**
By W. Stanley Jevons. Edited, with an Introduction, by H. S. Foxwell, M.A. Price 21s.

**JORDAN'S PRACTICAL INSTRUCTIONS ON THE FORMATION, MANAGEMENT, AND WINDING UP OF JOINT-STOCK COMPANIES.**
Price 5s.

**KINDELL'S AFRICAN MARKET MANUAL,**
Giving particulars of all Companies (African or otherwise) dealt in the African Market of the Stock Exchange. Price 5s.

**KING'S INTEREST TABLES,**
Calculated at Five per cent., exhibiting at one glance the interest of any sum, from one pound to three hundred and sixty-five pounds; and (advancing by hundreds) to one thousand pounds; and (by thousands) to ten thousand pounds; from one day to three hundred and sixty-five days. Price 7s. 6d.

**LOWNDES'S LAW OF GENERAL AVERAGE (ENGLISH AND FOREIGN).** Fourth Edition. Price 30s.

---

**LONDON BANKS, AND KINDRED COMPANIES AND FIRMS,**

Their Directors, Managers, Capitals and Reserve Funds and Dividends. By THOMAS SKINNER. Published annually. Price 10s.

---

**LAURIE'S HIGH-RATE TABLES OF SIMPLE INTEREST,**

At 5, 6, 7, 8, 9 and $\frac{1}{2}$ per cent. per annum, from 1 day to 100 days, 1 month to 12 months. Price 7s.

---

**LAURIE'S TABLES OF SIMPLE INTEREST,**

At 5, $4\frac{1}{2}$, 4, $3\frac{1}{2}$, 3, and $2\frac{1}{2}$ per cent. per annum. Also Tables of Compound Interest and Interest on large sums for a single day at the same rates. Price 21s., or, strongly bound half Russia, price 26s. 6d.

---

**LOUIS'S ANGLO-FRENCH CALCULATOR;**

A Ready Reckoner for facilitating Trade with France. Price 1s.

---

**LECOFFRE'S TABLES OF EXCHANGE BETWEEN FRANCE, BELGIUM, SWITZERLAND, AND GREAT BRITAIN.** Price 21s.

---

**McARTHUR'S CONTRACT OF MARINE INSURANCE.**

By CHARLES MCARTHUR. Price 16s.

---

**MERCES' INDIAN AND ENGLISH EXCHANGE TABLES.**

Rising by thirty-seconds of a Penny from 1s. to 1s. 6d., price 15s.; supplements 1s. to 1s. $0\frac{31}{32}$d., price 5s.; 1s. 1d. to 1s. $1\frac{31}{32}$d., price 5s.

---

**MERCES' INDIAN READY RECKONER.**

Showing Cost of Goods by number, weight, &c., including fractions of a Maund, at any rate from $\frac{1}{2}$ Pie to 250 Rs.; also Tables of Income, Weights, Exchange (1s. 2d. to 1s. 8d.), Interest, and Commission. Price 36s.

---

**MACLEOD'S ELEMENTS OF BANKING.** Price 3s. 6d.

---

**MACLEOD'S THEORY AND PRACTICE OF BANKING.**

2 Vols. Price 26s.

---

**MACLEOD'S THEORY OF CREDIT.** 2 Vols. 31s.

---

**McGOUN'S COMMERCIAL CORRESPONDENCE, BEING A COLLECTION OF LETTERS OF BUSINESS.**

Price 5s.

**MELSHEIMER AND GARDNER'S LAW AND CUSTOMS OF THE LONDON STOCK EXCHANGE,**
With an Appendix, containing the Rules and Regulations authorised by the Committee for the Conduct of Business. By RUDOLPH E. MELSHEIMER, Barrister-at-Law, and SAMUEL GARDNER, of the London Stock Exchange. Third Edition. Price 7s. 6d.

**MOXON'S ENGLISH PRACTICAL BANKING.** Price 3s.

**MATHIESON'S HIGHEST AND LOWEST PRICES AND DIVIDENDS PAID DURING THE PAST SIX YEARS.** Annually. Price 2s. 6d.

**MATHIESON'S PROVINCIAL HIGHEST AND LOWEST PRICES DURING 1894 AND 1895,**
As quoted on the following Stock Exchanges: Birmingham, Dublin, Edinburgh, Glasgow, Leeds, Liverpool, Manchester, Sheffield. Annually. Price 2s. 6d.

**MATHIESON'S RAILWAY TRAFFIC TABLES.**
Published monthly. Price 6d.; by post, 7d.

**MATHIESON'S AMERICAN TRAFFIC TABLES.**
Monthly. Price 6d.; by post, 7d.

**MATHIESON'S SIX MONTHS' PRICES AND DATES.**
Uniform with "Highest and Lowest Prices." Annually, in July. Price 2s. 6d.

**MATHIESON'S INVESTORS' HANDBOOK OF RAILWAY STATISTICS, 1879—1895.**
Annually. Price 6d.

**MATHIESON'S BRIGHTON RAILWAY STATISTICS.**
Annually. Price 1s.

**MATHIESON'S INDIAN RAILWAY COMPANIES FOR OFFICIALS, STOCKBROKERS, AND INVESTORS.**
Price 1s.

**OWEN'S MARINE INSURANCE NOTES AND CLAUSES.**
Third Edition. Price 15s.

**PALMER'S COMPANY PRECEDENTS SUBJECT TO THE ACTS 1862—1890.**
With an Appendix containing the Companies Acts and Rules. Sixth Edition. Part I, price 36s. Part II (Winding Up), 30s.

**PALMER'S SHAREHOLDERS', DIRECTORS', AND VOLUNTARY LIQUIDATORS' LEGAL COMPANION:**
A Manual of Every-day Law and Practice. Fifteenth Edition. Price 2s. 6d.

**PALGRAVE'S CHAIRMAN'S HANDBOOK.**
Suggestions and Rules for the Conduct of Chairmen of Public and other Meetings. By REGINALD F. D. PALGRAVE, the Chief Clerk of the House of Commons. Price 2s.

**PROSPECTOR'S (THE) HANDBOOK.**
A Guide for the Prospector and Traveller in search of Metal-bearing or other valuable Minerals. By J. W. ANDERSON. Price 3s. 6d.

**RAE'S COUNTRY BANKER; HIS CLIENTS, CARES, AND WORK.**
From an Experience of Forty Years. Price 7s. 6d.

**RANCE'S TABLES OF COMPOUND INTEREST**
For every ¼ from ¼ to 10 per cent., and for every year from 1 to 100 years. Second Edition. By THOMAS GEORGE RANCE. Price 21s.

**SKINNER'S STOCK EXCHANGE YEAR-BOOK.**
Published Annually (in December). Price 21s.

**SKINNER'S DIRECTORY OF DIRECTORS.**
A list of the Directors of the Joint-Stock Companies of the United Kingdom, and the Companies in which they are concerned. Published Annually (in February). Price 12s. 6d.

**SKINNER'S MINING MANUAL.**
Published Annually. Price 15s.

**THE STATESMAN'S YEAR-BOOK;**
A Statistical and Historical Annual of the States of the Civilised World for Politicians and Merchants. Revised after Official Returns. Price 10s. 6d. Published Annually.

**WALLACE AND M'NEIL'S BANKING LAW.**
Price 12s. net.

**WATT'S LAW OF PROMOTERS OF PUBLIC COMPANIES.** Price 5s.

**WILLICH'S POPULAR TABLES**
For ascertaining according to the Carlisle Table of Mortality the value of Lifehold, Leasehold, and Church Property, and various useful and interesting Tables. Price 10s. 6d.

# Royal Exchange Assurance.

INCORPORATED A.D. 1720.

## For SEA, FIRE, LIFE, and ANNUITIES.

Chief Office: ROYAL EXCHANGE, LONDON, E.C.

**FUNDS IN HAND** ... ... ... £4,000,000.
**CLAIMS PAID** ... ... ... ... £37,000,000.

## FIRE.

**nsurances are granted against Loss or Damage by Fire** on Property of almost every description, at moderate rates.
**rivate Insurances.**—Policies issued for Two Years and upwards are allowed a liberal discount.
**osses occasioned by Lightning** will be paid whether the property be insured for fire or not.

## LIFE.

ATEST DEVELOPMENTS OF LIFE ASSURANCE:—

1. **Settlement Whole Life Policies,** by which an income of 3 per cent. per annum is guaranteed on the Sum Assured.
2. **Pensions for Old Age,** returning all premiums with interest.
3. **Immediate Life Assurance without Medical Examination.**
4. **Optional Endowment Policies.**
5. **Loans on Reversions and Life Interests** carried out with despatch.

*Apply for Full Prospectus to* **E. R. HANCOCK, Secretary.**

---

## The Investors' Review

Edited by A. J. Wilson.
*Monthly,* 1s. *net;*
14s. *per annum, post free.*

This Review is indispensable to all who desire, not mere market tips, but the actual truth about public securities. It allows them to see the inside of London finance with a thoroughness and outspokenness no other publication of the kind attempts.

## The Investment Index

A Quarterly Supplement to the "Investors' Review."
*Price* 2s. *net;* 8s. 6d. *per annum, post free.*

"The compilation of securities is particularly valuable."—*Pall Mall Gazette.*
"A most valuable compilation."—*Glasgow Herald.*
"A most excellent and useful compilation which should be in the hands of every investor."—*Sketch.*

Subscription to the "Investors' Review" and "Investment Index," 21s. *per annum.*

**CLEMENT WILSON,** 29, Paternoster Row, London, E.C.

---

# PROVIDENT CLERKS'

## MUTUAL LIFE ASSURANCE ASSOCIATION,

27, MOORGATE STREET, LONDON, E.C.

# PROVIDENT CLERKS'

## UARANTEE & ACCIDENT COMPANIES, LIMITED,

61, COLEMAN STREET, LONDON, E.C.

**APPLICATIONS FOR AGENCIES INVITED.**

*Full information on application to Secretaries as above.*